This book is an historical study of the events of October 1941 in the Viaz'ma pocket, based on documents found in the Russian Federation's Central Archive of the Ministry of Defense in Podol'sk, Moscow Oblast', the German *Bundesarchiv*, and the US National Archives.

The author Mikhail Filippenkov describes the events that took place through the simultaneous, comparative analysis of Soviet and German combat reports according to time, and in the manner of reporting from the places of those events as they happened. The author writes about these events with chronological accuracy, not on the level of army headquarters and higher, but exclusively on the level of the combat formations down to the division-level, and with concrete geographical reference to the combat maps of those times.

Particular attention is given to the events that took place in the vicinity of Sychevka in Smolensk Oblast', since what happened there has never been deeply researched or examined by anyone in Russia. Unfortunately, research must rely primarily on the combat reports and combat documents of the units of the Wehrmacht's Panzergruppe 3, since almost no documents on the Soviet side have been preserved. They were either destroyed together with the units and formations trapped within the Viaz'ma pocket, or destroyed at an order from above to those units and formations which managed to escape encirclement more or less intact, in order to erase any record of the disaster.

Mikhail Filippenkov was born in Moscow in 1959. A lawyer by education and training, until 1991 he worked in a department of the USSR Ministry of Internal Affairs responsible for the struggle against embezzlement and speculation. In 1991, he was released from service in the rank of major of the militia. Until 1998 he worked in a business involved with the international trade of consumer goods. After 1998 and to the present, Filippenkov has been a legal advocate for civilian rights. Simultaneously, he has taken an interest in research into the history of Smolensk Oblast – his father's native land. Filippenkov is married and has a son, Aleksei Mikhailovich Filippenkov, an executive policy-maker and economist who is also busy with literary efforts, and who has recently written the novel *Voronka* [*The Shell Hole*] on the events of the First World War on the Western Front.

KONEV'S GOLGOTHA

Operation Typhoon Strikes the
Soviet Western Front, October 1941

Mikhail Filippenkov

Translated and edited by Stuart Britton

Helion & Company

Helion & Company Limited
26 Willow Road
Solihull
West Midlands
B91 1UE
England
Tel. 0121 705 3393
Fax 0121 711 4075
Email: info@helion.co.uk
Website: www.helion.co.uk
Twitter: @helionbooks
Visit our blog http://blog.helion.co.uk/

Published by Helion & Company 2016
Designed and typeset by Mach 3 Solutions Ltd (www.mach3solutions.co.uk)
Cover designed by Paul Hewitt, Battlefield Design (www.battlefield-design.co.uk)
Printed by Gutenberg Press Limited, Tarxien, Malta

Originally published as *Viazemskaia golgofa Generala Koneva* ['General Konev's
Viaz'ma Golgotha'] (Moscow: Veche, 2012).

ISBN 978-1-910777-37-4

British Library Cataloguing-in-Publication Data.
A catalogue record for this book is available from the British Library.

For details of other military history titles published by Helion & Company Limited
contact the above address, or visit our website: http://www.helion.co.uk.

We always welcome receiving book proposals from prospective authors.

Contents

List of Illustrations   vi

List of Maps   vii

Glossary of German Units and Formations   viii

Preface   ix

Foreword   xii

Introduction   xv

1   The Black October of 1941   19

2   The Wehrmacht Readies Itself for the Next Offensive   29

3   The Wehrmacht Strikes   41

4   The Defense of Sychevka   100

5   The Front Continues to Roll to the East   125

6   The Fall of Sychevka   135

Notes   155

Index   164

List of Illustrations

I.S. Konev – Commander-in-Chief of the Western Front.   93
I.V. Boldin – Commander of Operational Group Boldin.   93
I.I. Maslennikov – Commander of the 29th Army.   93
V.M. Sharapov – Chief of Staff of the 29th Army.   93
Friedrich von Bock – Commander-in-Chief of Army Group Center.   94
Georg-Hans Reinhardt – Commander of the XXXXI Panzer Corps.   94
Left: Wilhelm Keitel, chief of the OKW. Right: Hermann Hoth,
    Commander of Panzergruppe 3.   94
Erhard Raus – Commander of the 6th Panzer Division.   94
Soviet riflemen.   95
War comes to village by-streets.   95
German infantry and a panzer before an attack.   96
German anti-tank guns and their crews could not deal with the thick armor
    on Soviet tanks.   96
T-34 tanks knocked out by the enemy.   97
Smashed Soviet armor on a rural road.   97
A German soldier hastens to dig a foxhole in anticipation of Red Army
    counterattacks.   98
A dug-in German machine-gun crew.   98
The consequences of the 1941 encirclements – captured Red Army soldiers.   99
German officers in Viaz'ma.   99

List of Maps

In colour section

1 The German 3rd Panzer Group at the boundary between the 30th and
  19th armies. (Source: D.M. Glantz, *Atlas*)   i
2 Situation Eastern Theatre (according to German data) at the end of
  2.10.41 at 2000 hours. (Source: D.M. Glantz, *Atlas*)   ii
3 Counter-attack by Operational Group Boldin, 3-6 October 1941.   iii
4 Situation area of Viaz'ma on 5.10.41. (Source: D.M. Glantz, *Atlas*)   iv
5 Situation at 2000 on 7.10.41. (Source: D.M. Glantz, *Atlas*)   v
6 Situation at 2100 on 8.10.41. (Source: D.M. Glantz, *Atlas*)   vi
7 Situation on 9.10.41. (Source: D.M. Glantz, *Atlas*)   vii
8 Situation on 11.10.41. (Source: D.M. Glantz, *Atlas* – supplemented
  by author)   viii

Glossary of German Units and Formations

Abteilung – Battalion with less than five companies
Armee – Army
Artillerie – Artillery
Aufklärung – Reconnaissance
Bataillon – Battalion of five companies
Batterie – Battery
Division, Divisionen – Division, Divisions
Flak – Anti-aircraft
Heer – Army
Heeresgruppe – Army Group
Heeresgruppe Mitte – Army Group Center
Infanterie – Infantry
Kampfgruppe, Kampfgruppen – Combat or Battle Group
Kavallerie – Cavalry
Kompanie – Company
Korps – Corps
Kradschützen – motorcycle infantry
mot. – abbreviation for motorized
Panzer-Abteilung – armored battalion
Panzer-Division – armored division
Panzergruppe – Panzer Group
Panzertruppen – Armored troops
Pioniere – Pioneer
Radfahr – Bicycle mounted unit
Regiment, Regimenter – Regiment, Regiments
Schützen – Motorized infantry
Schwadron – Squadron
Zug – Platoon

Preface

The events of the Great Patriotic War [the Russian name for conflict on the Eastern Front of the Second World War] are receding ever further into the past, yet interest in the savage battles of that time is not flagging. Much has already been written about that war in both scholarly literature and memoirs by direct participants in those events, as well as by Russian and foreign scholars.

Fortunately, in recent years previously closed archives and materials have become open to all, which allows a fresh look at those severe trials that fell to the fate of our fathers and grandfathers, who are becoming fewer on this earth with every passing day. Thus, today documents are the primary, mute but impartial witnesses of that heroic era.

However, despite the fact that the Communist regime collapsed more than 20 years ago, for some reason access is still closed to the directives of the *Stavka* of the Supreme High Command; to documents of the Party and Komsomol [Communist Youth League] organizations and to the political communications of their leaders; to materials of the military procurators and tribunals; and without exception to all materials that contain maps on a 50-kilometer scale. Thus, it has been necessary to search through a mass of scattered documents and literally on the basis of fragments to assemble and analyze information that is simply impossible to refute. It has been possible to retrieve the long-forgotten names of people, who paid with their lives for the ambitions of those generals who had no gift in leadership or command. Documents have been preserved that point directly to the fact that the Red Army was adequately provided with weapons and equipment, which were in no way inferior to the enemy's in quality or number. The quality of staff work and the level of training of our staff officers were not inferior to those of their German counterparts, even with all their meticulousness and punctuality, and in many cases were superior. The military knowledge and command skills of commanders up to the division level in the majority of cases were sufficiently progressive for that time and in those circumstances. Our soldiers knew how to fight competently, and their tenacity and courage were repeatedly mentioned by the enemy in their summary reports and messages. But all of this was reduced to nil by the orders from the commands of *fronts* and higher. All too often, orders arrived from those levels that were simply absurd, and which had no logic or any connection with elementary military science, or with events as they were really happening; the cost of this was human lives. Plainly, for a long time now there has been no success in identifying who was the first, and with what aim, to conceive and express the notion of the Red Army's lack of readiness and weakness, and the German Wehrmacht's superiority over it.

Up until 1991, secret archival documents kept concealed the bitter and harsh truth about the abandonment of the ancient Russian city of Sychevka in October 1941 and its liberation in 1943; in 1991, the archives themselves became accessible for research. Only in the post-Soviet era have publications and historical studies begun to appear on the subject of the Rzhev – Viaz'ma operations; however, they are of a rather highly politicized nature and are seen primarily through the eyes of I.V. Stalin and G.K. Zhukov, as well as those commanders of the *fronts* and armies who directly organized and conducted the military operations, including that infamous Operation Mars. However, there has been no research at the level of the "trench perspective", in connection with the heroism and military honors of the simple soldier who remains anonymous. The tragedy of Sychevka still holds many secrets, and historical literature has still not touched upon it.

Having started my work in the archives, I collided with the fact that there are no documents in it relating to the Red Army formations and units that took part in the Viaz'ma battles of 1941. One can understand the absence of records from those formations and units that became encircled in the Viaz'ma area in 1941, but it is inconceivable why, and with what purpose, all of the documents of those units that came out of the encirclement, or those that avoided it in the first place, and were subsequently subjected to reforming, were destroyed back in November 1941. Only their numeric identification numbers are known today. Thus, in the first part of this dialogue, which is dedicated to the Sychevka tragedy of October 1941, to a great extent I've been forced to rely upon documents of the Wehrmacht's Heeresgruppe Mitte, 9. Armee and Panzergruppe 3, which were directly involved in seizing the city, and which were kindly given to me by foreign colleagues and scholars of the history of the Great Patriotic War.

In just the same way, the subject of the efforts to retake of Sychevka in 1942 and 1943 has been unjustifiably forgotten and absolutely untouched by research, even though this was a vital communications hub. In addition, the headquarters of the commander of Heeresgruppe Mitte's 9. Armee, Generaloberst Walter Model, was located there.

With the onset of the Red Army's counteroffensive in front of Moscow in December 1941, the adversary was thrown back from the capital by 150-200 kilometers, and as a consequence the Rzhev – Viaz'ma salient was formed, which the German high command and in particular Heeresgruppe Mitte (the 4. and 9. Armee, and Panzergruppen 3 and 4) thought to use as a staging area for a possible second strategic attack in the eastern direction. Thus, after the conclusion of the Battle of Moscow in April 1942, important offensive operations took place precisely around the Rzhev – Viaz'ma salient, which back in the Soviet era were assigned to the lengthy list of "forgotten battles", which failed to receive sufficiently full and objective coverage in the historical and memoir literature even later.[1]

The outline of this salient ran west of the city of Belyi, north of Olenino, north and west of Rzhev, east of Zubtsov and Gzhatsk [present-day Gagarin], and west of Iukhnov. This salient projected deeply into the Soviet defenses and encompassed a somewhat rectangular area created by the Smolensk – Viaz'ma and Viaz'ma – Sychevka – Rzhev – Olenino railroads, the latter of which extended further to Velikie Liuki. Supplies for Heeresgruppe Mitte ran along these railroads.

The depth of the Rzhev salient amounted to 160 kilometers, while the frontlines extended for 200 kilometers. It was separated from Moscow by 150 kilometers. In the *Stavka* and in the German General Staff, they understood that as long as the salient remained in German hands, there was the danger that it could serve as a "trampoline" for a new vault toward Moscow. This could not fail to make the Soviet command anxious. It repeatedly launched offensives with the aim of liquidating the main forces of Heeresgruppe Mitte and the salient they were holding. Unfortunately, they all failed to reach their objective. At the same time, a heavy fate fell to the towns and villages located within the salient and to the people that lived there, who had to endure bloody fighting and 17 months of German occupation. However, this is a subject for a different book.

In the process of my work, I studied the documents of the Red Army and the Wehrmacht that related to the same time frame, by means of a comparative analysis of the information they contained. The collected material prompted me to the thought of writing a book about those events, but to write it like a schedule of reports from the places of those events, citing only the documented facts of what was happening, while leaving final conclusions for the readers themselves to make.

The staff of the Russian Federation's Central Archive of the Ministry of Defense in Podol'sk, the Russian author and scholar Rostislav Aliev, and the Bulgarian historian and scholar Kamen Navenkin all gave me invaluable assistance in selecting and preparing the materials, and to all of them I wish to express my enormous and sincere acknowledgement and gratitude. In addition, I wish to acknowledge and thank Angelina Borisova, a graduate of Moscow's Russian University of the Friendship of Peoples, for her translation of German documents into the Russian language for me.

My father, the now deceased N.V. Filippenkov, who as an adolescent survived the German occupation in the village of Bol'shoe Krasnoe of Smolensk Oblast's Sychevka District, which was wiped from the face of the earth on 9 March 1943, prompted me to take up the research of my story. It is in the memory of my father that I have decided to write this book, which I leave to the judgment of its readers.

Filippenkov, M.N.
2012

Foreword

When Mikhail Filippenkov asked me to write the Foreword to his book, I gave a lot of thought as to what to say. What should I tell the reader? How to convince him or her to open his book for the first time? To persuade him or her that it is worthy of attention; and that it differs from the majority of all the other books? It really is different, and in many respects simply unique.

In the first place it must not be forgotten that in distinction from all the other military conflicts of the past, the Second World War still remains a political event, not a historical one. The First World War, the American Civil War, the Napoleonic Wars, the French Revolution, the subjugation of the New World, the Mongol invasions, the Crusades, the migration of peoples, and the military campaigns of Ancient Rome and the expeditions of Alexander the Great – all of these events are purely historical. People usually don't argue when they discuss them, politicians don't include them in their utterances, and there are no appeals regarding the "resurrection of the historical truth", the "defense of our heritage against ..." and so forth. They are all somewhere in the deep past, they are all settled facts, and they are all events which no longer give rise to pain in anyone.

With respect to the Second World War, everything is otherwise – arguments constantly swirl around it; it has turned into a favorite plaything of politicians; just the bare mention of it is capable of generating heated arguments, and thus it is still inflicts pain. All of the peoples of Europe suffered from it, and practically no one emerged as a victor from it. As a subject it still remains quite topical, because conflicts over it still haven't been settled.

As an author and historian, I've often had to give thought to how one should write about a war that *de facto* still continues. There is no universal formula, but likely, first of all one must write comprehendingly and with an abundance of reliable supporting facts. In the modern-day science of history, a reliable fact is first of all an argument referencing a documented source. Documents are the best friend of an honest historian and scholar, and a mortal foe to the charlatan historian, political lackey and manipulator of minds. There are no emotions in documents, and in the majority of cases, no distortions of fact. Politicians and public figures fear documents like the plague, and that is why quite often they even "repress" them – conceal "inconvenient" documents, classify them, and sometimes even simply destroy them. To the present day, for example, no one in London or in Moscow wants to give open access to the most intimate discussions between Churchill and Stalin (face to face or in correspondence). It also remains unclear what the *Stavka's*/Stalin's precise strategic plans were after the spring of 1943, when the Red Army began gradually to drive the forces of the Wehrmacht and its allies out of the Soviet Union's western lands. How deeply did they want to penetrate into Europe? Which countries did they want to "liberate" and which to leave under the control of the English and Americans? Where, when and with exactly how much force did they want to attack? After all, all of this is now in the past, and should be viewed as the historical past. But no, for someone or another, this is still the real present, and none of us will be alive when access will finally be given to these "inconvenient secrets".

Problems of such a nature also exist at the level of individual battles. Battles that lasted for many months, even entire operations from the time of the Great Patriotic War, which cost many thousands of soldiers' lives, still remain literally buried in the archives. Why? Because they were not won, or even worse – they were lost, and thus they've been excluded from the understanding of a "developed socialist society". Rather, it is preferred they be forgotten. No songs have been sung about them, no books written, no veterans decorated, no films made, no articles are published on their anniversary in the central newspapers and journals, and no matter how para-doxical, they aren't even studied in military schools and academies. Those who want to believe do so, and those who don't, do not; however, from the end of the Great Patriotic War up to the actual collapse of the Soviet Union, cases included in books published specifically for future officers of the Soviet Army were selected only from those operations that ended successfully …. Only in recent years in contemporary Russia has attention begun to be paid to battles that were "not won", or were "lost" by the Red Army, but since nothing has been written about them, the scholar must simply begin from scratch. Indeed, no matter how paradoxical, the hope that in the nearest future we, the lovers of military history, will read fresh research about unpop-ular, but still very interesting (from the point of view of drama and dynamics) battles of the Second World War is not very high – there are simply more "blank spots" than there are honorable scholars, capable of writing about them.

When talking about scholars who write books on topics of war (not only in Russia, but also in the "democratic" countries of the West), it must be stressed that for some unknown reason, the vast majority of them simple rewrite that which has been written in other books. In other words – they make books just like well-known international restaurant chains make hamburgers and pizza. Indeed, in the end, it happens that the "taste" for such books is also universally the same. Statistics, for example, show that in 2010 alone, not less than 11,000 people visited the Russian Federation's Central Archive of the Ministry of Defense in Podol'sk. However, it turns out that very few of them were actually writing books. In the same 2010, for example, less than 5% of all the books about the Great Patriotic War published in Russia contain references to archival sources. This means that the actual number of genuine historical studies is very, very small.

In the end, why did I decide to support Mikhail Filippenkov's book? Because in his book, I found everything that I as a scholar value in other studies. In the first place, this is respect for the facts. This is also the use of materials from both sides, which means as well a view from the opposing German side. Secondly, there is the absence of emotions and "politically convenient" conclusions and accordingly the author's own commentaries. The resulting book is unique – a historical "reality show". In it there is no excessive drama and pathos, but one can sense the smell of smoke, gunpowder, filth and blood, and the other common "attributes" of each battle of the 20th Century. They are there, in the lines of the messages and reports. The author also makes it possible for the reader to come to his or her own conclusion about what happened there, around Viaz'ma. He also describes this "forgotten" battle in great detail. Yet it was one of those battles of the Great Patriotic War, about which some men in the corridors of power very much wanted the rest of us to forget. For example, the "official" version of the Second World War, published in the 1970s under the editorship of Marshal Grechko, only states regarding the Viaz'ma pocket that "on the field of battle, many soldiers and commanders fell bravely". Yes, this is true, but what was the reality? What actually took place? I sincerely hope that Mikhail Filippenkov's book will help the reader find an answer.

Mikhail is not an official historian and doesn't serve any political interests. All that you will read here has only been written in the sake of his father's memory and on behalf of his own enormous personal desire to learn the entire truth of the catastrophe at Viaz'ma. I hope that in the future he will bless us with other honest and unembellished studies of "forgotten battles".

Kamen Nevenkin
Author and scholar of the history of the Second World War
Sofia, Bulgaria, 2012

Introduction

In the ancient past, on the steep left bank of the lovely Russian Vazuza River, along which in those times ran the water artery "from the Varangians to the Greeks", our ancestors, having cleared the surrounding forests, built their first homes. That's how the settlement on the Vazuza got started, which subsequently became known as Sychevka – the first city on the Vazuza River, located 80 kilometers from its source.

The region itself is mentioned in the Russian Primary Chronicle as the "Volkov woods" and belonged to the Smolensk fiefdom and to the subordinate Fominsk principality. This is how the Smolensk region historian B.A. Makhotin described the origination of the city's name in his 1989 book *K zhivym istokam* [*To living sources*]:

> The presence in the name of the component word "-ka" testifies to the relative youth of the village itself, which began as a small hamlet. Its advantageous location on the river path (Vazuza – Volga) contributed to its conversion at first into a palace village, and then, in 1776, into a district city.
>
> To the question as to when and how the name "Sychevka" arose, there is no unambiguous answer. There is the widely-held opinion that it stems from the common [Russian] name for the horned owl, *sych*. According to legend, the place at which the city of Sychevka is located was once covered with dense forests and swamps. Among them was the tiny hamlet of Sychi. This hamlet received its name, because back then there were plenty of horned owls in the area.
>
> It is also logical to view that Sychevka is named after its founder or first entrepreneur, who had the name of "Sych", or the surname "Sychev" (son of "Sych"). In the past, the ancient Russian proper name or surname "Sych" or "Sychev" was quite widespread in the land of the Rus'. Family names on their basis are also not so rare in the Smolensk area even in the present day. This suggests that the city of Sychevka and a lot of villages in the area, for example Sychevka, Sychevo and Sychiki, are related by their names not to horned owls, but to people, who had the surnames Sychi, Sychev or Sychikov.
>
> As in any other city in the Smolensk area, the toponym of Sychevka lives in its past and present. In the local regional history museum, there is a unique document – "The 1780 Plan of the City of Sychevka". In it, the city's bordering rivers are clearly visible: on its eastern and southeastern sides, the concave bend of the Vazuza River, and on its western side, its left-hand tributary, the Los'mina

River. The etymology of the name of the Vazuza River remains a puzzle even today. The etymology of the name of its tributary also isn't fully clear. Most likely, it must be searched with the help of a compilation of similarly-sounding river names in other regions of the country. For example, there is the Losma River (a right-bank tributary of the Mokshi River, which lies in the basin of the Oki River), which flows through the territory of an ancient settlement area of Finnish-language Mordovians. The comparison of the closely-sounding names of the two rivers suggests a common language origin, but the etymology remains unclear.

Much fell to the fate of the Sychevka land and the people who settled there. It is located at the juncture of the Smolensk, Tver', Rzhev, Rostov-Suzdal', Moscow and other fiefdoms. In the ancient past, the princes feuded among themselves. In connection with this, in 1216 Rzhev, Zubtsov and Vazuza are first mentioned in the chronicles. In 1238, returning from an unsuccessful campaign against Novgorod, the Mongols devastated many settlements in Sychevka region.

Mention is made of Sychevka and its volost' for the first time in the historical documents in 1473 (according to other sources, in 1478, but on both occasions for practically one and the same reason), and this was connected to a complaint by the Grand Prince Mikhail Viazemsky to the Polish King Kazimir IV that "men of the Tver' Prince Ivan (Ioanna) Molodoi, son of Ivan (Ioanna) III, have conquered the volost' of Prince Vasilii Byvalitsky Negomir' (subsequently Nemir'), and also Sychevka". In 1493, after Ivan III won Viaz'ma from the Lithuanians and absorbed it within the Moscow principality, Sychevka became a palace village of the Muscovite princes, and later – of the tsars. The village, like all of the Sychevka court volost', became part of the Viaz'ma district.

By the start of the 18th Century, the palace village of Sychevka had become a major trading center. Wharves, granaries and warehouses that belonged to the merchants who transported their goods by water had been constructed on the banks of the Vazuza. The river carried their grain, flax, hemp, resin, tar and building timber to Gzhatsk, Rzhev, Tver', Peterburg and other cities. On 22 February (5 March according to the new calendar) 1776, by a decree of Catherine II, the palace village of Sychevka was made a town with the same name, and became the center of the new Sychevka District. In 1780, Sychevka received from the Empress a letter of grant with the depiction of the city coat of arms in the form of a shield, split into two parts. In the upper portion is the emblem of Smolensk: in a silver field, a black cannon with a gold gun mount, and on it, the fairy-tale phoenix bird. In the lower part is the emblem of Sychevka – a horned owl perched on the trunk of a young tree against a blue background.

The conversion of Sychevka from the ranks of a village into a town, as well as the wharves that had been constructed on the banks of the Vazuza River, contributed to the further development of trade in the town. Simultaneously, local industry developed: a tobacco factory, a brick factory, a tannery and a winery operated there.

The people of Sychevka fought with Lithuania and the Poles, and conducted successful partisan operations against Napoleon's army in 1812. The French had arrived on the territory of Sychevka District on 18 August 1812. By this time, two partisan detachments had been created in Sychevka, which consisted of more than 400 townsmen and peasants. The detachment led by the village bailiff's wife Vasilisa Kozhina from the hamlet of Gorshkovo, which lies several kilometers from the village of Dugino, particularly stood out. Over two months and six days (from 19 August to 25 October), the Sychevka partisans killed 1,760 enemy soldiers and officers, and captured 1,009. The district's entire population rose up in struggle against the French conquerors.

In 1882, a railroad was laid down through the town. It contributed to a rapid development of the local industry, a rise in trade, and an increase in the population.

Today this district center has an area of 8 square kilometers and a population of approximately 7,500 people, and is located between the two now unnavigable rivers, the Vazuza and Los'mina, 234 kilometers east of Smolensk and 2 kilometers to the west of the "Old Smolensk Road". It is a major railroad station on the Viaz'ma – Rzhev line, 70 kilometers from Viaz'ma and 45 kilometers from Zubtsov.

Before the Great Patriotic War, 8,428 people were living in Sychevka, and in the surrounding rural area there were 40,793 people living in 418 settlements that were clustered into 25 rural councils. After the invasion of Nazi Germany, thousands of Sychevka citizens headed to the front. An enormous amount of work lay on the shoulders of those who remained in the rear.

In the connection with a breakthrough by the German Army to Moscow, the women, old men and adolescents had to dig dozens of kilometers of anti-tank ditches, trenches and communication trenches, and to construct a multitude of other defensive fortifications. Despite this, on 10 October 1941, Sychevka was occupied by the German Army. At the beginning of 1942, it wound up in the center of the Rzhev – Viaz'ma staging area which had been created by the Germans with the intention of a renewed offensive toward Moscow. The Soviet command undertook a number of offensives with the aim of eliminating this salient. Savage fighting took place on the Sychevka axis from January 1942 right up to the town's liberation. Over this time, the Soviets forces launched an entire series of offensive operations and liberated hundreds of populated places. Striving to retain possession of the strategically important lines, the German command was compelled to transfer reserves from other sectors of the front hastily to the area of Rzhev and Sychevka.

Combat operations took place on the territory of Sychevka District for one and a half years. Many of its villages changed hands more than once. Significant enemy forces were pinned down here for a lengthy amount of time.

On 8 March 1943, Sychevka was liberated from the German fascist aggressors. This liberation came at an excessively high cost. In no other area of the Smolensk lands were there such a number of intense and lengthy battles, in which such a multitude of rifle, cavalry and tank units and formations, as well as artillery and aviation, took part.

Thousands of citizens, who had been called up by the Sychevka military enlistment center, failed to return from the fronts of the Great Patriotic War. Practically each family in Sychevka experienced the pain of an irreplaceable loss. The Sychevka land was heavily saturated with the blood of tens of thousands of Soviet soldiers, who fought here between 1941 and 1943.

The citizens of Sychevka District also paid a heavy price for liberation; hundreds of populated places were destroyed. The district population by the end of the war amounted to just 21,171 people, including 3,152 in the town. The town of Sychevka itself lay in ruins.

1

The Black October of 1941

Reality and fantasy

After the destruction of the main forces of the Soviet Western Front in the Bialystok and Minsk pockets, the German command, wasting no time, made the decision to launch a new offensive on the Moscow axis with mobile formations alone, without waiting for the infantry divisions to come up. On this occasion, as had happened repeatedly in history, Smolensk wound up in the foe's path. There, between 10 July and 10 September 1941, savage fighting continued, in the course of which already on 17-18 July, separate sectors of the city repeatedly changed hands, By the morning of 19 July, the Germans nevertheless succeeded in taking the majority of the city, and on 28 July 1941, the Red Army fully abandoned Smolensk. Despite this, the battle for Smolensk became an important stage in disrupting the timetable of advance of the German forces toward Moscow. Soviet troops suffered enormous losses, but the German were also left bloodied and exhausted, having conducted heavy fighting for this major urban center.

Despite the fact that the city itself had been abandoned, this did not signify the end of the Battle of Smolensk, and already on 30 July 1941, the Wehrmacht high command ordered Heeresgruppe Mitte to go over to the defense with its main forces. Heavy fighting east of Smolensk continued until 10 September, and on 12 September Colonel General I.S. Konev was appointed as commander of the Western Front, in place of Marshal S.K. Timoshenko. He took command of the forces at the end of the Battle of Smolensk and adopted a defense on a line running from Lake Seliger to El'nia, at a time when the German command, having brought up supplementary forces and conducting a regrouping, had already readied a new offensive on the Moscow axis under the code name "Typhoon".

Having learned about the offensive being prepared by the Germans, the Western Front command began to bring up its reserves to the threatened sector, and on 30 September an operational group of commanders headed by the Front's deputy commander Lieutenant General I.V. Boldin was formed and sent to Vadino, in order to assume direct leadership of the forces on the Vadino direction. With this same aim, a signals hub was organized in Vadino, through which communications could be maintained with all the armies of the Western Front. The Western Front's main communications center at the Kasnia railroad station, because of the threat of Luftwaffe attacks, was removed from a single premise and scattered into bunkers on the directions of activity.[1]

Until 30 September, not only units of the Red Army that remained after the Battle of Smolensk underwent regrouping east of Smolensk. In addition, there were units from other areas that had been directed there after 22 June 1941 in order to build a line of defense.

At the height of the Battle of Smolensk, the full-strength 251st Rifle Division arrived in Baturino (Kholm-Zhirkovskii District in the north of Smolensk Oblast, 12 kilometers south of its border with Tver' Oblast) and became part of the 30th Army back on 15 July 1941. Together with other units that were under the 30th Army's command, it set to work constructing defensive positions on the Smolensk – Belyi line and giving combat training to the personnel. The 251st Rifle Division had been formed on 30 June 1941 out of units of the USSR NKVD [People's Commissariat of Internal Affairs] and reserve troops from Moscow Oblast. Colonel Stenin commanded it, and his chief of staff was Colonel Starovoitov. Having assumed a defense on the Viaz'ma axis, it was busy with constructing defensive fortifications and the training of its personnel; special attention was given to radio communications. All of the division's technical property was timely put in order.

From 30 September 1941, replacements began to arrive, which consisted, as it turned out, of completely raw new recruits. On this day, the 923rd Rifle Regiment alone received 1,000 men of a completely untrained replacement unit from Udmurtia, who had no idea that soon they alone would be one of the first to take on the powerful blow of the new German offensive.[2] We will find out about the actions of this regiment and its commander Major N.A. Guliaev a little later.

From the testimony of prisoners, it became known to Western Front headquarters that the Germans were preparing a general offensive toward Moscow, and 100 infantry divisions, 3,000 tanks and 1,000 aircraft were to take part in the operation. However in reality, according to the situation on 1 October 1941, the operational density of the two sides on a sector of the front 347 kilometers wide was assessed by the command of the Red Army's Western Front as follows (see Table 1):

The fact that already by the beginning of October the Germans had a superiority in force was explained by the command of the Western Front as the Soviet divisions' deficit in personnel (11% to 54% below their authorized strength), and by the average two-fold superiority of the Germans in combat equipment, especially in machine guns, anti-tank guns and artillery of all calibers, and tanks. After the start of the offensive it became clear that the Germans had assembled their main forces opposite the boundary between the Soviet 30th and 19th Armies. Here, the correlation of force was such that the Germans had twice the infantry, three times the artillery and tanks, and approximately 2.5 times the amount of aircraft than their Soviet counterpart. Considering such a concentration of Wehrmacht strength, the Western Front command nevertheless counted upon stopping its offensive.[3]

Table 1 Relative strength of the opposing sides as estimated by the Western Front command

	USSR	Germany
Number of divisions	27 rifle divisions	34 infantry divisions
Frontage in kilometers of each rifle or infantry division	approximately 13	11.9
Density of guns (excluding anti-tank guns) of all calibers per kilometer of front	5.9	11.9
Density of anti-tank guns per kilometer of front	1.6	3.0
Density of armor per kilometer of front	1.2	2.0

So that the reader will not be confused in the future by the numeric designations of the armies and units, below I present the total composition of the opposing sides:

The Wehrmacht:
Heeresgruppe Mitte (Generalfeldmarschall Fedor von Bock)
9. Armee (Generaloberst Adolf Strauß)

On the left (northern flank) of Panzergruppe 3:
XXIII Armeekorps (General der Infanterie A. Schubert): 251., 102., 256. and 206. Infanterie-Divisionen
Panzergruppe 3 (Generaloberst Hermann Hoth)
VI Armeekorps (General der Pioniere O.-W. Förster): 110. and 26. Infanterie-Divisionen
XXXXI Panzerkorps (General der Panzertruppe Georg-Hans Reinhardt): 36. Infanterie-Division (mot.), 1. Panzer-Division and 6. Infanterie-Division
LVI Panzerkorps (General der Panzertruppe Ferdinand Schaal): 6. and 7. Panzer-Divisionen, 129. Infanterie-Division
V Armeekorps (General der Infanterie Richard Ruoff): 5., 35. and 106. Infanterie-Divisionen

On the right (southern flank) of Panzergruppe 3:
VIII Armeekorps (General der Artillerie Walter Heitz): 8., 28. and 87. Infanterie-Divisionen
XXVII Armeekorps (General der Infanterie A. Wager): 86., 162. and 255. Infanterie-Divisionen
9. Armee Reserve: 161. and 14. Infanterie-Divisionen (mot.)
4. Armee (Generalfeldmarshall Günther von Kluge)
IX Armeekorps (General der Infanterie G. Gejer): 137., 263., 183. and 292. Infanterie-Divisionen
XX Armeekorps (General der Infanterie F. Materna): 268., 15. and 78. Infanterie-Divisionen

VII Armeekorps (General der Artillerie W. Farmbacher): 7., 23., 197. and 167. Infanterie-Divisionen

Panzergruppe 4 (Generaloberst Erich Hoepner):
LVII Panzerkorps (General der Panzertruppe A. Kunzen): 20. Panzer-Division, 3. Infanterie-Division (mot.) and the SS Division *Das Reich*
XXXXVI Panzerkorps (General der Panzertruppe Heinrich Gottfried Otto Richard von Vietinghoff): 5. and 11. Panzer-Divisionen, 252. Infanterie-Division
XXXX Panzerkorps (General der Panzertruppe Georg Stumme): 2. and 10. Panzer-Divisionen, 252. Infanterie-Division
XII Armeekorps (General der Infanterie W. Schrot): 98. and 34. Infanterie-Divisionen
2. Armee (Generaloberst Maximilian von Weichs)
XIII Armeekorps (General der Infanterie G. Felber): 17. and 260. Infanterie-Divisionen
XXXXIII Armeekorps (General der Infanterie Gotthard Heinrici): 52. and 131. Infanterie-Divisionen
LIII Armeekorps (General der Infanterie W. Weisenberger): 56., 31. and 167. Infanterie-Divisionen
2. Armee Reserve: 112. Infanterie-Division
Panzergruppe 2 (Generaloberst Heinz Wilhelm Guderian)
XXXXVII Panzerkorps (General der Panzertruppe Joachim Lemelsen): 17. and 18. Panzer-Divisionen, 29. Infanterie-Division (mot.)
XXIV Panzerkorps (General der Panzertruppe L. Geyr von Schweppenburg): 3. and 4. Panzer-Divisionen, 10. Infanterie-Division (mot.)
XXXXVIII Panzerkorps (General der Panzertruppe Werner Kempf): 9. Panzer-Division, 16. and 25. Infanterie-Divisionen (mot.)
Gruppe 34 (General der Infanterie G. Mez): 45. and 134. Infanterie-Divisionen
Gruppe 35 (General der Artillerie R. Kempfe): 95., 196., 262., 293. Infanterie-Divisionen, 1. Kavallerie-Division
Heeresgruppe Mitte Reserve: 19. Panzer-Division, 900. Lehr-Brigade (mot.) and Regiment *Grossdeutschland* (mot.)
Rear Security of Heeresgruppe Mitte: 339. and 707. Infanterie-Divisionen; 221. 286., 403. and 454. Sicherungs-Divisionen [Security Divisions], SS-Kavallerie-Brigade
Luftflotte 2: Generalfeldmarschall Albert Kesselring

The Workers' and Peasants' Red Army
Western Front: (Colonel General I.S. Konev)
22nd Army (Major General V.A. Iushkevich)
29th Army (Lieutenant General I.I. Maslennikov)
30th Army (Major General V.A. Khomenko)
19th Army (Lieutenant General M.F. Lukin)
16th Army (Lieutenant General K.K. Rokossovsky)
20th Army (Lieutenant General A.A. Vlasov)

Reserve Front (Marshal of the Soviet Union S.M. Budennyi)
In the first echelon:
24th Army (Major General K.I. Rakutin)
43rd Army (Major General P.P. Sobennikov)
In the second echelon:
31st Army (Major General V.N. Dalmatov)
49th Army (Lieutenant General I.G. Zakharin)
32nd Army (Major General S.V. Vishnevsky)
33rd Army (Brigade Commander[4] D.N. Onuprienko)

Briansk Front (Colonel General Ia.T. Cherevichenko)
50th Army (Major General M.P. Petrov)
3rd Army (Major General Ia.G. Kreizer)
13th Army (Major General A.M. Gorodiansky)
Operational Group of Major General A.N. Ermakov

However, not all of the above formations and commanders will be of interest to us, but only those that were directly involved in the combat operations on the Sychevka axis. They were the Wehrmacht's Panzergruppe 3 (and to a great extent only its 1. Panzer-Division, which took Sychevka), and correspondingly the units of the Red Army's 29th, 30th and 31st Armies that opposed it.

Subsequently, the *fronts* would change, the armies would be repeatedly re-subordinated, and the commanders reshuffled, but since none of this is the aim of our study, we will not be drawing the readers' attention to it.

Panzergruppe 3 prepares

Colonel General Hermann Hoth's Panzergruppe 3 was to attack along the Viaz'ma axis, having the seizure of the important communications hub of Sychevka as one of its main tasks. Without taking this city, the further advance of the panzer group toward Moscow would be seriously hampered, since the problem of keeping the rapidly advancing units supplied and the transfer of reserves would arise, because there were no other major transportation hubs on this axis.

From 22 August to 1 October 1941, Hoth's panzer group had been sentenced to a period of inactivity after the heavy defensive fighting against the Red Army's strong counterattacks in the Smolensk area with large masses of infantry and powerful artillery support. Units of Panzergruppe 3 suffered large losses, since in the course of the combat operations its panzer divisions were gradually replaced with infantry divisions that came up from the rear. Subsequently, the infantry divisions were also pulled out of combat in greatly weakened conditions. Losses, particularly in junior command staff, proved to be much heavier than in preceding offensive operations. The re-assignment of the available motorized divisions to infantry corps led to the improper use of these divisions and to the further loss of equipment.

However, at the moment Sychevka still lay ahead, and the totally unsuspecting Heeresgruppe Mitte headquarters was undisturbedly located in the backwaters of the war in the village of Ripshevo, in Smolensk Oblast's Dukhovshchina District. This was a period of waiting, which for it and for the arriving 7. Panzer-Division, 14. Infanterie-Division (mot.) and 900. Lehr-Brigade (mot.) was exceptionally discomforting. This was because of the overall operational situation on the Soviet-German front.

After the rapid breakthrough by Heeresgruppe Mitte to Smolensk, the center of operations shifted to the north in the direction of Leningrad, and then to the south, toward Ukraine. The major operational successes achieved by the Wehrmacht in the process demonstrated how unexpected these decisions were to the Red Army command, and it proved unable to implement any satisfactory countermeasures against such flexible, highly-maneuverable tactics of the German command. Yet the Western Front command evidently believed that it could contain the central grouping of German forces attacking through Smolensk toward Moscow. However, this was a delusion, which subsequently had to be paid with soldiers' lives.[5]

The Red Army's higher command shifted its forces too slowly, and sent forces to the south and to the north only when it was already too late, while at the same time the central front was left too weak. After the destruction of the armies under the command of Voroshilov in the north and of Budennyi in the south, Heeresgruppe Mitte was to resume the offensive toward Moscow with the aim of destroying the forces of Western Front, with a decisive breakthrough to Moscow.

The availability of major panzer formations prompted the command of Heeresgruppe Mitte to the thought of using them for the purpose of a double envelopment of the Red Army's opposing forces. Based on the experience of past battles, it seemed that a concentric offensive with the deep envelopment of Western Front's forces made sense, since its command was showing little reaction to a threat to its rear, and had kept its front static for a long time. Thus, Panzergruppe 3 and 4 were given the task to seize Viaz'ma.

For this purpose, Panzergruppe 3 was made operationally subordinate to 9. Armee, which had the initial task to rupture the Red Army's lines between the Smolensk highway and the Bor – Belyi road. Subsequently, it was to breach the Soviet reserve defensive positions along the Dnepr River, and having broken into the depth of this position, to attack in the general direction of Viaz'ma in order to destroy the entire Western Front grouping in conjunction with 4. Armee, which would be attacking toward Viaz'ma from the southwest.

Preparing for this operation, the command of Panzergruppe 3 on 9 September issued a directive to its subordinate forces, giving them the task in cooperation with 2., 4. and 9. Armee and Panzergruppe 2 and 4 to destroy the Western Front. Not simply to shove it aside, but to destroy it, because at the given moment, the primary objective was not Moscow, but the destruction of Konev's Western Front.

When planning this offensive operation, even by the end of September, the German command was still uncertain about how to conduct it, whether by means of a double envelopment and subsequent encirclement of Western Front's forces, or by means of a single thrust with a decisive attack into the flank and rear of the ruptured Soviet front. In order not to exhaust its mobile divisions during the breakthrough phase, in this case an enveloping offensive seemed more sensible to the command of Heeresgruppe Mitte, and it was precisely Panzergruppe 3 that was supposed to conduct it as far as possible to the north, best of all from Lake Il'men to the southeast. In so doing, it was anticipated that an offensive from Toropets (in Tver' Oblast, located west of the Valdai Hills at the source of the Toropa River out of Lake Solomeno, 332 kilometers west of Tver') would strike the flank of the Soviet defensive positions, whereas an offensive out of the Bor – Vasil'evo area would constitute a frontal attack.

The German command initially planned for the panzer groups to conduct a broad envelopment of the Western Front's forces at Kalinin and Tula in the general direction of Moscow, but subsequently it was forced to reject this plan, since in connection with the past experience of the Red Army's method of conducting of combat operations, it was concerned that such a plan would not ensure the rapid destruction of Western Front, and in this case it might keep hold of its defensive positions or be able to offer resistance right up until the onset of winter.

The analysis of intelligence data and the assessment of the current situation conducted by the command of Heeresgruppe Mitte led to the discomforting conclusion, that if its shock groups targeted near objectives in the area of Viaz'ma, because of their deeply-echeloned formation the Red Army's major forces might not be fully enveloped, whereas with any breakthrough to deep objectives, the ring of encirclement would be insufficiently strong, in which case major forces of the Western Front might break out, and thus a significant amount of time might be necessary to bring the operation to a successful conclusion. However, the time available to the Germans before the onset of winter was limited. When calculating the distance to possible objectives beyond the assumed defensive positions of Western Front, the German command resolved that the objectives must be closer to the jumping-off positions for the offensive, moreover because German intelligence was informing its command that the Red Army had 60 divisions on the front facing Heeresgruppe Mitte, and another 12 reserve divisions were in the process of forming up in the suburbs of Moscow.

The German staff officers planned to target the Western Front's weakest sectors with a concentration of force and a deeply-echeloned formation on the main axis of attack, either in the event of an enveloping offensive, or even more so in the case of a frontal assault. The infantry corps and panzer groups were allocated specific offensive sectors, and it was planned to achieve the greatest possible cooperation between the infantry, motorized and panzer divisions by subordinating infantry directly to the panzer corps.[6]

The command of Heeresgruppe Mitte didn't doubt that the Red Army intended to keep any German offensive in check in front of Moscow, and believed from past experience that it would launch numerous heavy counterattacks with major forces from out of their previously prepared defensive positions behind the Dnepr. The German determined that the focal points of these counterattacks would be in the areas east of El'nia and east of Smolensk, and they had no doubt that the command of Western Front attached great significance to regaining possession of Smolensk. This assurance of the German command was bolstered by the Red Army's recent successes at El'nia and in the sector of VIII Armeekorps, as well by the fact that the threat to Moscow on the central axis had become clear to the Red Army high command. In addition, the recent successes by the Germans on the Leningrad and Kiev directions made it possible for the German command to conduct an offensive that would outflank the defensive positions that had been prepared by the Soviet side on the Moscow axis.[7]

In the opinion of German staff analysts, the Red Army command had recently handled its forces rather clumsily, and it showed a lack of sensitivity to threats of an attack into their flank and rear; it also didn't fear encirclement, because its forces had been trained to break out of encirclement before the war. Confidence in this assessment had been gained by looking at the initial stage of the war, when the Red Army command had reacted slowly in shifting its forces from the front to threatened flanks, as for example had been the case during the breakthrough by the German forces in the offensive toward Toropets and Dubno.

On the basis of these analytical conclusions, the German command, held prisoner by the stereotypes that had arisen, expected that after the encirclement of Leningrad and the latest defeats of the Soviet forces of the Southwestern Front, the Red Army command would view the threat to Moscow as coming from the south and north, and it would take corresponding countermeasures. The German command was convinced that the Red Army command had available as reinforcements only the small forces at Volkhov and east of Leningrad; the reserve divisions forming in the suburbs of Moscow; and forces which might be made available from other sectors of the front.

Thus, in order to complete the preparations for the offensive, the matter of ascertaining the behavior of Western Front's forces and the operational intentions of its command acquired exceptionally important significance for the German command. German intelligence intended to establish this in the shortest amount of time possible by using every available means (aerial reconnaissance, particularly nighttime aerial reconnaissance, and ground observation; its network of agents; radio intelligence; and the seizure of prisoners), after which it would receive an answer to all the questions of interest to the command of Heeresgruppe Mitte:

1.   Would the Western Front command withdraw its forces from the front and would the Red Army retreat to the east?
2.   Was the Red Army intending to defend behind the Dnepr, the Oka or the Volga Rivers?
3.   Were there any signs that the Red Army intended to counterattack the German forces?

In the event that it became clear that the Red Army would continue to hold its present front lines, the Germans accordingly sought to establish the weakest and most vulnerable spots in their lines, which were already assumed to be in the areas of Ostashkov, Butaki, Belyi and Rzhev. The Germans believed that given its rudimentary forms of command and control and its elementary forms of staging combat, the Western Front command would continue strongly to cover and defend the main roads leading to Moscow with major forces: the Warsaw – Moscow highway as well as the road between Leningrad and Moscow. Thus, the German forces were prepared to meet the strongest opposition from the Red Arm along these main roads.[8]

Returning to the Panzergruppe 3, it should be noted that the condition of its divisions' motorized pool was on such a level, that by their mobility and number they were fully capable of conducting an enveloping offensive. The fact as well that a purely frontal offensive by the panzer divisions would require the same panzer strength, but be more costly and given the limited time available to the Germans, still ultimately require an eventual exploitation using the maneuverability of the panzer group, spoke in favor of an enveloping offensive. The panzers' maneuverability to outflank and bypass knots of resistance would be on full display from the outset, which would not be the case during a frontal assault or even during a breakthrough.[9]

Use of the panzer group was planned according to the condition of the road network and its trafficability, and it was projected that if the group was going to act in a concentrated manner, then each panzer corps would have no more than one route. Given poor weather, a number of the roads would become totally unsuitable for movement, and in this case, the troops attacking along poor roads would doubtlessly be compelled to halt their offensive or would spontaneously divert to the few good roads, and thereby disrupt the planned route assignments. Flowing from these considerations, the separation of the panzer group from the main mass of attacking divisions was recognized as quite desirable.[10]

In addition to all the above, the Germans planned the offensive based on the fact that behind the Dnepr, around Sychevka and in front of Rzhev, the Western Front had an elaborate defensive belt, and that major populated places, like Rzhev, Sychevka, Viaz'ma and Gzhatsk would in the Russian custom be defended stubbornly. Therefore it was preferable not to assault them directly, and it was recognized that a better approach would be to bypass them. Consideration was also given to the large forested, swampy tracts between the cities of Belyi and Sychevka, as well as south of Belyi. Higher ground in the areas of Sychevka, Viaz'ma and Gzhatsk thus became important objectives in the planning stage.[11]

For the German command right up until the start of the offensive, it was still unclear whether the Red Army would cling to its positions or retreat; thus it was believed that the direct route to Moscow running through Smolensk and Viaz'ma, and as well as the route running from Moscow to Leningrad through Kalinin, would be defended, which would allow the Soviet side to gain time and delay the German advance. On the basis of these prognoses, ultimately the German command opted to conduct an enveloping offensive into the Soviet rear so as to destroy the Western Front, not simply to push it back, rather than make a direct assault into the Red Army's front or flank, and this was transmitted to the panzer group command. In addition, given the lack of time and the consideration of the Red Army's methods of giving battle that had already become known to the Germans, it was determined that the enveloping attack should target a near objective. Thus, Panzergruppe 3 consisting of the XXXXI and LVI Panzerkorps and the V and VI Armeekorps, currently concentrated in the Toropets area, would prepare for an offensive with the task to attack through the city of Belyi with its two subordinate infantry corps on the left flank of the army group, and with one corps further south, through Kholm-Zhirkovskii on the Dnepr River [130 kilometers northeast of Smolensk and approximately 38 kilometers north of the main Warsaw – Moscow highway], with an eventual emergence at Viaz'ma.[12]

2

The Wehrmacht Readies Itself for the Next Offensive

We will begin our promised chronology of events from the end of September 1941, since by this time the deployment of the opposing forces had already crystallized. In addition, we will not torment the reader with an excessive amount of data and statistics, as many contemporary scholars do, because in the first place, numbers cannot always be considered the Gospel truth because many documents are missing and because many documents on the Soviet side are still classified; and in the second place, because an excessive amount of statistical data obscures the conception of the reality of what happened in one interval of time or another. Moreover, numbers will always provoke many arguments and can serve as a means of manipulation by ill-intentioned scholars.

As I said from the beginning, I set my task as examining exclusively tactical moments, while the statistics and strategy of what happened have already been rather scrupulously gathered and exhaustively analyzed by the scholar L.N. Lopukhovsky in his major work *1941. Viazemskaia tragediia* [This highly acclaimed book has been translated by Stuart Britton and published by Helion in July 2013 under the title *The Viaz'ma Catastrophe, 1941: The Red Army's Disastrous Stand against Operation Typhoon*]. Moreover, just figures alone make definitive conclusions impossible for one simple reason: they are usually doctored by the losing side for the sake of justifying their failure, while for those on the winning side it simply makes no sense to lie, but it also doesn't hurt to fib a bit for the sake of hastening the acquisition of already deserved honors and awards.

So, the date of 25 September 1941 has arrived, and henceforth only documents will be speaking. Please note that the German documents will be using Berlin time, while Soviet documents use Moscow time. Berlin time is two hours behind Moscow time.

25 September (Thursday)

The day began as had all the preceding days; it was cloudy, but warm and dry. Local combat to improve positions were going on along the entire front of Heeresgruppe

Mitte's 9. Armee and of its Panzergruppe 3 in particular, but the headquarters at every level were already working feverishly, preparing to implement the plan of Operation Typhoon – the offensive toward Moscow -- which had already been confirmed long before.

Little time remained before the start of the offensive, but much still had to be done. Moreover, in reality there wasn't adequate strength and it was necessary for the Germans somehow to offset their numerical shortcoming with quality and the concentration of available force on particularly important directions.

At the staff level, the offensive in essence was already in motion, and there was no longer any way to stop the process. There were still few who knew the details of what had been planned, but a wave of information, orders and instructions was now flowing along invisible channels, from top down, to the unit headquarters. Yet if there they could still permit themselves a few hours of rest at night, at the level of the panzer group command, and even more so at the army level command such a luxury had already been forgotten. A great burden rested on the rear support services, since not only the fate of individual combat units, but also that of the offensive as a whole depended on the smoothness and performance of their work.

The command of Panzergruppe 3 was already fully-aware that the headquarters of Heeresgruppe Mitte was in control of the preparations for the offensive, and would be monitoring the completion of assigned tasks. Thus it was clear that units of the panzer group would be expected to continue to hold their previously-seized positions on the Dnepr, while simultaneously attacking to the east, north and south.

At 0930, a telephone rang in the headquarters of Panzergruppe 3; Heeresgruppe Mitte's headquarters was calling in order to express its concerns that the 36. Infanterie-Division (mot.) would not arrive in time to replace the understrength 8. Panzer-Division, and for support it was proposing to use ordinary infantry divisions: 129. Infanterie-Division from the LVI Panzerkorps and 6. Infanterie-Division from the XXXXI Panzerkorps; and at that only at the outset of the operation, since the primary objective remained establishing a bridgehead over the Dnepr River. Thus, the army group command further proposed to coordinate their actions with the 14. Infanterie-Division (mot.) from XXXXI Panzerkorps.[1]

It is necessary to make clear that a conference had taken place back on 22 September in the headquarters of the 129. Infanterie-Division involving the commanders of the division's units, at which it was announced that 4. and 9. Armee were to destroy "Army Group Timoshenko" (actually, I.S. Konev had taken control of the Western Front on 12 September 1941 in place of Timoshenko; it isn't clear why the Germans didn't know about this), for which purpose 9. Armee was to break through the Soviet positions strictly to the east between the roads leading from Dubovshchina and Bor to Belyi. The offensive was generally directed toward Kholm-Zhirkovskii and Bol'shevo, which were located on the Dnepr River; from there it was to advance to an area 30 kilometers southwest of Sychevka, before pivoting to the southeast in the direction of Viaz'ma. Having taken that objective, the offensive would continue to an area northeast of Roslavl' in order to link up with 4. Armee.[2]

While the staff officers of the panzer group dealt with the 6. and 129. Infanterie-Divisionen, by noon the commander of XXXXI Panzerkorps General der Panzertruppen Georg-Hans Reinhardt and the corps' chief of staff Oberst Roettiger had familiarized themselves in detail with the forthcoming tasks, but didn't hurry to confirm the sequence of the corps' shift from Osotnia to Smetishcha, because this would require the cooperation of LVI Panzerkorps. However, its commander and chief of staff had only just left in order to drive to their headquarters' new location in order to conduct their own meeting at 1400.

At 1545, 9. Armee's headquarters called Hoth to express its bewilderment over the fact that his 106. and 129. Infanterie-Divisionen were continuing to push to the east, abandoning the Vop' River on their left, and believed that they must be stopped in order not to weaken the positions of his panzer group, because the assembly area for VIII Armeekorps had been altered. Hoth had not been timely informed of this.

At 1630 a conference began in Panzergruppe 3's headquarters. There, the commander of the 12. Flak-Division Generalmajor Eibenstein and Hoth discussed the possibility of the broader use of the Flak units in ground combat operations, in view of their superiority over the field artillery against Soviet tanks.

Only at 1800 did it become known in the headquarters of 9. Armee that the final command regarding the start time of the offensive would be issued only on the eve of the offensive, but this would complicate final planning with respect to air support, because it would be necessary either to take advantage of the early morning mists when starting the ground offensive, which would prevent air support, or start later, thus enabling air support once the mists had dissipated around 0930 in the morning. Learning of this, Hoth made a request over the telephone to the headquarters of Heeresgruppe Mitte regarding the possibility of being notified about the start time of the offensive not on the evening before D-Day, as was planned, but on the morning of the day prior, and for the announcement to be repeated at noon on the same day. He received the answer that everything would depend on the activity of the Red Army. At the same time, Hoth was informed that with the aim of preserving secrecy, all of the markings on the army's working maps that showed the positions of the forward Armeekorps in fact didn't correspond to their real locations, and accordingly they would not match the daily reports that he would receive from them.

The German Army command considered it improbable the Soviet command would remain unaware of the regrouping for the forthcoming offensive. The Red Army air force became greatly more active after 23 September.

By 2200, 1. Panzer-Division managed to reach Nevel', while 6. Panzer-Division at the same time was already located west of Demidov. The XXXXI Panzerkorps halted in Seleski, directly to the east of Zagoskin, while the LVI Panzerkorps stopped in Konoplianiki southeast of Maetskaia.

There were no further changes in the Panzergruppe 3 for the rest of the day.[3] Of course, to the great joy of 6. Panzer-Division's supply and maintenance chief, a long-awaited batch of spare parts arrived from Smolensk, among which fortunately were spare parts for the "Skoda" Pz. 35(t) tanks that comprised the majority of the division's tanks. This delivery was to be the last, since production of these tanks had ceased even before the start of the war. In the division, there was the understanding that it would be re-equipped with new tanks, but this had been promised only after the loss of the remaining Pz. 35 tanks.[4]

The day was coming to an end, but even with the onset of darkness the Russian artillery continued to conduct fire, and in the sector of VI Armeekorps, its activity even intensified. It seems that the 9. Armee command had legitimate concerns regarding the Soviet side's awareness of the pending offensive.[5]

26 September (Friday)

After the encirclement of the four Soviet armies at Kiev and their month-long resist-ance, by 26 September their remnants laid down their arms and capitulated. In the course of this time period, all the other major operations on the Eastern Front had ceased.[6]

Now the hands of the command of Heeresgruppe Mitte had been freed, and with the arrival of the new day, the commander of 9. Armee Generaloberst Adolf Strauß as his first step confirmed for Hoth the objectives of his panzer group's offensive: "… cut the Viaz'ma – Rzhev railroad and penetrate deeper to the east beyond the Dnepr along the highway to Viaz'ma. Keep the guns silent at the front until the concrete directions of the offensive have been determined, as well as in connection with the fact that the Russians should not be given advance notice of the offensive."[7]

At dawn it was cloudy, but by noon the sun emerged, visibility improved, and the commander of 6. Panzer-Division Generalmajor Landgraf headed out on a reconnaissance trip together with his chief of staff Major Count Kielmansegg.[8] At the same time, the Western Front commander Colonel General Konev reported to Moscow about the results of a conducted reconnaissance, which were indicating that the next German offensive would begin on 1 October, but the *Stavka*, the highest command organ on the Soviet side, didn't take this information seriously. The Soviet leadership didn't believe that the Germans would launch any major operation so soon after the battle for Kiev. It was expecting that the arrival of the seasonal *rasputitsa* with its dissolution of roads into mud would paralyze all move-ment. It still couldn't comprehend that the Germans were capable of moving so quickly, owing to a great degree to their organizational skills. The *Stavka* leaders were underestimating their opponent.

Meanwhile the German command, directed in their turn by the canons of classical military theory, believed that given the presence of only a few hard-surfaced roads in the region west of Moscow, the Red Army would block them as the first order of business, and they correspondingly took this factor as well into their planning.[9]

By 1200 Hoth had reached a preliminary decision that in the sector of his panzer group's offensive 14. Infanterie-Division (mot.) would go on the offensive first. Meanwhile, mobile teams for removing obstacles on the roads had been formed in the march groups of 1. Panzer-Division, thanks to which already by nightfall it was able to reach its assembly area west of Velizh without delays.[10]

In the course of the entire day, Russian artillery continued to shell the entire front of 9. Armee without a pause. In the vicinity of the roadway leading to Kholm-Zhirkovskii, the artillery fire had even increased.[11]

27 September (Saturday)

Overnight, VI Armeekorps had occupied the ground between Lake Chudo and Velizh with all its mobile units.[12] The neighboring 6. Panzer-Division had also fully arrived in its designated sector, but among its personnel, justifications for a return home to Germany already by Christmas had appeared, since in their opinion, the division's old and worn-out equipment, which required constant maintenance and repairs even outside of combat, was simply no longer suitable for lengthy marches. Yet despite the condition of its armored vehicles, the division all the same received an order to launch an offensive on 2 October with Viaz'ma as its ultimate objective. However, given the condition of the division's combat vehicles, it was decided to form a separate panzer brigade under the command of Oberst Koll from 6. and 7. Panzer Divisionen and make it ready for the offensive on this axis. It included their Panzer-Regimenter 11 and 25, Major Aschoff's leichte [light] Artillerie-Batterie 76 and the halftrack-equipped 8./Schützen-Regiment 114. Koll's brigade was given a concrete task; it was to breakthrough to the Dnepr beyond Kokosh' in the direction of Kholm-Zhirkovskii.[13] There were no other changes in the other dispositions of the panzer group's headquarters and units on this day.[14]

The day turned out to be cloudy, but dry; a chilly wind began to blow and the day was cooler. Even though not everything was ready for the offensive, it was risky to delay its launching, because winter was no longer distant. All of the preliminary measures had to be completed as quickly as possible. The flywheel of the offensive's preparations began to unwind even more quickly, because once started, it would be too late to prepare anything else. Thus, already at 0700 an order from 9. Armee command arrived at Panzergruppe 3, requiring 36. Infanterie-Division (mot.) to move out to the north and to arrive in the area of Bor and Liapkino simultaneously with LVI Panzerkorps. Then, if necessary, it was to move out behind 14. Infanterie-Division (mot.) directly toward the city of Belyi.

Three hours later, Hoth flew off to the location of VI Armeekorps, so as to discuss how to use it with its command, but already by noon, a final decision reached him: "Consider 2 October as the start date for the offensive and (if a separate order does not ultimately arrive by the evening of 28 September), Panzergruppe 3 and VIII Armeekorps should be ready by this date, while XXVII Armeekorps must be ready by the next day, except for the group's left wing, which should immediately follow behind the attacking VIII Armeekorps. The XXIII Armeekorps should begin the offensive only upon receipt of a special order from 9. Armee headquarters."[15]

By 1400 all of Panzergruppe 3's units were already waiting for the order regarding the start time of the attack. It was planned to begin the final deployment of the infantry directly into their attack formations simultaneously with the opening of the preparatory artillery fire, which was to continue for just 10-15 minutes. Of course, such a brief artillery barrage conducted directly by the panzer group's own forces might prove inadequate for an immediate attack against the Russian positions; thus, VIII Armeekorps was designated to offer supplementary artillery fire for another 30 minutes, but it was only to open fire at the request of the panzer group command and to cover its units for just this short time.

Everything was proceeding according to plan, and there were not even any hitches in the timetable. However, the appearance of the Soviet air force, especially in such cloudy weather, came as a complete surprise. At 1500, units of the panzer group that were located in Prechistaia came under an attack by bombers that were flying at an extremely low altitude due to the low layer of clouds. The anti-aircraft gunners were having a meal, and thus didn't have time to react; the first bombs struck their positions and knocked out the anti-aircraft defenses. Immediately following this, the main bombing attack targeted the supply dumps, where a portion of the food stores was completely destroyed. This event slightly disheartened the command of Panzergruppe 3. However, they took solace from the unpleasant attack at a phone call from 9. Armee headquarters at 1550, which informed them that the 36. Infanterie-Division (mot.) had already arrived in Opochka, and that it would move from there in the direction of Nevel', which it expected to reach by the next day.

At the next meeting, which took place at 1630 in the headquarters of Panzergruppe 3 and included the commander of 9. Armee Generaloberst Adolf Strauß and the commanders of the V and VI Armeekorps, the issue of the complete lack of readiness of the full 1./Panzerjäger-Abteilung 8 to offer support to the tanks arose, in connection with which even the question of cancelling the code signal for the offensive for the entire panzer group was discussed.

In its wake there followed a report from Reinhardt, the commander of XXXXI Panzerkorps, that his units, even with tracked transport, were still making slow progress toward Vitebsk, and thus the concern arose that the deployment plan was falling behind schedule. However at 1900 there arrived another report that it had nonetheless arrived in time, and that the 36. Infanterie-Division (mot.) had already been dispatched to the distant Bazary – Toropets area, which in turn came as a surprise to the 9. Armee command. However, it made no attempt to block this move.

It was initially assumed that the XXIII Armeekorps would serve as 9. Armee's reserve; however, on the basis of arriving intelligence reports, there was an increased concentration of Red Army units in the vicinity of a dock on the Semets River, which argued for the need to pull the corps out of the reserve and to employ it in the offensive. Agreement for this move was received, but Hoth was ordered nevertheless to set aside one motorized division from the offensive and to keep it for defensive purposes.

At 2200, confirmation arrived in all the units from headquarters of 9. Armee that the offensive would begin on 2 October, but it was clarified that the start hour for the offensive would be earlier than planned. By this time, all of 1. Panzer-Division's wheeled vehicles had arrived at the designated place of assembly.[16]

As on the day before, Soviet artillery conducted constant fire throughout the day in the sector of 9. Armee's prepared offensive. Toward the evening, it became even livelier.[17]

September 28 (Sunday)

The weather was as before favorable. Partial cloudiness and the lack of rain made the roads dry and passable, albeit dusty.

At 0930 Hoth over the telephone requested 9. Armee headquarters not to rush with the use of the 36. Infanterie-Division (mot.) from XXIII Armeekorps, but instead proposed to create a reserve out of the 14. and 36. Infanterie-Divisionen (mot.) in order to support XXXXI Panzerkorps on the army's northern wing while keeping the entire 14. Infanterie-Division (mot.) in reserve. For this Hoth also proposed shifting the 14. Infanterie-Division (mot.) to join with 1. Panzer-Division. Satisfied with this discussion, he flew off to the 129. Infanterie-Division. However, despite even his written objections, it was decided by 9. Armee headquarters to subordinate 36. Infanterie-Division (mot.) to the XXXXI Panzerkorps, and to hold 14. Infanterie-Division (mot.) in its current area.

The quality and trafficability of the roads were not sufficient to hasten the movement of troops and rear services, and therefore in the shortest amount of time, a special railroad was laid down parallel to the Maetskaia – Prechistaia – Bor road, over which units of the VI Armeekorps consisting of the 6., 26. and 110. Infanterie-Divisionen began to move, thus no longer hindering the established timetable of shipments and movement of the panzer group. The 5., 35., 106. and 129. Infanterie-Divisionen were added to the roster of V Armeekorps. The 161. Infanterie-Division was transferred to the army reserve.

Simultaneously, the final meeting took place in Velizh with the participation of representatives of the VIII Fliegerkorps regarding air support for the offensive, at which it was separately stipulated that this meeting among representatives of the army, the panzer group and the Luftwaffe's corps would be the last one prior to 29 September. Here, it was first brought to the attention of the air corps that 2 October had been designated as the start date for the offensive. The march of the panzer divisions into their final jumping-off lines would begin on 29 September, but 7. Panzer-Division had already set off on its march that day.

While the meeting was taking place, Soviet air raids began at 1400. The rear elements of the panzer group in Ripshevo were subjected to attack in two of the five raids by seven low-flying aircraft with bombs and on-board machine guns. Bombs were also dropped on other of the group's dispositions. The plane that had delivered the commander of the VIII Fliegerkorps to the meeting received slight damage. In 7. Panzer-Division, three men of Panzer-Regiment 3 were killed. However, on this occasion the air raid was not such a surprise, and two Soviet aircraft were shot down over Prechistaia by the fire of VI Armeekorps' anti-aircraft artillery. As a result of this airstrike, and indeed in connection with the growing activity of the Soviet air force, concerns arose within the 9. Armee command that the presence of German units even in Vitebsk might be revealed during a bombing raid.[18]

In the afternoon, the commander of 6. Panzer-Division General Landgraf issued assignments to Panzer-Regimenter 11 and 25 and separately to the commander of Panzer-Regiment 11 Major Löwe, who would be first to launch the attack. In 6. Panzer-Division's journal of combat operations it was written that Landgraf emphasized: "Responsibility for the further success of Heeresgruppe Mitte's offensive rests upon the forward divisions of Panzergruppe 3. Crossings on the Dnepr River have been set as the initial objective, and then only forward, since the main task remains the speediest possible destruction of 'Army Group Timoshenko', in connection with which the units and elements have been informed of the undesirability of being drawn into frequent, prolonged battles."[19]

Despite the activity of the Soviet air force, the movement of the units of 9. Armee that had been designated to participate in the offensive was not interrupted. In the afternoon, even special units were detached from the LVI Panzerkorps to assist with the overall process of deployment. For example, at two stages of the process 1. Panzer-Division was offered equipment for transporting its tanks. Tracked vehicles had already arrived according to an analogous order from 6. Panzer-Division. Meanwhile, the 36. Infanterie-Division (mot.) still remained in Nevel'.

Toward the end of the day, the units of the Red Army opposing Panzergruppe 3 noticeably increased their activity; constant artillery fire and small arms' fire came from their side. Fire and the shifting of Soviet units opposite the group's right wing became particularly noticeable.

According to German intelligence, the Red Army were assembling a large force opposite the center of V Armeekorps' front, and this also became perceptible in the density of the fire being conducted. On the front of VI Armeekorps, however, the situation was opposite; Soviet fire was rather light and the positions of the Soviet units were unchanged.[20]

By the end of the day, the command posts of Panzergruppe 3 and of the XXXXI and LVI Panzerkorps had still not changed their locations. However, the command post of V Armeekorps had moved to Diablovo, and that of the VI Armeekorps to Dubovitsa.[21]

In Moscow, they were still expecting renewed German activity only with the onset of winter. Therefore Konev, having received this information from the *Stavka*, decided to adopt a rigid defense, which subsequently in fact allowed the Germans to encircle the Soviet Western, Briansk and Reserve Fronts. Receiving such guidance, in the headquarters of Western Front they had no inkling that Operation Typhoon would come in two stages: first, the penetration of the front and the encirclement of the Russian forces in front of Moscow; and then, just as before, to crush the remaining armies in tank battles. After these concluded, Moscow was supposed to fall into the hands of the victor like a ripe apple. It was planned to conclude the first stage by mid-October and to seize Moscow already by the beginning of November. Plainly therefore Panzergruppen 2, 3 and 4 were counting on celebrating Christmas already on the Volga.[22]

29 September (Monday)

The morning brought no other substantial changes. The weather hadn't changed, but it was perceptibly warmer. In Panzergruppe 3, since yesterday evening and all through the night, depending on the behavior of the Russians, a stealthy regrouping of units and the issuing of orders to them had been in process. The VI Armeekorps was ordered to advance toward Etkino with the aim of a future envelopment of Belyi from the north.[23]

The commander of 129. Infanterie-Division Generalmajor Rittau ordered his Infanterie-Regiment 427 to attack in three waves and the regiment's I. and II. Bataillon had spent the night preparing once again for an offensive. North of the division, Schützen-Regiment 18 of the 6. Panzer-Division was to attack, which had been attached to 1. Panzer- Division for the start of the offensive.

The regiment took up a position in the woods northwest of Ershovo, with the task to break into the Russians' positions, seize the heights around Zhidkii, and subsequently those northeast of Dolgoe, and having crossed the Dnepr River at Osomen'e, it was to cut the Konnoe – Liubashino road. To the north of the regiment's sector of attack between Shelepy and Ershovo, the direction was being secured only by a motorized battalion of 1. Panzer-Division. It was assumed that in the event of a threat to the left flank, the regiment's breakthrough beyond Shelepy wouldn't be endangered thanks to its echeloned formation. It had been promised that artillery would support the seizure of the flanking Hill 220 1 kilometer west-southwest of Zhidkii by 1. Panzer-Division. It was clear that the success of this attack was important not only for the regiment itself, but also in general for 1. and 7. Panzer-Divisionen. Already in the morning, the headquarters of Infanterie-Regiment 427 had relocated into a ravine south of Retka, in order to be closer to the action.[24]

By 1100 the commanders of 1. and 6. Panzer-Divisionen had gathered in Semtsovo and Demidova, after which they decided nevertheless to discuss the desires of Panzergruppe 3 for air support with the VIII Fliegerkorps, for which purpose they made a special trip to Velizh. This time, the concrete requests of the panzer units for support of their units from the air during the offensive were given.[25]

At the direction of the 9. Armee commander, Hoth at 1230 informed the commander of LVI Panzerkorps over the telephone that one and a half hours before the start of his offensive, it had been planned for V Armeekorps to make a local attack east of his area of assembly. Thus, the LVI Panzerkorps, having launched the offensive with the Infanterie-Regiment 430 of the 129. Infanterie-Division 30 minutes after the start of V Armeekorps' attack, would secure the latter's flank from a counterattack, which would ensue according to all the canons of classical military theory. In case of the emergence of a threat to V Armeekorps' left flank, where 35. Infanterie-Division was located, the LVI Panzerkorps would step off earlier.[26]

However, Hoth was assessing the Red Army differently than the commanders of his subordinate divisions. He didn't believe there were strong reserves in the depth of the Russian defenses, and thus recommended to the commander of Infanterie-Regiment 430 to start the attack simultaneously with the tanks; however, at the same time he advised caution, because there were no longer any reserves behind Panzergruppe 3.

In the middle of the day, Oberleutnant Pollex of Panzergruppe 3's operations department made the command of 9. Armee aware of Panzergruppe 3's readiness on the Viaz'ma axis and on the availability of up to 1,000 tons of fuel, though even 500 tons would be adequate to be ready within an hour's time. Thus, on 1 October all the divisions of the panzer group had up to 5-7 refills of fuel. Food provisions were also adequate.

The developing situation was so encouraging that 9. Armee's quartermaster was recommending the postponement of the issuance of winter clothing (with the exception of sweaters) until the operation's completion, because at the given moment this wasn't urgent and might have an adverse effect on the realization of the issued orders. The distribution of winter gear would require time and bring about a postponement of the offensive.

At 1400 the units of Panzergruppe 3, which were now stood ready for the offensive, were issued a written order, which directed that XXXXI Panzerkorps' 36. Infanterie-Division (mot.) would step off on the offensive first.

Having returned at 1730 (Berlin time) from 9. Armee headquarters, Hoth informed his staff officers that at his recommendation, the start time for the offensive had been set for 0600 in the morning, but he was upset because the Luftwaffe wouldn't be able to take part, albeit temporarily, because VIII Fliegerkorps was promising to be ready only by 0700. It was supposed to inform about its readiness 6 hours before the start of the offensive.

The day was coming to an end without any more unpleasant news, when suddenly, at 2230 it was unexpectedly made clear that 14. Infanterie-Division (mot.) on the northern wing wasn't ready for the offensive, while once again the Russian artillery had opened up a lively and heavy artillery fire along the entire front of V Armeekorps. In addition, at midnight Soviet infantry again became active in the center of the corps' position. Artillery fire also intensified against the positions of 26. Infanterie-Division.

However, opposite 6. Infanterie-Division, the Soviet infantry's activity was low as before, but constant harassing fire of field artillery was falling, supplemented by small-arms fire. In the course of the day, and especially with the onset of darkness, German observers were noting greater activity of Russian infantry and aircraft on the entire front opposite XXXXI Panzerkorps.

By the end of the day, all of the tracked vehicles of 36. Infanterie-Division (mot.) were fully assembled in Velizh, and all of its streets were jammed. The 6. Panzer-Division had assembled south of Ripshevo; 7. Panzer-Division with its attached units was in the Prechistaia area, while 1. Panzer-Division was still in its former location.

The command posts of other units had still not changed their position. Deployment for the offensive was continuing.[27]

30 September (Tuesday)

Even on this day, the weather didn't betray the Germans. Although it was cloudy, just as before it was warm, the roads were dry and their trafficability fine. Over the preceding night, 5. and 35. Infanterie-Divisionen had finally taken up their sectors for the offensive and were waiting for the order to attack.

At 1030, Generalfeldmarschall Kesselring and the commander of VIII Fliegerkorps arrived at Panzergruppe 3 headquarters. Hoth confirmed the objective and his group's schedule of actions and raised questions regarding VIII Fliegerkorps' support, because lacking this support, problems would arise for the ground units, which would inevitably entail the loss of time and excessive casualties. He stressed the particular importance of covering the northern flank, as well as protection of Kokosh' and the bridges across the Vop' River. He had been promised the support of Luftflotte 2 and VIII Fliegerkorps. True, the first air strike was planned to arrive not until 15 minutes after the start of the offensive due to the thick early morning fog, which wouldn't dissipate until after sunrise. Accordingly, the offensive's start time was postponed by 15 minutes. No one could say how the Russians would react. So the decision was taken to begin with an artillery preparation in the fog, and from 0615 wait upon the appearance of the Luftwaffe for the attack, despite the fog. In connection with this, Kesselring recalled only that "airstrikes had been planned primarily along the roads, in order to prevent counterattacks against the center of the front, and targets for a raid against the airbase in Belyi had been selected."[28] He was basing his stance on the fact that all of VIII Fliegerkorps hadn't yet arrived from the northern front, and thus the attacking units would have to rely primarily on their own fire support, accompanied only by Ju-87 Stuka dive bombers. For his part, Hoth was insisting that "the situation of his units on the Dnepr was excellent; given full Luftwaffe support, everything would go well."[29] In the end, Kesselring's position for more limited support was accepted. He had no spare aircraft to do anything more.

After the meeting ended, in a telephone conversation at 1115 with the headquarters of Heeresgruppe Mitte, Hoth declared that he was awaiting the start of the offensive with some unease, but that he was nevertheless fully confident of the outcome, because never before had a panzer group started with so many tanks concentrated in such a narrow sector. He was anxious only because of the possibility of the threat of a counterattack from the north into his rear, just as the panzer group was pushing to the east, and he'd been given only the 26. and 110. Infanterie-Divisionen as rear security. The army group command rationalized this by the fact that in this area, the Dnepr turns to the south and would provide an excellent natural obstacle to any Soviet flank attack.

The situation was favorable for XXIII Armeekorps to conduct a strong demonstration attack, and the headquarters of 9. Armee expressed its agreement with

Hoth's intentions to make it. However, despite the fact that XXIII Armeekorps had nothing more in the way of artillery to offer other than its available mortars, the 161. Infanterie-Division was given the mission to make an attempt to enter Belyi with the support of tanks. For additional support, an infantry regiment from *Grossdeutschland* was activated by a special order.

At 1200, a message arrived from the panzer group's quartermaster, which revealed that in the Nebelwerfer regiment, there were only enough shells for 15-16 salvoes. In the rest of the group, the resupply of units and elements was going according to plan, although from some units there were wishes for an improvement in the quality of the rations.

At 1335, the commander of Heeresgruppe Mitte personally confirmed to Hoth over the phone that the artillery of XXXI Panzerkorps' training brigade was ready to make the first attack, but with his next phone call at 1700 (Berlin time) he directed: "14. Infanterie-Division (mot.) already today is to be prepared to march to the Il'ino area, but it is to release a certain portion of the troops from participation in the offensive in order to combat partisans; this prompted alarm in view of the uncertain schedule of replacements."[30]

At 2130, Hoth requested two more light artillery battalions of the 14. Infanterie-Division (mot.) from the 9. Armee commander in order to support the initial attack of the XXXXI Panzerkorps; his request was granted. However, despite the fact V and VI Armeekorps were weak in artillery, on the northern wing of V Armeekorps tasks were set to seize Russian positions.

As if having premonitions of the approaching catastrophe, throughout the day the Soviet air force was rather active, even more so than on the preceding days[31], and in the afternoon low-flying Soviet aircraft struck the headquarters of 6. Panzer-Division in Vorosovo and the positions of the division's Artillerie-Regiment 76, leaving one man killed and four wounded in the artillery regiment.[32]

In the course of the day, the Soviet artillery subjected the units of XXVII Armeekorps in their jumping-off positions to a heavy artillery barrage. At the end of the day, an unexpected report arrived in the headquarters of Heeresgruppe Mitte based on VIII Fliegerkorps' aerial reconnaissance, which revealed "the movement of a large amount of Russian artillery 45 kilometers west of Viaz'ma"[33], followed a little later by another report: "In the course of the day it has also been established by reconnaissance and observation that constant visual surveillance over the units of Panzergruppe 3 is being conducted by the Russian side."[34] There could no longer be any doubts that the offensive was no longer a secret.

3

The Wehrmacht Strikes

1 October (Wednesday)

From the morning onward, the sun again peeked out between patches of clouds. It was still warm, and hopes appeared in the attacking German units that the road conditions would improve even more.[1]

Since the evening before, 129. Infanterie-Division had become subordinate to LVI Panzerkorps, while 6. Infanterie-Division was attached to the XXXXI Panzerkorps. In the early morning hours of 1 October, 36. Infanterie-Division (mot.) began moving up into its jumping-off position.

A message was received in the headquarters of the Panzergruppe 3 that Nebelwerfer-Regiment 51's Nebelwerfer-Batterie 111 would arrive from 16. Armee within 2-3 days and would become available to XXXXI Panzerkorps in order to support its own tank attack. One of the two sections of rocket launchers had been transferred to LVI Panzerkorps and was already in its firing positions. Considering that the relocation of the rocket launchers could be implemented only at night, they still hadn't arrived in the XXXXI Panzerkorps.[2]

A Luftwaffe liaison officer, Leutnant Papenberg, who arrived at the headquarters of 6. Panzer-Division that morning, announced that "one squadron of Ju-87 dive bombers, two squadrons of fighters, and up to two squadrons of fighter-bombers had been allocated for Panzergruppe 3 for all of its four shock groups. Their first objective had been set for them – the Dnepr River 100 kilometers to the east of Kholm-Zhirkovskii."[3]

From 1100 units of XXXXI Panzerkorps headed into their jumping-off positions along the Dnepr in order to prepare for the offensive, and already at 1200 the corps commander General Reinhardt began to coordinate over the telephone with the command of LVI Panzerkorps, since his Nebelwerfer battery[4] still hadn't deployed; moreover, at this time, LVI Panzerkorps was still on the march.

At 1700 the commander of V Armeekorps reported to the panzer group's headquarters that VIII Armeekorps hadn't yet arrived on his right flank, and he was expecting it after 0600, and this might create a threat to his right wing. However after a number of queries to 9. Armee headquarters, the concerns disappeared, because it became clear that VIII Armeekorps would still be able to arrive by the set start time for the offensive.

In the course of the day, the Soviet artillery kept up a lively fire, more intense than on the preceding days, along the entire front of the panzer group, with the exception of 110. Infanterie-Division's sector. The artillerymen of XXXXI Panzerkorps, which had just managed to set up in their new positions, were partially suppressed by the Soviet artillery fire. There were no signs of a lull on the Soviet side. Because of this artillery barrage, delays began to arise in the deployment of the 14. Infanterie-Division (mot.) because of disrupted lateral movements of the units.

During the evening, the forthcoming missions of the VIII Fliegerkorps' units began to be planned, which would be issued to them only that night. Primarily, the overall plan involved attacks upon the headquarter locations of Red Army units; troop positions in Belyi and Kholm-Zhirkovskii; the airbase in Rzhev; and artillery positions in Krapivna, Baturino and Kopyrivshchina. In addition, direct cooperation with 6. Panzer-Division and its support from the air were specified. Fighters and "free hunters" were to oppose the Soviet air force in the areas of Korytna, Kholm-Zhirkovskii and Belyi and to cover the German forces attacking on this axis.[5]

Both sides were preparing for the clash. The offensive's engine had already been started by the German command, and there was now no way of stopping it. There remained only to wait for its outcome. The Wehrmacht was waiting, as was the Red Army.

Just a single night remained before the start of the offensive, and no one could say how the morning would be or what it would bring. By the end of the day, both sides had completed all of their preparations. The Germans had prepared for an offense; the Russians, for the defense.

2 October (Thursday)

Panzergruppe 3 was putting the final touches on its preparations, and by 0100 all its corps reported to headquarters on the completion of their deployment. On this final night, there were surprisingly few exchanges of fire between the opposing sides. Soviet artillery primarily targeted the position of 26. Infanterie-Division. Everything froze in expectation, as if having an omen of something bad. The echoes of a distant cannonade carried from the south, and the flashes of distant explosions were visible on the southern horizon; somewhere, death had already started its harvest. Only later did it become revealed that Operation Typhoon had already begun; Guderian had put it in motion with his Panzergruppe 2. However, in the sectors of Panzergruppe 3 and 4, it was still relatively calm. Morning was approaching. The command staff of 9. Armee and Panzergruppe 3 were counting upon an improvement in the autumn weather by morning, so that the offensive could still begin with Luftwaffe support. Their hopes were not betrayed; the morning proved to be sunny with a few patchy clouds. In fact, for the rest of the day the sky remained clear and sunny, and the temperature rose to 10 C. [50 F.].[6]

At midnight, reports arrived in the headquarters of 129. Infanterie-Division from its subordinate regiments. The infantry and field artillery of Infanterie-Regiment 427 were ready, as had been foreseen. Earlier that evening [1 October], the regimental command post had relocated into a ravine 800 meters southwest of the Shelepy heights, where prior to this the headquarters of the regiment's II. Bataillon had been located. That same evening, the regiment had been given Pionier-Battalion 2, which immediately set to work clearing passages in the minefields. Everything was ready for the attack. In the sector occupied by the division, the typical schedule of fire had been maintained that night, and routine patrols sent out. On the Soviet side as well, no changes had been identified.[7]

As of the evening before, the personnel of the Red Army's 119th Rifle Division, which had still not received their combat baptism, and the labor battalions that had been attached to the division, numbering approximately 5,000 people, had finished work on the fortified area that the division was defending. There, it began its combat path and on this same day of 1 October 1941, it had become part of the 29th Army.

The division was a regular one and had formed up back in 1939 in the city of Krasnogorsk, on the basis of the remaining elements and materiel of the 94th Rifle Division, which had then departed for Mongolia, where it remained as part of the Siberian Military District until the start of the war. From 1939, regular army commanders Major General A.D. Berezin and his chief of staff Colonel M.I. Shchedrin had commanded the 119th Rifle Division.[8]

Although the division was located in the second echelon, it was fully-armed and ready to meet the enemy. True, this would happen only on 8 October, and jumping ahead, I want to inform the reader that it avoided encirclement and destruction. It conducted a fighting withdrawal, preserving its combat formations and inflicting damage upon the enemy. Its commander A.D. Berezin would later be killed in combat in July 1942, but this is a very different story and we will return to this division several days later in our narrative. Let's now return to the morning of 2 October 1941.

As if in anticipation, a half-hour before the start of the German offensive Soviet artillery opened a heavy fire with 122-mm and 152-mm howitzers along the entire sector of 9. Armee, which proved rather unpleasant for the Germans. The Soviet artillery operated most actively against IX Armeekorps of Günther von Kluge's 4. Armee, and there it became even necessary to open observed counterbattery fire, corrected by an aerial spotter.[9] Yet at 0600, the artillery fire transitioned to a general artillery preparation against the Soviet positions, which began according to plan on the entire front of 9. Armee.

The early morning fog that blanketed the ground gradually dissipated. With the sunrise, 196 German heavy-caliber guns opened fire and sustained it for 15 minutes, after which the rocket launchers fired several salvoes. The aircraft of VIII Fliegerkorps were already in the air.

During the artillery preparation, in the 129. Infanterie-Division, pioneers of the assault companies of Infanterie-Regiment 427 continued their work. Despite the suppressing artillery preparation that had taken place, which after 15 minutes gave way to aerial bombing runs, the Soviet positions proved to be unsuppressed, and after Infanterie-Regiment 427 went on the offensive, the Russian artillery responded with heavy fire, which resulted in serious losses, particularly in the second and third attacking waves. The fog, smoke and rising sun was seriously hindering observation, even though the German and Soviet positions were separated by just 80 meters.

The soldiers of I./Infanterie-Regiment 427, which were assaulting the Soviet defenses atop Hill 220 north of Staro-Selo, encountered diligently prepared positions and camouflaged bunkers, in which, as later became clear, the commanders and soldiers of the 720th Rifle Regiment were continuing to defend stubbornly, despite the German artillery fire. Its positions were superbly equipped with barbed wire obstacles and covered with minefields deep in the defense's depth, and together with several dug-in tanks they inflicted significant losses in personnel, horses and arms on the attackers. The German attack from the march was a failure and further frontal assaults were halted; in order to avoid excessive casualties, the decision was made simply to encircle the defenders. The II./Infanterie-Regiment pivoted in that direction as reinforcement, while I Bataillon closed the ring on its eastern side, isolating the defenders and blocking their retreat.

Despite this, one separately encircled forward Soviet earth-and-timber bunker continued to hold out stubbornly. As soon as fire from it finally ceased (plainly, the defenders' ammunition had been exhausted), the Germans that entered it discovered no one left alive. It isn't possible to ascertain who was carrying out their oath to the end, since none of the documents on the Soviet side were preserved, while the Germans kept records only on the division level and higher, where even there, only this scant information was uncovered.[10]

Even though these positions were in fact taken by II./Infanterie-Regiment 427 before 0800, this was only after the use of Nebelwerfer rocket launchers, as a consequence of which those defending there suffered particularly heavy casualties. After a short hand-to-hand struggle, a small portion of the Red Army defenders that remained alive succeeded in breaking out to the east through tenacious hand-to-hand and bayonet combat. However, not everyone was lucky; the larger portion of the survivors, the majority of which were wounded, were taken prisoner. The Luftwaffe played no role in this action, since the dive bombers had been directed to suppress the Red Army's rear positions, which the 129. Infanterie-Division still had yet to take.[11] The successful breakthrough and the further development of the attack prompted the commander of Infanterie-Regiment 427 Oberst Danhauser to shift II./Artillerie-Regiment 129 to new positions in the area east of Shelepy.

Following the effective artillery support, 7. Panzer-Division went on the attack at 0615 with one panzer regiment at the Kokosh' and Vop' Rivers. However, before the panzers went into motion, the 129. Infanterie-Division was supposed to throw the Russians' forward positions back beyond the Kokosh' River and to reach the Vop' River.

In the first stage of the offensive, 7. Panzer-Division had been given the primary mission to prevent a counterattack by units of the Red Army and to prevent them from regaining their lost positions on the Dnepr River. The 6. Panzer-Division was attacking on its right, the 1. Panzer-Division on its left. The latter not long before the start of the operation had been hastily transferred from a point near Leningrad in order to reinforce Panzergruppe 3.[12] The 1. Panzer-Division had also begun to attack at 0615 after a powerful, 25-minute artillery barrage and the salvoes of rocket launchers that followed it.[13] After the very first attack, Leutnant Krefft of 6. Panzer-Division's Artillerie-Regiment 76 jotted in his diary: "With the fire, our artillery and rocket launchers are sowing death in the ranks of the foe, which has been caught by surprise. The enemy is conducting counter fire. The next wave of our bombers and dive bombers is approaching." This first attack cost the division only 2 men killed and 8 wounded, but in return 500 prisoners were taken, as well as six guns and five tanks that were abandoned undamaged.[14]

After 10-15 minutes of artillery fire, the German infantry had totally ruptured the Soviet defenses in the entire sector of the offensive's *schwerpunkt*. Only insignificant forces were offering resistance. Within 20 minutes from the start of the offensive, 106. Infanterie-Division was already 500 meters east of the village of Staro-Selo, 335. Infanterie-Division was 300 meters east of Gorodno, while 6. Infanterie-Division had even reached the eastern edge of the swamp in the area, having ruptured the Soviet defense from the march.[15]

The first fragmentary reports began to arrive in the headquarters of Panzergruppe 3 that Kotovo had been taken by the 26. Infanterie-Division at 0705, and 45 minutes later the commander of LVI Panzerkorps reported that "the Russians are trying to place strong blocking fire with their artillery on our jumping-off positions, but were too late, because no one was any longer there."[16]

By this time 106. Infanterie-Division had passed through Morozovo; Pochinok had been taken by XXXXI Panzerkorps, and a bit earlier, back at 0715, the arriving tanks of the panzer corps had also seized a bridgehead in Morozovo. Having reported the seizure of Hill 220 east of Shelepy, the 129. Infanterie-Division, without stopping, next took Sechenki from the march. On the basis of the intelligence coming into the headquarters of the units and formations of Heeresgruppe Mitte, an alarming question began to arise: "Were the Russians retreating to the east or not?"[17]

About this same time, 129. Infanterie-Division lost contact with its Infanterie-Regiment 428, which at the decision of its headquarters had diverged from the left because of strong resistance and had unexpectedly wound up on the division's right. As a result of this, the left flank of Infanterie-Regiment 427 remained exposed, and the regiment was seriously suffering from Soviet artillery fire from a hill near Zhidkii. Nevertheless, its regiment commander Oberst Danhauser ordered: "Absent flank formations and contact [with neighbors], exploit the success and continue the offensive in the direction of Hill 220 in Gulievo."[18]

At 0815 the seizure of a bridgehead on the northern bank of the Osmiaia River began with elements of Hauptmann Wittman's II./Infanterie-Regiment 427, consisting of Leutnant Bormann's bicycle company, reinforced with an assault gun, two combat engineer groups and a platoon of field artillery. For this Wittman reinforced 2. Kompanie so that with its help after the seizure of the hill in Gulievo he might make a rapid advance south of the bridge in Lukshino to the northern bank of the Osmiaia, and from there advance through the river valley south of the line Lukshino – Smetishche to take and hold the bridge north of Sonino. Then, despite increasing resistance, Wittman intended to double back and take the bridge in Lukshino, hold it, and do everything possible to organize a bridgehead now on the southern bank.

This decision initially to bypass the bridge in Lukshino led to one hitch in the German offensive. Everything went smoothly until the battalion with its attached elements pivoted toward Lukshino, where it ran into strong resistance at the bridge that they were supposed to take. By this time, regimental pioneers under the command of Leutnant Frank, with the support of the assault gun and the regimental artillery, were already to have removed demolition charges on the bridge, but it still hadn't been seized. The defenders at the bridge were strong in number, yet use of the assault gun and artillery had been forbidden due to other matters. Leutnant Bormann ordered a halt to the bicycle company's advance and established observation over the river opposite Smetishche, now in the sector of the 1. Panzer-Division's offensive.

The 1. Panzer-Division, which was attacking on the left, initially ran into problems as well, because it could advance only by using a dam across the Osmiaia River directly to the southeast of Smetishche. Von Hey's shock group of the division also required special support, in order to clear a path across the causeway to the northeast, but it had been promised no earlier than 1100.

By this time, Infanterie-Regiment 427 had seized a passage to Efremovo; thus the city of Kholm-Zhirkovskii on the Dnepr River was set as the mutual objective for the 129. Infanterie-Division and 7. Panzer-Division. Meanwhile, II./Infanterie-Regiment 427, staggered to the left, had penetrated deeply to the east and was attacking toward Hill 220 in Gulievo. All available small arms, heavy caliber machine guns, heavy 120-mm mortars, field guns and a platoon of heavy 150-mm infantry support guns (two such guns) were committed into the battle, as a result of which the resistance of the defenders was rather quickly broken and the hill was taken.

The regiment's headquarters relocated to the seized hilltop. Its III. Bataillon was combing through the woods east of Fochino; I. Bataillon radioed about the position of Wittmann's II. Bataillon on the northern bank of the Osmiaia River beyond Smetishche, and since he with his 5. Kompanie was a little north of I. Bataillon, the regiment command agreed to a crossing of the causeway east of Smetishche with his battalion, which was necessary in the emerging situation.[19]

Bitter fighting developed in the vicinity of Otria, where the Red Army's 244th Rifle Division was opposing 35. Infanterie-Division. In a message, the Germans succinctly wrote: "The Russian infantry is defending fiercely, but their artillery fire, directed against the eastern outskirts of Otria, which has been taken by us, is relatively light."[20]

Unfortunately, such a knot of resistance couldn't stop the tidal wave of the German offensive. The Red Army's defenses were not continuous and were based on isolated strong points, which the Germans sought to avoid assaulting with frontal attacks; wherever flashpoints of resistance appeared, they simply bypassed them, leaving the defenders in encirclement. Thus, the seizure of Borki by VI Armeekorps was praised by the Panzergruppe 3 command, and in its wake, the 26. Infanterie-Division took Ostrye Luki at 0845. Reports from the corps were expected at 0830, but it was known already that its 110. Infanterie-Division with one regiment was already in Mezha and had simultaneously seized Stolby.

Although the offensive was in fact developing mostly according to plan, even after the analysis of the first reports it still wasn't clear whether the main forces of the Red Army were opposing them or only rear guard detachments. After all, from the beginning the entire plan of the German offensive was based upon the encirclement and destruction of the main forces opposing them.

At 0905 the next report arrived from 129. Infanterie-Division, informing that its Infanterie-Regiment 430 had taken the hill south of Gordeenka. Its flanks were being secured by the 6. and 7. Panzer-Divisionen. The division command had the impression that this time the Russians had retreated immediately after the first attack.[21]

At this same time Koll's panzer brigade went on the offensive with its forward detachment, and 45 minutes later Generalmajor Raus's infantry brigade linked up with it and moved on in the wake of the tanks. In his summary account, Leutnant Krefft of the headquarters of 6. Panzer-Division's Artillerie-Regiment 76 noted: "A roaring and howling filled the air. It was impossible conceive of anything better than the sight of hundreds of tanks before your eyes; the scene was unique in its scale, and the soldier's eyes had never seen anything more impressive."[22]

Major Aschoff was located in his command tank in the first wave of the panzer attack, in order to have the possibility to control the actions of his attacking elements. His first attack was repulsed. Later, in his account Aschoff wrote:

> We succeeded in breaking into the Russian positions only on the second attempt, and this time with the support of infantry, since most of the tanks were lightly armored. Indeed, the terrain wasn't helpful for an offensive, since it was barely passable because of the numerous swamps and hillocks, and in addition to maps, only the remains of tanks, destroyed trucks, abandoned weapons of all types, the corpses of people and animals and smashed fortifications could serve as a guide marker.[23]

According to intelligence already obtained from prisoners by this time, the commander of V Armeekorps decided that the Red Army's defensive line to the west of the Votria River had been breached. Moreover, at this time they had received intercepted Russian radio messages: "There are no reinforcements, hold the positions?", "I have assumed command, the commander has been killed.", and "There is no possibility to hold on, the portable transmitter has been destroyed." All signs of the consequences of a powerful offensive were evident.

In the opinion of the corps command, the Soviet artillery fire had slackened, because it was under strong pressure from German artillery fire; in addition, as soon as German aircraft appeared overhead, the Russian guns fell virtually silent.

However, despite the overall successful advance of V Armeekorps, its right wing back at the start of the offensive had become bogged down because of minefields and vertically embedded log posts, as well as mortar fire from the south. But on the whole the corps made headway and maintained its direction of advance, thus this ground as well had already been taken back at 0730 in conjunction with the northern flank of VIII Armeekorps.[24]

By 0930 the first prisoners taken by VI Armeekorps were saying that back on 29 and 30 September, the withdrawal of combat-capable units from the front had been conducted in order to defend the city of Belyi. However, despite this, the units that remained in their positions were continuing to offer stubborn resistance.

The 35. Infanterie-Division back at 0900, leaving the village of Shukovo behind on its left, had advanced to the Votria River. Units of the 5. and 35. Infanterie-Divisionen were moving like a water current, flowing around knots of resistance. According to intelligence, the German panzer units should anticipate the next opposition at the Vop' River.

Since 0930, after taking Dobrosel'e, 35. Infanterie-Division had been advancing directly to the east without encountering any Soviet units, and the Panzergruppe 3 command was hoping that this would continue. In the headquarters of the panzer group, reports had begun to arrive about the detection of disorganized columns of retreating Russians, which normally signifies a general retreat. However, it was still too early to say whether the Russian rear guards were falling back with the main forces. According to one of the reports, by this time units of VIII Armeekorps had taken Losevo.

In the V Armeekorps' sector, the advance by 106. Infanterie-Division slowed in the area of Kudinovo at 0930, where the infantry had been held up by wooden obstacles on the line Shatuny – south of Gunino. However, despite this, the division's main forces already by 1000 took Markovo and continued to advance further without stopping. The 35. Infanterie-Division was continuing to push toward Karpovo, leaving behind volunteers from among its number of Hiwi volunteers to the left of itself in Il'ino.[25]

A bit before this, back at 0945, 129. Infanterie-Division's II./Infanterie-Regiment 427 had reached the Mikhailovshchina – Glievo road, but already just 5 minutes later the battalion bumped up against a causeway almost simultaneously with the tanks. South of it, 5./I./Infanterie-Regiment 427 was initially checked when Soviet sappers managed to blow up part of the causeway there, but after a quick inspection Leutnant Frank reported that the damage wasn't significant and he quickly repaired it with his combat engineers. The desired bridgehead was nonetheless taken. Everything that had happened demonstrated the competence of the German junior officer staff and the prompt cooperation between the elements.

However, the euphoria of the success didn't last long; soon II./Infanterie-Regiment 427 stopped, having run into stubborn resistance in strong field fortifications north of the Osmiaia River in the sector of the 1. Panzer-Division's offensive, which brought a halt to any further advance. The battalion had to fight savagely before it managed to break through these positions and to seize the more or less densely populated places of Ekaterinino, Khotno, Potenovo and Shemelovo, and the territory south of the river.

Before mid-day, the headquarters of Infanterie-Regiment 427 had already moved into Shemelovo. Since the second and third waves were attacking without having any obstacles in front of them, the regiment's artillery was in the process of changing locations even before the start of the attack toward Kokosh'. With the support of the artillery, the forced crossing of the river with the same name from north to south took place without any hindrance.

Southeast of Gordeenka, at the boundary with the Infanterie-Regiment 428, to the northeast of Pod'ezzhalovo, south of the position of II./Infanterie-Regiment 427, the command post of the Soviet 627th Rifle Regiment was discovered and captured by a German reconnaissance tank. In the vicinity of Krapivino to the south, the LVI Panzerkorps had passed a crossroads, and subsequently its command post spent the night between the 129. and 35. Infanterie-Divisionen.

Even before the onset of darkness, Infanterie-Regiment 427 was dug into the positions along the Kokosh' River that had been abandoned by the Russians, but the bulk of its II. Bataillon had even crossed it in the Efremovo area. The 5. Kompanie on the left was crossing the Osmiaia, in order to seize a bridge west of Bol'shoe Skachkovo. The 6. and 7. Kompanien were fording the Kokosh' River, but on the other bank ran into strong resistance in flawlessly camouflaged pillboxes and moderately developed field positions in Efremovo, which they managed to overcome in close combat from the march. At the same time, a special kampfgruppe that had been sent crushed the fierce defense in pillboxes east of Shestaki and Byshovo, and at the last moment prevented the demolition of the bridge that had been prepared in Bol'shoe Shakhovo. This presented the opportunity to take Hill 206.8, and by 1700 every objective that had been set before Infanterie-Regiment 427 for the day had been reached.[26]

In the sector of VIII Armeekorps' offensive, the Soviet units were making a fighting withdrawal to the east. At 1030, the corps' northern wing had passed through Lopachiki. Only at Iartsevo did Soviet heavy artillery give support to the units defending their positions.[27]

At 1045, 129. Infanterie-Division's reconnaissance battalion received an order to scout the axis of Infanterie-Regiment 427's forthcoming actions in difficult terrain east of Shelepy. The division's panzerjäger battalion was shifting to the area of Ivkino and at this same time, the division's headquarters had already moved out to the area of Staro-Selo.[28]

By 1300, the first mandatory reports on the attained results began to come in. It became clear that in the sector of XXXXI Panzerkorps' offensive, the plank roads through a swamp had been blown up and thus the advance of 1. Panzer-Division had slowed down. A portion of the corps' divisions had halted in the Shelepy – Smetishche area, thereby creating a gap with the LVI Panzerkorps, which at this time was already advancing from Smetishche to the north.[29]

The strongly developed positions that were being stubbornly defended on the eastern bank of the Kokosh' River had been seized by 129. Infanterie-Division without aerial reconnaissance or air support. By 1100, the division with one regiment, with the support of heavy and field artillery, had advanced almost 18 kilometers, having taken according to preliminary estimates approximately 900 pillboxes, bunkers and field fortifications, more than 1,000 prisoners, four field and one long-range gun, several 150-mm mortars, 21 light and 12 heavy machine guns, 500 rifles, as well as numerous transport vehicles and equipment.[30]

Oberleutnant Lösch's special group and the special group of Oberleutnant Darius's of 1. Panzer-Division's Panzer-Regiment 1, with the support of motor-cyclists of the 3./Panzer-Aufklärung-Abteilung 4, seized the Osotnia – Bakh causeway southeast of Smetishche with a sudden and fierce attack, and already by 1300 had cleared a path for 1. Panzer-Division to the northeast. Baturino was taken by the same motorcycle company; there, the defense proved to be relatively weak. Then Lösch received a message that his soldiers had taken a windmill on a hill southeast of Storozhok, and he arrived there in person. By noon the forces of 1. Panzer-Division's Schützen-Regiment 18 had taken Ershovo and broken through the strong Soviet defenses at Osotnia without any particular difficulties. So even though the offensive was complicated by the poor condition of the majority of roads, wooden planks were quickly made and laid down by pioneers, which prevented the pace of advance from slowing.[31]

In the morning, given the fine weather, the Luftwaffe conducted its first raid on the city of Belyi, and in particular targeted the positions of the second-echelon 119th Rifle Division. The division still hadn't tasted combat, but as a result of the aerial attacks suffered its first casualties.[32]

In order to increase the pressure, Oberst Koll's panzer brigade, which consisted of Panzer-Regimenter 11 and 25 of the 6. and 7. Panzer-Divisionen, was put in motion by Hoth. Around noon, the brigade quickly reached the Krapivnia – Sonino road, and soon its headquarters established itself in Krapivnia.[33]

By 1310 Koll's panzer brigade managed to get across the Kokosh', and without stopping it began to move toward Korytno. However, here suddenly complications arose, because the woods east of the road were passable only for tracked vehicles. The 6. Panzer-Division had also been compelled to move east of the road, where traffic bottlenecks were created together with the vehicles of 7. Panzer-Division. As a result, 6. Panzer-Division was lagging behind the vehicles of the 129. Infanterie-Division.[34]

Not long before this, Koll was reporting suspected strong resistance on the Vop' River, which in fact was broken from the march by his panzer brigade without encountering any particular opposition. To his surprise, his panzer brigade calmly crossed the river and headed toward the Sveta River, where a regrouping was planned with the onset of darkness. Subsequently, by midnight an infantry brigade arrived as support for him.[35]

Once Panzergruppe 3's panzer units forced a crossing of the Kokosh' River, the Soviet defensive line had been fully ruptured. A bit earlier, 35. Infanterie-Division, having crossed the Vop' River, reached Zamosh'e by 1300, 5. Infanterie-Division entered Repnia, while the northern wing of the 106. Infanterie-Division with its

Hiwi volunteers was in Zavivnaia, but the capture of Kudinovo was depending on its southern wing. The VI Armeekorps was still fighting for Svity and Frolovo.

In the Belyi area, in view of the stubborn opposition, the offensive of the LVI Panzerkorps had bogged down, and its headquarters began to ask Hoth over the telephone about the possibility of redirecting at least one panzer division toward Komary, bypassing Belyi, since in their opinion the Soviet defenders in the city had no intention of retreating.

From Krapivnia, 6. Panzer-Division, in place of its planned route of advance, had been forced to pivot sharply to the northeast in connection with the absence of roads suitable for its wheeled transport. Therefore its infantry units had also been compelled to look for an alternate route north of the fringe of the forests, since the exploitation of their success was important in order to prevent the panzer units from coming under possible counterattack.[36]

At 1430, at the request of the commander of V Armeekorps, Hoth made the decision to leave two guns of a battery of heavy field howitzers with the corps, and a battery of II./Artillerie-Regiment 51 with LVI Panzerkorps, while two companies of infantry artillery would assist the forcing of the Vop' River with the support of one motorized battery. For V Armeekorps this was a form of the higher command's recognition of its rapid advance and actions in defense of the bridges across the Dnepr on the southern flank of the panzer group. The slow advance made by 26. Infanterie-Division in front of Kholm-Zhirkovskii spoke to the fact that 1. Panzer-Division had earlier been delayed by the defending Soviet units north of Kholm-Zhirkovskii.

Despite all expectations, it turned out that the Soviet units made no attempt to defend their positions on the Vop' River, except in the sector of LVI Panzerkorps' offensive. Moreover, the Panzergruppe 3 command simply could not understand why the retreating enemy didn't destroy the bridges across the river behind it.[37]

By 1500, 129. Infanterie-Division's Infanterie-Regiment 427 had seized a bridgehead north of Bol'shaia Skachkovka, after which it was given an order to seize yet another bridgehead in Skachkovka itself for 7. Panzer-Division, which was being held up by the terrain and traffic congestion. This had to be done quickly, in order to cover the left flank of LVI Panzerkorps against attacks from the northwest, north and northeast.[38]

Disruptions in the timetable of movement of the German units on this axis began to arise because of numerous traffic jams on the available roads, along which the panzer units, without encountering any sort of resistance were all converging on the Smolensk – Belyi highway at the same time after the breakthrough of the Soviet defenses on the line Dobrosel'e – Mikhalevo at 1200. However, not everywhere was there such an unhindered advance. Having broken through the defenses of the first echelons of the Soviet 30th Army back at 1200, 129. Infantry marched on toward Kokosh'. However, in the neighborhood of 1400, its Infanterie-Regiment 428 unexpectedly collided with the forward units of the 251st Rifle Division, which was positioned in the 30th Army's second echelon. In the division's sector of defense, in the village of Liada, Major N.A. Guliaev's 923rd Rifle Regiment took on the first attack.[39]

The use of aircraft precisely where the 923rd Rifle Regiment was defending isn't supported by German documents[40], although in the documents of the 251st Rifle Division it is stated that "the first combat for the regiment began with an enormous number of German aircraft that struck the defenders from the air and a massive artillery preparation."[41]

It is impossible to explain the causes for such a discrepancy in view of the absence in the archive of the majority of documents of the Red Army's units. Thus, as was stated at the beginning of the book, I must rely on the information found in the more complete German sources. Moreover, the attackers always have a much greater possibility to prepare summary documentation, because the retreating side, to put it gently, can't be bothered with formalities, and all the accounts are written much later in a more peaceful setting. It also can't be excluded that such post-hoc accounts might even have been written deliberately with the intention to escape responsibility for any miscalculations or blunders, at a time when there is no longer anyone or any way to refute what has been written. However, this is all in the future; meanwhile, the 923rd Rifle Regiment was in combat readiness in its positions, waiting for the enemy's approach.

The Infanterie-Regiment 428 received an order to resolve the situation in Liady with its II. Bataillon, and thereby create an opportunity to cross the entire 129. Infanterie-Division over the Kokosh'. For this purpose, III. Bataillon was to outflank the village on both sides, in order to establish a bridgehead on the other bank after crossing the Vop' River.[42]

On the approach to the line of defense of Guliaev's regiment, the German tanks opened direct fire at our poorly-camouflaged firing points, and thereby for a certain amount of time disorganized the defense. Considering that communication means between the defending units was by telephone cable and rather rare, the Germans overwhelmed the first trenches from the march. However, Guliaev managed to rally his men and to dig in with his entire regiment in the second line of trenches, which lay 400 meters behind the first. The absence of anti-tank artillery was sorely felt in the struggle with the German tanks; the soldiers had to be satisfied with grenades. As a result, by 2000 the tanks, with infantry support, approached the western outskirts of the village, having simultaneously occupied the neighboring Bol'shaia and Malaia Korytnia and reached Efremovo. At 2200 they also broke into Liady.

For unclear reasons, Guliaev's regiment hadn't been furnished with adequate ammunition from the outset, and when Guliaev radioed the division headquarters about the developing situation, he received an order directly from the division commander: "Hold out to the last man!" Only at 2300, at a point when the Germans were already on the western outskirts, did another order follow: "Fall back to the line of Nikitinka Station."

Fortunately, the regiment had been equipped with an adequate number of RB radio sets; communications with both the rifle battalions and the division headquarters were uninterrupted during the battle. Given that the telephone lines had been severed at the start of the battle and there had been no success in repairing them, the radios were a vital aid.

After receiving the order to retreat, Guliaev together with his radiomen, covered by a rifle platoon, abandoned the line of defense only at 2330, at a moment when German tanks were already in the village, while enemy infantry had outflanked it on both sides and were already just 200-300 meters away from the regiment's observation post. It was the final defensive position held by Liady's remaining defenders.

The Germans weren't expecting to encounter any further resistance, and now considering the village their own they were searching through all that remained of the village's structures and the regiment's former defensive positions. In places, shots were still ringing out; plainly, it was those men who hadn't been able or hadn't had time to retreat with the rest of the regiment. It was precisely at this moment that the fighting flared up with renewed strength directly in the vicinity of the regiment's observation post. Everyone still there at this time, including the radiomen, took part in it. The defense was being led by Guliaev himself, who personally shot four of the Germans who approached too closely. Even though the regiment's signals service was fully staffed, the majority of its personnel were untrained for combat actions, and the riflemen among them were so-so. However, despite this, the Germans halted their advance for a time, which was sufficient to allow those remaining alive to escape and to carry away the wounded together with them. In this combat, the radiomen Iudin and Lozovsky, who not only maintained communications to the very last, but also simultaneously took part in the combat, particularly distinguished themselves.

Fortunately, the signals equipment in the regiment was adequate, and given the presence of radio sets, problems with communications didn't arise, even though 18 telephones and 14 kilometers of telephone cable were lost. The only thing is that in view of the compulsory retreat, the Soviet side wasn't successful in taking any loot from the Germans.[43]

In the rifle division's preserved documents, everything was tabulated and regret was even expressed about the absence of booty; however, information is absent about those who were holding this final defensive position at the observation post, about whom the Germans themselves later recognized: "Infanterie-Regiment 428 is attacking the bristling Russian hedgehog positions in Liady from three directions."[44]

In the future, Guliaev would continue to command his regiment as part of this same division, and later fought valiantly and took part in the liberation of the Sychevka area in 1943. However, this is a subject for further research, so meanwhile, so as not to disrupt the chronology, let's return to 2 October 1941.

By 1500, the German forces had reached the following lines:

V Armeekorps was at a line 3 kilometers northeast of Shakhlavo – 3 kilometers southeast of L'vovo and Markovo – the bridge across the Vop' River east of Repino – bridgehead at Zamosh'e – 3 kilometers east of Pochinok. The corps commander requested of the panzer group that if 106. Infanterie-Division in the given situation could not pursue the Soviet units retreating to the east, then it should remain as before under the command of the corps.

LVI Panzerkorps with its panzer units had stopped on the line Bogdanovo – Kokotnia – Brokhovo.

XXXXI Panzerkorps was in the process of moving into a bridgehead east of Ostrov and to the northeast. Its infantry was at a line running from east of Iasennaia to east of Spirichina. There were still no combat clashes southwest of Zhidkii.

VI Armeekorps was fighting in front of Svity. A portion of the corps was pushing toward Zaruch'e, and another portion to the east and north. Frolovo had been taken with combat. North of the Los'mianka River, Russian field positions had been detected in Azarovo. The 110. Infanterie-Division was attacking Borki from two directions and from the east of Zakeevo.[45]

From 1600, Panzergruppe 3's panzer units became engaged in heavy combat in Bogdanovo and were making little headway. At this same time, 7. Panzer-Division was dealing with traffic jams and beginning to move along the road that had previously been seized by 1. Panzer-Division, intending to push as far as possible toward Skachkovo by nightfall. The LVI Panzerkorps was anticipating that the entire 6. Panzer-Division with the support of approaching elements of 7. Panzer-Division, would on the next day strike in the direction of the Kokosh' River. After arriving at the Dnepr River, the corps would still retain its former axis toward Kamenets and Viaz'ma.

At 1640, by an order of the panzer group's headquarters the position of 106. Infanterie-Division of V Armeekorps was changed according to plan. The strong Soviet defense in Iartsevo was demanding a transfer of force to the south, and at the same time it was necessary to make sure the flanks didn't become too extended. The German command remained concerned about flank counterattacks by the Red Army.[46]

At 1700 the commander of VI Armeekorps made a request for dive bomber support for an attack he planned to make early on the morning of 3 October against Soviet positions northeast of Frolovo that had been detected by reconnaissance.[47] Without putting in a request in advance, the ground units could not expect air support, unless an extremely critical situation was developing.

At this same time, 7. Panzer Division had at last fully reached the Vop' River, while its Panzer-Aufklärung-Abteilung 37 was even able to force a crossing of the Dnepr River and was fighting there in order to secure a possible bridgehead.[48]

At 1845, XXXXI Panzerkorps reported that it had taken Baturino and announced that 1. Panzer-Division had made it through the swamp west of Storozhek. The corps command was hoping to push it forward a little more, since 1. Panzer-Division had been especially trained for night attacks. Reinhardt proposed to transfer part of 36. Infanterie-Division (mot.) to the Belyi area, since in his opinion this would hasten the encirclement and capture of the city. This assumed the combat employment of the battalions of that division's Infanterie-Regiment 26 in Svity. Hoth approved this proposal, but believed that frontal attacks by the motorized forces should be avoided, and thus it was preferable to adjust the maneuver of LVI Panzerkorps' 14. Infanterie-Division (mot.) toward Smetishche through Bogdanovo. Thus Hoth requested that he be informed when on 3 October 14. Infanterie-Division (mot.) would arrive in the Prechistaia – Bor area for the link-up, because in the event that there were no Soviet counterattacks the next day against VIII Armeekorps, 106. Infanterie-Division should remain subordinate to V Armeekorps. Simultaneously, in order to defend the northern flank of LVI Panzerkorps, tracked vechicles were directed through its rear area toward the city of Belyi.

By 2000, 26. Infanterie-Division with the headquarters of Infanterie-Regiment 1, infantry and combat engineer battalions, as well as artillery of 36. Infanterie-Division (mot.) had assembled in readiness to take the Svity – Demekhi road in expectation of an order from XXXXI Panzerkorps to attack toward Demekhi from the west. It was thought that the division was capable alone of conducting the assault and seizing the village, after which it would advance in full strength toward Belyi. At 2030, a message arrived from VIII Fliegerkorps' aerial reconnaissance that some formation of German panzers had been spotted 5-6 kilometers to the west of the railroad line in the area of Mamonovo, but in the darkness it could not be identified. At the same time, the pilots were confirming that the Russians were continuing to hold on the Dnepr and no signs of a retreat had been observed.

By 2200, in XXXXI Panzerkorps' zone, the plank road through the swamp had again become unserviceable and heavy vehicles and equipment was unable to move along it, especially because night was falling. In connection with this, it was decided to leave one of the panzer divisions, which hadn't yet made it through the swamp, in the sector of LVI Panzerkorps' offensive, and move it on the following day toward the Shelepy – Smetishche area.

At 2300 it unexpectedly became clear that despite the order given by Hoth, 14. Infanterie-Division (mot.) was still unready to march to the Prechistaia – Bor area, which prompted the dissatisfaction of the headquarters of 9. Armee. Hoth issued a rebuke to its commander. However, in the rest there were no further glitches of any sort. Infantry of 6. Panzer-Division was positioned on a hill near Bogdanovo[49], while the forward infantry units of 7. Panzer-Division had earlier that evening reached the Kokosh' River at Efremovo, and later that night took Malinovka.

By the end of the day, the bridgehead seized by 129. Infanterie-Division's Infanterie-Regiment 427 had been expanded, and the regiment headquarters together with I. Bataillon settled in for the night in Brekhovo; III. Battalion had stopped east of Liady and to the right of Efremovo, while II. Battalion remained in reserve north of Byshovo. Infanterie-Regiment 428's III. Battalion was assembled on the eastern edge of Shipki; it had been unable to seize the village of Dresta lying to the east of the Vop' River.

A reconnaissance patrol of the division's Aufklärung-Abeilung 57 sent out that night wound up in a swamp in the darkness, where it was forced to hunker down until morning. Only the passivity of the Russians prevented the possibility of it being wiped out.

As a result of the day's fighting, 129. Infanterie-Division alone had taken 1,108 prisoners, including 8 commanders. In addition, 41 rifles, 4 field and 4 anti-aircraft guns, 4 tractors, 10 tanks, 70 submachine guns and 30 trucks had been taken. The division itself on this day lost 3 officers killed and 7 wounded, 47 junior officers and soldiers killed and 245 wounded, and 3 men missing in action. In Krapivnia, a lot of abandoned tanks and trucks had been seized by the forward units of the neighboring 6. Panzer-Division.[50]

By evening, units of Panzergruppe 3 had assembled on the attained lines:

> V Armeekorps: Brigolovo – bridgehead on the Vop' River east of Drozdovo, east of Slisino, east of Repino; and on the line Krasnaia Gora – north of Pokikino.
> LVI Panzerkorps: 129. Infanterie-Division on the eastern bank of the Kokosh' River between Grigor'evo and Skachkovo; forward units of the 7. Panzer-Division east of Skachkovo.
> XXXXI Panzerkorps: 1. Panzer-Division had reached an area directly south of Kholm-Zhirkovskii; the 6. Infanterie-Division was in field positions after the attack on Spirichina and with support units at Baturino.
> VI Armeekorps: It had been decided not to enter Svity; moreover, in the gathering twilight it was going to be difficult to take the Russian fortified positions in Azarovo, and thus the request had been made for Luftwaffe support on the following morning. The 110. Infanterie-Division was in the vicinity of Borki, while its left wing was 3 kilometers west of Koshchenki Station.

By the end of the day it had also become clear that the losses in the preceding days and the lack of time to repair vehicles, which could not withstand the poor roads, were telling on the combat strength of 1. Panzer-Division and 36. Infanterie-Division (mot.). The vehicles were often compelled to move off-road; to the Germans' good fortune, the weather was still favorable for this.[51]

Summing up the results of this day, in the headquarters of the panzer group they believed that few Russian units were in front of them and their weak resistance might be based on one of the following factors:

* Given an attack against their positions, the troops had a standing order to retreat without combat; however, because of the surprise offensive, they weren't always able to do this;
* The Red Army was ready for a retreat, or was already in the process of retreating;
* The combat capabilities of the Red Army had fallen significantly.

The results of the fighting over the day indicated that the Red Army was making less use of field artillery than it had previously, and sparing use was being made of tanks and infantry. The air force, on the other hand, was operating actively, but only in the sector of V Armeekorps' offensive.[52]

In Panzergruppe 3's account for the command of 9. Armee, the following was written:

> Although the Soviet command could not have been unaware of the assembly and deployment of our powerful forces for the offensive, the start of this offensive apparently came as a complete surprise to it. The mobile formations and infantry divisions (especially of V Armeekorps) after a brief artillery preparation seized the enemy's forward positions and quickly crossed the Votria, Vop' and Kokosh' Rivers. The resistance of the defenders was weaker than expected; especially the artillery, the fire of which was lighter than previously. Our offensive was so successful and vigorous, that from the beginning fears arose that this was the cover of deliberately weak rear guard detachments. The majority of prisoners were indicating that in the positions occupied by their divisions, in places all preparations for winter had been made. On the other hand it seems probable that after such a blow by mobile formations, the Red Army retreated, since it should have become recognizable that the decisions of its high command before our offensive were incorrect.
>
> According to reports of aerial reconnaissance, security is absent on the path of the enemy's march columns on the roads to the east or behind them. It is possible that this conduct of the Russians was even premeditated, but in any case, their rare opposition was less fierce than before; apparently in view of the constant failures on the defense, the offensive and the retreats, and apparently having overestimated their own ability to resist, they fell apart.
>
> The command is convinced that the joint action of the two panzer regiments and of the panzer brigade composed out of 6. and 7. Panzer-Divisionen had a particularly strong and effective influence on the enemy. In addition, for the breakthrough the combination of an infantry division and a panzer corps was used. Support on the part of aviation was particularly strong. The dry weather was favorable for movement along the bad roads and pathways, and even through the relatively impassable woods in the Mamonovo area. Only on the left flank of Panzergruppe 3's offensive was progress slow, since the advance of XXXXI Panzerkorps was hindered by the weak artillery support of light artillery and the difficult terrain; thus on the first day it was unable to reach the assigned area southwest of Kholm-Zhirkovskii.
>
> VI Armeekorps was also successful in the northern direction, albeit slowly. The Russians as always are particularly stubbornly defending the main roads and major towns, and thus there is the supposition that that there will be no strong resistance at the Mamanovo land bridge.[53]

By the end of 2 October, it had become evident that Panzergruppe 3 with its northern wing had broken through the Soviet front at the boundary between the Soviet 19th and 30th Armies in the direction of Kholm-Zhirkovskii, and partially toward Belyi. Meanwhile, General Erich Hoepner's Panzergruppe 4 had breached the sector of defense of the 43rd Army, south of the Warsaw highway.

Subsequently, Panzergruppe 4 overran the Soviet units and launched an attack now against the Reserve Front's second echelon – against forces of the 33rd Army. Unfortunately, at this moment all of the attention of the *Stavka* of the Supreme High Command was fixed upon the Orel and Briansk directions, as well as on the situation in the Khar'kov area. By this time, Guderian's Panzergruppe 2 had already made a deep penetration into Briansk Front's sector of defense, but the situation in the Viaz'ma area still wasn't viewed as critical.

The Soviet Supreme Command was slow to react to the changing situation and prevent a further breakthrough by the German motorized formations. At this time, the Red Army General Staff was still receiving positive reports regarding the successful defensive actions of the 16th, 20th and 24th Armies of the Western and Reserve Fronts, and few could believe that German tanks had already reached the Spas-Demensk – Iukhnov highway, thereby outflanking the bulk of the main group of Soviet forces.

As subsequently became clear, by 2 October the Germans in the sector of their offensive had actually concentrated up to 35 infantry divisions in the first echelon opposite the troops of the Western Front, which in fact had been the previous estimate of the Western Front headquarters, but on the directions of advance of interest to us, more specifically the enemy had the following groupings opposite the Soviet fronts:

29th Army – 4 infantry divisions;
30th Army – 5 infantry divisions, 1 motorized division and 1 panzer division, altogether 7 divisions;
20th Army – 3 infantry divisions.[54]

The offensive's first day had come to an end and in Daily Summary No.109 on the situation on the Eastern Front, the 4th Oberquartermeister of Germany's OKH succinctly reported: "On the front of 9. Armee, the enemy is offering stubborn resistance only in places."[55] For the coming morning, the command of Panzergruppe 3 directed the continuation of the offensive across the Dnepr and toward Belyi.[56]

3 October (Friday)

The second day of the German offensive was dawning; as before, it was dry, which was especially beneficial for the conducting of the planned operations. For the rest of the day, the sky was clear and sunny, and the high temperature held at 10 C. [50 F.].

Overnight, the Soviet air force had periodically bombed the positions of Panzergruppe 3. However, this didn't particularly affect the implementation of the designated plans, and with the sunrise, the offensive resumed on the same axis. However, situations that weren't taken into account by the plan constantly brought adjustments. For example, because of the great expanse of woods east of the Vop' River, V Armeekorps' 5. and 35. Infanterie-Divisionen were forced to circumvent them to the north.

Overnight, nothing significant had happened at the front, with the exception that on the Kholm-Zhirkovskii – Tikhanovo road, units of the 6. Panzer-Division had to repel frequent counterattacks by Soviet forces. As on the previous morning, the German forces moved out at around 0600 and like a water current, flowing around any Red Army strongpoints that continued to offer resistance, they advanced further to the east.[57] The roads had dried out over the preceding days of good weather, and it was easy to move along them. Roads that were becoming impassable were constantly being repaired by pioneers.[58]

At 0630, according to the request made by the commander of VI Armeekorps on the previous evening, a powerful airstrike hit the Russian positions northeast of Frolovo, after which few there could have survived. However, the soldiers that were readying for the attack were nevertheless being told by their commanders that they still faced a stubborn defense in order to keep them alert and motivated.[59]

The night before, a report had arrived in 129. Infanterie-Division's headquarters from VI Armeekorps that Kholm-Zhirkovskii had fallen, so its commander Generalmajor Rittau already at 0400 issued a command to his headquarters' staff to begin relocating into wooded terrain 1.5 kilometers southeast of Lekhmina, which was completed by 0730. Having taken this decision, Rittau simultaneously ordered all his units to push ahead toward the town. However, as soon as the forward units, around 0500, had reached the first buildings on the outskirts of Kholm-Zhirkovskii, they were greeted with not only small arms' and machine-gun fire, but also with fire from field artillery.

The report that Kholm-Zhirkovskii was in German hands proved to be false, and there was not a single German soldier in the place. The report had appeared after some hasty message to the corps that six motorcyclists had caught the Russian bridgehead in Tikhanovo by surprise with an unexpected attack, as a result of which the defenders there had abandoned their positions and fled. Next, the reports claimed that having merged with the tail end of a retreating Russian column, the motorcyclists had crossed the Dnepr over a bridge and had subsequently opened fire from the opposite bank in the reverse direction. However, no one in the corps knew that the bridge had been wired for demolition, and in fact the river crossing took place much later, and only after the explosive charge had been disarmed by combat engineers of the arriving units. Not a single German soldier set foot on the opposite bank of the Dnepr River in this place prior to this.[60]

With the sunrise the first German reconnaissance aircraft appeared overhead, and already at 0750 they had spotted the movement of a large number of Soviet troops toward Kamenets, north of Tver', which gave the command of Panzergruppe 3 pause to consider – was something unexpected being prepared there? While the headquarters was pondering this, within an hour a proposal arrived from XXXXI Panzerkorps, suggesting that the artillery of 14. Infanterie-Division (mot.) and 900. Lehr-Brigade (mot.) in their present places of assembly be withdrawn from their parent units and unified into an independent combat unit, because their slow rate of march from the outset was restraining the corps' rapid advance. The panzer group headquarters had to agree with this, since there appeared to be no alternative. However, the panzer group headquarters reserved for itself the right to issue an order to hasten the march of 36. Infanterie-Division (mot.) toward Belyi in the event this would be necessary, and moreover, agreement was reached with the headquarters of VI Armeekorps and XXXXI Panzerkorps that 26. Infanterie-Division would remain off-road to the west of the route of advance, since the road would now be restricted to the use of only heavy transport vehicles.[61]

The arriving dawn brought heavy fighting to the 1. Panzer-Division in Baturino, where the Soviet units had been defending stubbornly since the evening before. It was decided to attack in two waves, one following immediately after the other, for which purpose Major Eckinger at 0815 began to form a vanguard shock group led by von Hey consisting of I./Schützen-Regiment 113, II./Artillerie-Regiment 73, 3./ Panzer-Aufklärung-Abteilung 4, and a single panzer battalion of Panzer-Regiment 1.

Heavy and field artillery, which had set up their firing positions in woods northeast of Baturino, opened up first. The combat was hard, and von Hey's kampfgruppe failed to break into the Soviet positions from the march. However, the defenders' resistance already by 0900 was broken by the second attacking wave consisting of the remaining panzer battalions of Panzer-Regiment 1 and Oberleutnant Elias's two flame-throwing panzers, supported by Major Neumann's II./Artillerie-Regiment 73.[62]

At 0930, a message arrived from VIII Fliegerkorps' aerial reconnaissance, which once again prompted great surprise in Panzergruppe 3's headquarters. It turned out that the bridge across the Dnepr in Glushkovo, like the one previously in Tikhanovo, was still intact. At 0940, reconnaissance pilots spotted the movement of a large column of Soviet infantry toward Kholm-Zhirkovskii north and south of the Dnepr, while according to obtained aerial photographs, the ground north of Veselovo, 5 kilometers south of Kholm-Zhirkovskii, appeared suitable for tanks. Thus, a group of Hiwi volunteers was sent there, which took up positions on the outskirts of Zabegaevka.

Based on the intelligence supplied by aerial reconnaissance, the panzer group command was compelled to acknowledge that the Red Army had sufficient strength and Hoth reasonably conjectured that the Germans would face tough resistance at Kholm-Zhirkovskii.[63]

The 6. Panzer-Division spent the first half of the day idle because of a lack of fuel, and only by noon, after refilling the fuel tanks, were the panzers capable of attacking further. Koll's panzer brigade even succeeded in seizing a bridge across the Dnepr intact and created a bridgehead on the opposite bank.[64]

At 1200, at an order from 9. Armee's headquarters, 106. Infanterie-Division, which had remained in V Armeekorps' reserve, was directed to Vasil'evo. At this same time, VIII Armeekorps according to plan was on the panzer group's southern flank on the line Kolkovichi – Neelovo. The XXIII Armeekorps was on the panzer group's northern flank, which hadn't been approved in advance by 9. Armee's command; however Hoth was able to convince it that this was not simply OK, but even desirable.[65]

The 129. Infanterie-Division's Infanterie-Regiment 427 in the course of the day acted in support of 1. and 7. Panzer-Divisionen in the Efremovo – Bolshaia Skachkovka – Byshovo bridgehead, where in the morning the Soviets conducted several aerial attacks against the newly rebuilt bridge in Efremovo; however, all the bombs missed the target. On the next raid at 1300, the Soviet aircraft struck a column moving toward the bridge, and five were shot down – three by an anti-aircraft gun and two by Bf-109 fighters that had been called up to cover the column.[66]

On the Belyi axis, 1. Panzer-Division ran into bitter resistance from units of the Soviet 107th Motorized Rifle Division.[67] Back on the evening before, the commander of the Western Front's 30th Army Major General V.A. Khomenko had ordered a special detachment of this division consisting of a battalion of medium tanks to move to the Khalomidino and Podselitsy area. It consisted of 19 T-34 tanks and 3 KV tanks, a full-strength motorized rifle battalion of the 237th Motorized Rifle Regiment, a platoon of combat engineers and an anti-tank battery. Major Shil'diaev, the commander of the 143rd Tank Regiment, and Battalion Commissar Maksimov headed the detachment. Already at dawn, at 0700 Shil'diaev's detachment attacked units of 1. Panzer-Division that were moving along the Baturino – Belyi highway. The Germans opposed the detachment with a panzer and motorized infantry regiment, supported by light artillery.

With this Soviet attack, the attempts by the Germans to break through to Belyi along the road were thwarted, after which the command of 1. Panzer-Division, leaving behind a covering screen of panzers, motorized infantry and artillery, turned his main forces toward Presnetsov, Berezovka, Sergeevo and Chalyshevo. In the action on the Baturino – Belyi road, Shil'diaev's detachment lost 14 tanks and 267 men killed alone. The combat, which had subsided by 1430, resumed 30 minutes later when the 237th Motorized Rifle Regiment and the 118th Anti-tank Artillery Battalion, which had been directed to this place aboard vehicles by the 30th Army command, entered the battle from the march. They were opposed by up to two battalions of German infantry, supported by 25 tanks and two battalions of field artillery.

The remaining units of the 107th Motorized Rifle Division also collided with German tanks and motorized infantry at 1530 south of Aleshkovo. The Soviet 120th Motorized Rifle Regiment, a battalion of T-26 tanks numbering 26 machines, a battalion of the 118th Artillery Regiment, and an anti-tank battery attacked German-occupied Volynovo, but unsuccessfully, since major forces of the German 1. Panzer-Division were there.[68]

However, we'll leave the face-off between these two divisions for a spell, because for the rest of the day no substantial change took place. There would be exchanges of fire and fruitless attacks, without any particularly high casualties, and the opposing sides essentially held their respective positions.

At 1500 aerial reconnaissance pilots of VIII Fliegerkorps reported that German tanks were already approaching Kholm-Zhirkovskii, but up to 1,000 Russian infantry troops were moving to the north along the road from Pogoreloe to Kholm-Zhirkovskii. This was evidence that a retreat had partially already begun. The movement of approximately 300 Russian vehicles from Neelovo to Pogoreloe was detected. The pilots acknowledged that they hadn't seen such aggregations since the Bialystok pocket.[69] Analyzing the received intelligence, the Panzergruppe 3 command understood that the offensive should indeed continue according to plan, but maneuver would be absolutely essential in order to obtain a greater success.

To this point, except for opposite Panzergruppe 3, the behavior of the Soviet units was still unpredictable everywhere. The V Armeekorps and LVI Panzerkorps were meeting relatively light resistance, but VI Armeekorps and XXXXI Panzerkorps had gone over to a tactical defense because of Soviet counterattacks. Soviet aircraft had increased their activity in the area of XXXXI Panzerkorps.

For the command of the panzer group, it had ultimately become clear that a tenacious defense of Belyi was being readied, because intelligence had established the movement of forces to that place by railroad from Koshchenka Station lying 3 kilometers to the north. Moreover, despite German attempts to contain them, some Soviet units had nevertheless been able to break through to Kholm-Zhirkovskii.

By this time V Armeekorps' 106. Infanterie-Division was 3 kilometers east of the Vop' River, while 35. Infanterie-Division was attacking field positions in Paksha and covering the area 7.5 kilometers east of Pochinok. The 5. Infanterie-Division was following behind the 35. Infanterie-Division.

The LVI Panzerkorps was attacking northwest of Kholm-Zhirkovskii and south of Matrenino. The 129. Infanterie-Division, as before, was 2 kilometers east of Mamonovo.

The XXXXI Panzerkorps had linked up with 1. Panzer-Division during the advance to the northeast toward Alekshovo, following the division's combat with Soviet tanks in Podselitsa. The 6. Infanterie-Division was in the process of moving through Tereshino toward Proshkino. The full-strength 36. Infanterie-Division (mot.) was in the Nikol'skoe – Timoshevo area. Forward infantry units of 6. Panzer-Division were advancing 10 kilometers west of Kholm-Zhirkovskii.

VI Armeekorps was tied up in heavy combat 4 kilometers northeast of Svity and west of Okolitsa and Bor. Despite this, its 110. Infanterie-Division succeeded in taking Borki and Koshchenka Station from the march.[70]

South of Kholm-Zhirkovskii was Major Löwe's Panzer-Regiment 11 of 6. Panzer Division, which had detected Russians that were quite nearby. Suddenly it came under heavy fire simultaneously from three directions from a well-camouflaged and well-trained enemy. In this close combat, his panzer regiment lost 28 armored vehicles, among which were 14 tanks and 3 armored halftracks that were destroyed in the fusillade. Eleven more tanks were lost due to mechanical breakdowns. Grasping the lack of prospects, Löwe halted further fruitless attacks and reported to higher command that "owing to his regiment's resolve, two bridges have been rebuilt and an attack by Russian tanks from the south prevented; however, after such losses it is no longer possible to attack, and it is better to resume the division's offensive together with the attached 129. Infanterie-Division somewhat further to the south."[71]

At 1700, 9. Armee command directed Panzergruppe 3's particular attention to the Dnepr River, and thus 1. Panzer-Division received an order to halt its advance toward Belyi, but instead to pivot to the east toward the Dnepr south of the city. Its attached 36. Infanterie-Division (mot.), to avoid the loss of command and control, was ordered to move to Liapkino, and from there turn directly to the east, and leave Belyi to be taken by infantry alone.

At 1725, having encountered a strong Russian anti-tank defense, the panzer group succeeded in grabbing a bridgehead across the Dnepr at Glushkovo with an outflanking maneuver.[72] In the vicinity of the southern bridge, a bridgehead was established by one panzer regiment of 6. Panzer-Division after the single Soviet tank unit located there, declining combat, hastily retreated from Kholm-Zhirkovskii to the south, and in the area of the northern bridge by one regiment of 7. Panzer-Division from Koll's composite panzer brigade. Meanwhile, the command of 129. Infanterie-Division was promising that the division would take Kholm-Zhirkovskii on the next day, and its units were already on the march there.[73]

However, it turned out that already by that evening, the second bridge in Kholm-Zhirkovskii, and subsequently the entire city itself, had in fact been taken by Raus's kampfgruppe from the 6. Panzer-Division. The bridge was captured by Leutnant Wissemann's 2./Kradschützen-Abteilung 6, which had merged with the tail of the retreating Russian column and had crossed the bridge together with it, and then had stopped and taken it undamaged.[74]

In the course of the entire day of 3 October, 7. Panzer-Division was involved in heavy and unproductive fighting in Martynovo; however, only after the onset of darkness, it nevertheless managed to take the village at 1945. Meanwhile, one panzer regiment of 7. Panzer- Division, which had crossed the Vop' River the day before, was now already closing on the Dnepr River. The units positioned in Glushkovo (east of Kholm-Zhirkovskii on the Viaz'ma – Belyi road) were subordinated to it, in order to create an additional bridgehead across the Dnepr.[75]

A difficult situation developed by evening for 1. Panzer-Division in the area of Kniazh'e, 18 kilometers from Belyi. Oberleutnant Elias, Leutnant Gittermann and several officers of II./Panzer-Regiment 1 lost a significant number of field and Flak guns destroyed and had no success. The commander of 7. Panzer-Kompanie Oberleutnant Zollmann was lightly wounded. In order to achieve success, the remnants of II. Panzer-Abteilung were attached to Oberleutnant Oferweg's II./Schützen-Regiment 113 and a portion of Leutnant Katzmann's III. Bataillon of the same regiment, which having regrouped, launched another attack. The infantry advanced at an interval behind the panzers, which rendered it unable to support the tanks effectively with fire, and thus didn't allow the panzers to break into the Russian trenches and eliminate the pockets of infantry resistance. The 2. Kompanie of Oferweg's II. Bataillon was committed to bolster the attack. It had an experienced commander; taking command upon himself and having organized the forward group of their tanks and remaining armored halftracks of Leutnant Gayen's company, he attacked the stubborn Russian positions. With this, the group managed to break the resistance and take Kniazh'e by nightfall.

After refueling, a forward detachment of Panzer-Regiment 1 headed by Oberleutnant Darius attacked directly toward Belyi, while the rest of the panzer regiment together with I./Schützen-Regiment 1 and Major Born's I./Artillerie-Regiment 73 pushed on toward Glinkovo through Berezovka. Leutnant Erdmann's platoon was expected by twilight.[76]

As the sun started setting, the Germans grew more cautious. Unfamiliar with the terrain and in the euphoria of the initial successes, it would be too easy to stumble into some Russian strongpoint among the hillocks and hills. Thus, the command of 129 Infanterie-Division halted its attacking units, and at 2025 sent the reconnaissance battalion out ahead, in order to determine who had possession of Hill 241.5 north of the village of Vnukovka to the north of Kholm-Zhirkovskii.[77]

While the probing of the terrain lying up ahead was going on, the command of Panzergruppe 3 at 2045 issued a directive to XXXXI Panzerkorps on the need to take up a position south of Belyi on both sides of the Dnepr River around Spas-Demensk. The VI Armeekorps, which was near Belyi at this time, was to take measures to defend the eastern and northern flanks of the panzer group. In addition, it was expected that on 5 October, 14. Infanterie-Division (mot.) would shift location from Bor to Liapkino between midnight and 0800, and remain there in reserve under the control of the panzer group. Meanwhile, 161. Infanterie-Division, positioned in 9. Armee reserve, would join VI Armeekorps on 6 October and first take Bor under control.[78]

The reconnaissance conducted around Vnukovka indicated that Hill 241.5 was unoccupied, and at 2130 129. Infanterie-Division's Infanterie-Regiment 430 pushed on toward Kholm-Zhirkovskii with the order to seize this hill and to dig-in there strongly. Considering the constant maneuvering, no telephone cable was laid down and only radios were used for communication.

The division's Infantry-Regiment 427 was holding the bridgeheads on the Efremovo – Bolshaia Skachkovka – Byshovo line. In order to strengthen the division's left flank, the regiment's I. Bataillon was activated. In the course of the day, the bridge in Efremovo was subjected to several aerial attacks, but again without success. The anti-aircraft cover of the bridge was preventing any low-altitude bombing.[79]

After exhausting fighting, the infantrymen of 1. Panzer-Division under the command of Hauptmann Richtofen pushed too far ahead and had to spend the night on open ground. For elementary security, they had to surround their nighttime location with barbed wire and to deploy outposts.

That same evening, the division's operations chief received a preliminary report from Major Kielmansegg of 6. Panzer-Division about the situation north of Viaz'ma: "We detected a boundary, and then broke through to a hill south of Kholm[-Zhirkovskii]. From there, we undisturbedly pivoted toward Belyi."[80]

After an evening conference with Hoth, the 129th Infanterie-Division received an order at 2200 to push on to Kholm-Zhirkovskii even with a compulsory night march and to link-up with the panzer and infantry units located there, though without weakening security on the southern flank. In addition, for the next day a schedule for the withdrawal of the panzer units from Kamenets to the south toward Viaz'ma was foreseen, while the command of 14. Infanterie-Division (mot.), bypassing its superior XXXXI Panzerkorps headquarters, was to coordinate its actions instead directly with the LVI Panzerkorps.

The enlivened activity of the Luftwaffe throughout the day made a significant contribution to the success of the entire operation, and already at 2230, all of the possible requests for the next day to pin down the Soviet units in the Dnepr staging area had been transmitted to VIII Fliegerkorps, and it was also given the task to monitor all of the enemy's movements in the Belyi area.

For the morning, with the exception of the decisive success regarding the seizure of the two bridges across the Dnepr River and the weak Russian positions along it, the panzer group command had planned the following:

> V Armeekorps has been greatly weakened by fierce resistance, and having halted combat operations, has started the regrouping of its remaining forces. From 1800 106. Infanterie-Division was already moving from Shivarino to the east, in order by morning to seize the Vlasovka – Skripenka area. The 35. Infanterie-Division should by morning reach the area 3 kilometers north of Novika, while 5. Infanterie-Division at 1800 should move out toward Glissnitsa behind 35. Infanterie-Division.
>
> LVI Panzerkorps with 7. Panzer-Division has stopped 4.5 kilometers east of Matrenino, but its 129. Infanterie-Division is continuing its movement, since according to the latest order, it should reach the hills at Kholm-Zhirkovskii by nighttime.
>
> XXXXI Panzerkorps with the forces of the 6. Panzer-Division is continuing to attack Russian field positions east of Tereshino, and together with 1. Panzer-Division is engaged in night combat with tanks of the Soviet 107th Motorized Rifle Division on the line Podselitsa – Kniazh'e – Chalyshevo.
>
> VI Armeekorps is moving unhampered along the Bor – Belyi main road toward Demekhi.
>
> Today's undertaken offensive toward Belyi went better than anticipated. Moreover, as a result of the day's fighting, units of the panzer group seized 150 guns and 6,600 prisoners.[81]

By evening, Kholm-Zhirkovskii was fully in German hands. They had also succeeded in creating two bridgeheads across the Dnepr River to the east of the town, from which on the next day an offensive toward Belyi was planned, and even beyond it if possible. The day's attempt to take the city with a quick attack had been roughly handled as a result of the units of the panzer group being unready for it, and direct attacks had been stopped to avoid heavy losses.[82] In addition, the expansion of the Dnepr River crossings on the Pigulino – Kamenets line was designated for the next day. The attack of XXXXI Panzerkorps toward Komary, Ivashkovo and Mol'nia, and across the Dnepr River toward Spas-Demensk, had been prepared. The outflanking of the city of Belyi by VI Armeekorps proved possible only with the support of units of XXXXI Panzerkorps.

The command post of the LVI Panzerkorps shifted to Verkhov'e, while the XXXXI Panzerkorps' headquarters was 2 kilometers south of Bor, and that of V Armeekorps was in Repino. The situation was unchanged for the remaining units.[83]

4 October (Saturday)

It finally became clear to the German command that the Soviet forces were not conducting a deliberate withdrawal to reserve positions, but instead were continuing to defend in place, albeit with varying amounts of resistance. Moreover, the Red Army command was continuing to hold the ground between the German break-throughs, and still didn't realize that it had already missed the last opportunity to withdraw its forces from the forming pocket the evening before. Now it was no longer possible to conduct an organized retreat. The armored spearheads of Panzergruppen 3 and 4 were continuing to exploit in the direction of Viaz'ma, enveloping the forces of the Western and Reserve Fronts with a concentric offensive. However, even in spite of this, throughout the previous night Soviet bombers had again been very active in the sector of Panzergruppe 3's offensive.[84]

Since the prior evening, 1. Panzer-Division and 36. Infanterie-Division (mot.) had encountered fierce opposition from Soviet infantry and tanks in the Aleshkovo – Lukino – Iur'evo sector. Here, the Soviet 107th Motorized Rifle Division was continuing to resist the Germans stubbornly, and by dawn its 120th Motorized Rifle Regiment had managed to retake Shchelkanovo and Volynovo. This had happened because overnight, the main German forces had pulled back from these places to regroup, leaving behind only light covering detachments. Having no time to rest, the regiment was compelled to carry out the division's urgent order to continue to attack toward Kholomidino in order to link-up with the 237th Motorized Rifle Regiment. This need had arisen because the Germans had begun to outflank the division on the right through Lukino and Aleshkovo, without encountering any opposition on this axis, and having reached the road to Belyi, were now threatening the division's flank and rear. They had encountered no opposition because the neighboring 250th Rifle Division that had been defending Svity, Chernyi Ruchei and Okolitsa had retreated on 3 October without notifying the command of the 107th Motorized Rifle Division. It grew aware of this only after small groups of commanders and men of the retreating division had begun arriving at its command post during the night. It became totally clear that morning when the commander and commissar of the 918th Rifle Regiment appeared, who had managed to lose contact with their subordinate regiment. As a result of what happened, already by the morning of 4 October the path of retreat of the 107th Motorized Rifle Division to the city of Belyi had been severed, and it fell into encirclement. The division's command post was located in woods 1 kilometer northeast of Aleshkovo, and here the 20th Separate Reconnaissance Battalion, an engineer company, a traffic control company, the signals battalion and a reserve tank company of 8 T-26 tanks had assembled. The Germans had thus far not troubled them, and there was the possibility to ponder a withdrawal from encirclement.[85]

Leaving the 107th Motorized Rifle Division alone for a time, pursuant to orders 1. Panzer-Division's I./Schützen-Regiment 113, reinforced with panzers, as a kampfgruppe's forward detachment was given the task to set out from Kniazh'e and to break through the Russian front in the northeast direction through dense woods on Hill 250.7 southwest of Mazury. Prior to this, Leutnant Katzmann with his platoon of the same regiment, supported by Strippel's platoon from III./Panzer-Regiment 1, had managed to break through to Mazury and seized it, and were to hold it until the arrival of the reinforced I./Schützen-Regiment 113 aboard armored halftracks. Eckinger's group had spent the night in the same place. Meanwhile, the rest of the division's Panzer-Regiment 1, in the vicinity of Medvedovo, had come under attack by Soviet tanks, which were destroyed in heavy combat by the artillery accompanying the regiment, after which Panzer-Regiment 1 itself launched a counterattack. Exploiting this counterattack and with the aim of beginning to create the pocket, the panzer regiment with the support of I. Bataillon (minus its 1. Kompanie) and a forward artillery spotter pivoted toward Lukino, and having attacked it from the march, seized the village.[86]

The reinforced battalion of 129. Infanterie-Division, which had set out back at 0600, was lagging behind all the rest, and was still slowly advancing on foot, significantly hampered by the swampy and sandy terrain and the narrow bridges along the roads badly worn by the heavy traffic of the motorized columns.[87]

By morning, fragmentary, cut-off Red Army groups retreated to Kholm-Zhirkovskii and took it again. Thus, when the bridgehead of the 129. Infanterie-Division at Tikhanovo came under attack by infantry and tanks at 0700, it became clear that Kholm-Zhirkovskii was once again in Russian hands. Simultaneously, Soviet artillery opened heavy fire from a thickly forested area east of Pushkovka, and a tank attack involving several heavy tanks was launched from the same place. Prior to this, all of this equipment there had been so well-camouflaged, that the German side didn't even suspect they were there. As a result of this attack, units of the 129. Infanterie-Division lost 15 armored vehicles and 3 halftracks destroyed, while the Soviet side lost 25 tanks.[88]

This was a full-fledged and well-planned attack, as a result of which the German bridgehead at Tikhanovo wound up virtually isolated, while the Soviet artillery pounded the only road leading to it. In order not to lose the bridgehead, Panzergruppe 3 command made the urgent decision to send Panzer-Regiment 11 of LVI Panzerkorps' 6. Panzer-Division to the relief of 129. Infanterie-Division.[89] Its attack managed to cut the road to Kholm-Zhirkovskii and to halt the advance of the Soviet units.

However, in the meantime the commander of 129. Infanterie-Division Generalmajor Rittau and his higher ups remained completely unaware of this situation, because the news that the Russians were in Kholm-Zhirkovskii and were maneuvering with tanks had been sent with two armored halftracks of 6. Panzer-Division. However, on the way, one of them received a direct hit, forcing the other to stop and render aid to the injured men in the knocked-out halftrack, and thus the information was slow to arrive.

Having received the delayed information about the situation in Kholm-Zhirkovskii, Rittau at 0800 personally led the available units at hand into a counterattack, as a result of which three Soviet tanks were knocked out, while the rest retreated. Despite this success, the increasing counter-activity shown by the Red Army raised an enormous threat to the entire right wing of the LVI Panzerkorps. As a consequence, Infanterie-Regiment 403 was ordered to alter its route and to break through to the southern outskirts of Kholm-Zhirkovskii with its reconnaissance battalion. [90]

At 0810 in a telephone conversation with Hoth, Generalfeldmarschall Kesselring stressed the importance of Viaz'ma, and in particular the necessity of doing everything possible to take it that day, since according to information from aerial reconnaissance crews, there were few Soviet forces in this area at the present time, and moreover, no movement of any sort of fresh reinforcements from the north had been spotted. Kesselring announced that the air force was capable of controlling all possible movements of the Russians, the forces of which east of the highway were insufficient to stop the developing German offensive.

Already at 0830, Heeresgruppe Mitte's operations chief over the telephone brought Hoth's attention to the fact that the second line of the Russian defense east of the Dnepr River seemed rather strong, and this was being confirmed by aerial reconnaissance photos. Thus, in accordance with a proposal from Generalfeldmarschall von Bock, Panzergruppe 3's command was to focus its efforts along the road to Kostino. To Hoth's question, whether Viaz'ma was worthwhile in this respect, he was told that according to an order from above, everything had already been decided, everything was ready west of Viaz'ma, and the available force was fully sufficient for this. At the same time he was informed that XXXXVI Panzerkorps would be operating in the general direction of Ugra, while XXXX Panzerkorps was already advancing in the direction of Mozhaisk, and would pivot to the north after reaching Iukhnov.

At 1130 Kesselring again called Hoth and began to press him regarding the advance to Viaz'ma. He particularly wanted to begin the reinforcement of the offensive from the flanks, because word had come from the neighboring 4. Armee about its slowing progress.

At noon, having been briefed on the situation, the commander of LVI Panzerkorps issued an order to his corps to advance to the second line of the Russian defense at Pigulino and Kamenets, and bypassing Khmelita on both sides, to the highway leading to Griaznoe. Everything had already been closed off there from the east and the west. In addition, powerful forces had moved to Spas-Demensk, 20 kilometers north of Viaz'ma, for an attack against the city, or if possible to emerge even east of it. [91]

By noon, attacking units of 7. Panzer-Division, including the separate Aufklärung-Abteilung 37, together with forward units of a panzer regiment had created the bridgehead that had been designated the evening before. [92] Also at 1200, 106.

Infanterie-Division of V Armeekorps launched an attack 2 kilometers east of Zalaznia, while 5. Infanterie-Division joined battle 3 kilometers north of Noviki.

By around 1300 on 4 October, 129. Infanterie-Division regained possession of Kholm-Zhirkovskii. Generalmajor Rittau then shifted his headquarters to the fork in the roads 1 kilometer northwest of the town.[93] At this time it was passed down from the headquarters of 9. Armee that the units of Panzergruppe 3 were not to halt, and at the given moment it was necessary first and foremost to reach the highway to Griaznoe, and if possible, it was necessary to take the village that day.

The advance of LVI Panzerkorps south of the Dnepr and the withdrawal by the Russians of all their forces from the right through Staroe Menshchikovo to Chupchugovo was reducing the threat to the portion of Panzergruppe 3's southern flank to the west of the Dnepr River, and thanks to this V Armeekorps was able to cross the railroad line east of Noviki without hindrance; its 35. Infanterie-Division made major progress to the east and reached an area 4 kilometers east of Otpisnaia by 1345. At the same time, XXXXI Panzerkorps radioed LVI Panzerkorps that it soon would also be approaching the Dnepr River at Spas-Demensk in order to provide immediate cover for the latter's northern flank south of Sychevka.

Yet for 6. Panzer-Division the day went badly from the very morning, when at sunrise its marching columns were struck by Soviet aircraft, which in truth didn't inflict much damage, since it seems the attack wasn't adequately organized. Even so, in the afternoon 6. Panzer-Division was forced to stop as a result of a strong counterattack against its forward units by the Soviet 101st Tank Division to the south of Kholm-Zhirkovskii and Tikhanovo.[94]

As a result, Oberleutnant Strohteicher's 8./Schützen-Regiment 114 was completely destroyed. It had moved out in front together with a forward platoon of Panzer-Regiment 11 with the aim of breaking through beyond the Dnepr. However, quickly after starting out they suffered losses from heavy anti-tank fire. The commander of Panzer-Regiment 11's forward platoon received a direct hit to his tank and was burned alive inside it. Strohteicher, a participant in many dashing attacks, was killed when his halftrack took a direct hit. His driver was also killed. The halftrack of the commander of 1. Zug [platoon] Leutnant Mikus was also hit, and Mikus himself received several wounds, but remained in position together with his crew.

Leutnant Scheller under the hurricane of fire at first attempted to pull back under the cover of his artillery, but this attempt failed, and when attempting to restore the situation, he was forced after Strohteicher's death to take command of the company and attempted to break through some woods to the encircled forward platoon of Panzer-Regiment 11. However, he didn't know that in those same woods, a well-camouflaged anti-tank trap had been set for his vehicles, and he was compelled to retreat even despite an order from his commander Major Löwe, who then quickly withdrew the entire kampfgruppe out of the battle. Remnants of the encircled forward platoon later with difficulty managed to break out and returned to the battalion. Both knocked-out armored halftracks were also evacuated, and within two days they were back in service.

Thus, 6. Panzer-Division suffered its first defeat. Over two days of fighting, its 8./Schützen-Regiment 114 alone lost 7 killed and 25 wounded. Only 4 armored halftracks remained operational. On this same day, the commander of Panzer-Regiment 11 Oberstleutnant Zollenkopf was also wounded, and Oberstleutnant Linnbrunn had to take command.[95]

Things went better for other units. The 7. Panzer-Division's advance toward Glushkovo was going smoothly, and its command was even planning to direct Schützen-Regiment 4 to Viaz'ma. The 129. Infanterie-Division was continuing to attack toward Kholm-Zhirkovskii from the south with two regiments, and had reached the line Kholm-Zhirkovskii – Olad'ino, which is 5 kilometers southwest of the town.

Experience had demonstrated that with the defensive battles to hold bridgeheads; the bad roads; and the Wehrmacht's constant difficulties with fuel supplies, a quick victory in the east was impossible. However, despite this, the divisions' progress over the past two days had been particularly good.

The LVI Panzerkorps had driven back all the attacks by infantry and tanks south of Kholm-Zhirkovskii and against the bridgehead at Tikhanovo east of Kholm-Zhirkovskii, while south of the town the forward regiment of 129. Infanterie-Division without any form of support was trying to achieve a rapid success with its own forces. The XXXXI Panzerkorps and the right wing of VI Armeekorps were continuing to attack 10 kilometers southwest of Belyi.

The 6. Infanterie-Division back at 1100 had arrived northeast of Andreikovo, and then entered Komary without encountering any resistance.[96]

The 1. Panzer-Division and the 36. Infanterie-Division (mot.), as before, were locked in a tough battle with the Soviet 107th Motorized Rifle Division in the Aleshkovo – Lukino – Iur'evo area. In the afternoon, several German tanks with infantry loaded in halftracks attacked the command post of the 107th Motorized Rifle Division with the support of field artillery in the sector held by the 20th Reconnaissance Battalion. The combat action was fleeting, and the attack was repulsed.[97]

In the woods south of Kholm-Zhirkovskii, on the approach to the road running north from the western bank of the Dnepr River, at 1320 aerial reconnaissance spotted 40 Soviet tanks with a large quantity of infantry. Only later, after the liquidation of the pocket, did it become revealed that the 28th Tank Regiment, supported by the 18th Motorized Rifle Regiment of the 101st Motorized Rifle Division was located there. In their rear were the 101st and 202nd Tank Regiments, as well as artillery and anti-aircraft battalions. It was impossible to find out more details about these units in view of the absence of any sort of documents that touch upon them in the open archive.

The infantry of 129. Infanterie-Division came under their fire, followed by a storm of fire from the tanks and artillery positioned southwest of Kholm-Zhirkovskii in the Bochanska area. The 35. Infanterie-Division's Infanterie-Regimenter 109 and 111 that were attacking from the west, and its Infanterie-Regiment 34 attacking from the north, also came under this fire.[98] The progress of the German units in this area came to a stop.

The situation was different in the Belyi area, where 2 kilometers southeast of the city VI Armeekorps' 26. Infanterie-Division was continuing its unhindered pursuit of retreating Soviet units, while 110. Infanterie-Division, having completed a totally unobstructed operational maneuver, at 1400 reached the northern bank of the Mezha River and continued a free march to Rog.[99]

At this same time, Panzergruppe 3 received a report from the VIII Fliegerkorps chief of staff about the results of aerial reconnaissance flights over the Viaz'ma area, and it became clear that a retreat along the Smolensk – Viaz'ma highway had been initiated by the Russians. Having received this information, the fliegerkorps and the panzer group asked 6. Panzer-Division to get moving to reach the bridgehead to the right of the bridge and on this same day push on along the road to Mikhailov.

Approximately 1600, German armored vehicles began advancing out of the forested area on the right flank of 1. Panzer-Division, with the support of massed artillery and tank fire. In the first attack, a medical halftrack of I./Panzer-Regiment 1 that was carrying the regiment's surgeon Schmidt took a direct hit. Two medics were killed. Schmidt and other members of the crew were wounded. The wounded were left without aid, some confusion arose, and the attack faltered. To avoid excessive losses, the attack was stopped and air support was summoned. Ju-87 dive bombers and fighter-bombers of the VIII Fliegerkorps supported the halted panzer regiment so effectively that after a second attack, the Soviet resistance was quickly broken.

The commander of the division's forward panzer battalion Major Mast led this second attack. At first he came under flanking fire from Soviet field and anti-aircraft artillery, but with a strong swerve to the right and the excellent support of a team of artillery spotters from Artillerie-Regiment 73, his further advance went well. Soviet infantry was defending stubbornly; however, nothing could withstand the German flamethrowing tanks. Those defenders remaining alive were taken prisoner and sent to the rear under the escort of infantrymen and one motorcyclist, headed by Leutnant Maltzan. The regiment pushed on without stopping and already at 1615, it seized Shiparevo 10 kilometers to the west of Belyi.

Simultaneously, Oberstleutnant Korr's divisional scouts established that the Russians were still occupying Dubrovka, and a reconnaissance-in-force with 8./Panzer-Regiment 1 under the command of Oberleutnant Düntsch was planned. In connection with this, a further advance to the east was strictly forbidden by the regiment command, since the success of this operation depended on the possibility of still entering Zhizhino before the onset of darkness.[100]

As had been planned, the infantry of 129. Infanterie-Division went on the attack at 1630. The division's Infanterie-Regiment 430 shifted its headquarters to the southern outskirts of the previously-taken Kholm-Zhirkovskii, and despite bitter opposition, before sunset I./Infanterie-Regiment 430 took Kolshansk. The II. Bataillon was unable to take Hill 229.5 and dug into its eastern slopes. Infanterie-Regiment 428 had its headquarters in Baranova, and made a penetration to the southwest of the Dnepr, while its II. Bataillon captured Cherenovo. Again and again, the German soldiers witnessed seized Soviet positions, dug-in tanks, machine-gun nests and dead

Red Army soldiers in their trenches. Here there was also a heavy-caliber gun and a lot of damaged, abandoned automatic weapons. Columns of prisoners were moving to the rear.[101]

At 1750, the units fighting in the Dnepr bridgehead were informed by the headquarters of Heeresgruppe Mitte that it was necessary for them to finish the battle as soon as possible, in order to be in Griaznoe before the morrow's sunrise. At 1800 an urgent message arrived in the headquarters of Panzergruppe 3 that VI Armeekorps had entered Belyi, and that its 110. Infanterie-Division had been designated to take the city. It seemed that the city was no longer being seriously defended. Prisoners taken there were indicating that the Western Front headquarters still had three fresh divisions in reserve, one of which, the 101st Tank Division, was preparing to restore the situation specifically in Kholm-Zhirkovskii. This prompted nervousness among the German command, because intelligence hadn't passed along anything on this subject, and accordingly no one was able to anticipate when the counterattack by these forces might be launched.

At 2030 1. Panzer-Division was still locked in combat with the Soviet 107th Motorized Rifle Division northeast of Liapkino, and the quantity of knocked-out Russian tanks had increased to 33, including two heavy tanks.[102]

By 2300, the operational situation was as follows:

V Armeekorps with 106. Infanterie-Division has reached the area south of Vasil'evo; only slight changes in the 5. and 35. Infanterie-Divisions. In the corps' sector of the offensive, everywhere there is serious resistance by Russian units.

LVI Panzerkorps with 129. Infanterie-Division is on a line 2 kilometers south of Kholm-Zhirkovskii – Olad'ino, while 7. Panzer-Division has reached especially poor roads in Glushenkovo.

XXXXI Panzerkorps with 6. Infanterie-Division is moving directly to the south from Komary. Its 1. Panzer-Division as before is in combat on a line 2 kilometers northwest of Vysokoe – Zhutchinovo, and partially still in Podzelika and Kniazh'e. The 36. Infanterie-Division (mot.) is advancing southeast of Belyi in the direction of the Belyi – Komary highway.

VI Armeekorps with 26. Infanterie-Division is to the north of Belyi. The 110. Infanterie-Division, having met light resistance in Ust'e, crushed it and moved on further to the east. In Borki, 500 prisoners were taken by units of the division, and 300 bodies of dead Soviet soldiers and commanders were counted. Its left wing at Koshchenki Station at the army's command was detached for further use to the southeast in order to support XXIII Armeekorps' 206. Infanterie-Division.

The city of Belyi has been fully occupied by troops of VI Armeekorps. Encircled forces of the Red Army with increasing attacks were gradually undertaking ever more fierce attempts to break out of encirclement; however, they were all repelled with very high losses for them.[103]

By the end of the day to the right of 6. Panzer-Division, 129. Infanterie-Division had turned its front to the south and was mopping up the area south of Kholm-Zhirkovskii. The artillery and tanks of 6. Panzer-Division were ready for further offensive actions. The division itself was poised to advance to Viaz'ma and would start this, once the reinforced 129. Infanterie-Division had reached the line that had been designated for it and all the approach routes had been made absolutely safe. In addition, 6. Panzer-Division was filling a large gap, which had been created after the withdrawal of its Panzer-Regiment 2 to Liapkino to assist 1. Panzer-Division and the forward movement of the 129. Infanterie-Division.

As on the Briansk axis, the German breakthroughs to Viaz'ma were implemented after the corresponding working over of the Soviet defenses by the Luftwaffe. German aircraft were operating in large groups, inflicting mass attacks upon units of the Red Army. The Germans had plain superiority in the air. On 4 October alone and only in the Belyi – Sychevka – Viaz'ma triangle, the formations of the VIII Fliegerkorps conducted 152 missions by dive bombers and 259 raids by bombers.

On the front of the attacking German 9. Armee, units of the Red Army were continuing to offer varying amounts of resistance, although on the front of LVI Panzerkorps' offensive, they had already been thrown back beyond the Dnepr. In their summary accounts for 4 October, the Germans noted strong counterattacks by the Red Army along the entire bridgehead that they occupied east of Kholm-Zhirkovskii.[104]

The Soviet units south of Kholm-Zhirkovskii had been for the most part destroyed, and the Germans had begun an unobstructed advance out of their bridgeheads toward the highway leading to Griaznoe. XXXXI Panzerkorps had advanced to the Dnepr south of Belyi, while VI Armeekorps, securing the northern flank of the panzer group, had already closed on Egor'e.

By the end of 4 October 7. Panzer-Division had once again halted for want of fuel. Its route of advance was such that it was only possible to supply it by air. For this, the division command demanded the urgent support of VIII Fliegerkorps on 5 October. Temporary field airstrips in the area of Rudakovo northwest of Kholm-Zhirkovskii were established as the place for the unloading of fuel. Simultaneously, the securing of air support against the Soviet remnants south of Kholm-Zhirkovskii and against the Soviet positions north of the bridgehead was planned.

The operations department of the Panzergruppe 3 headquarters moved to Korytno. It was decided to conduct the relocation of headquarters at night, since by day the roads were too congested. The weather on this day hadn't let anyone down; it had been sunny and clear.

The command posts of XXXXI Panzerkorps and VI Armeekorps were unchanged; the LVI Panzerkorps' headquarters was in Babinki, while that of V Armeekorps was in Bykovo.[105]

One more day of Operation Typhoon had come to an end. Over the three days of the offensive, 8,400 prisoners had been taken by units of Panzergruppe 3, and 103 guns and 77 tanks captured.[106]

5 October 1941 (Sunday)

For the morning, an attack by 7. Panzer-Division in the direction of Viaz'ma out of its staging area in Glushkovo had been designated. German reconnaissance established that in the sector of the division's attack, the Russian positions were moderately developed and well-camouflaged on the fringes of forests and seemed ready to defend stubbornly against attacks by the division's Schützen-Regiment 6, which had been reinforced by a portion of a panzer regiment on the right flank and Panzer-Regiment 25 on the left flank. As always, the ground forces had been guaranteed strong air support.[107]

Throughout the preceding night, Soviet field artillery had placed harassing fire on the northern outskirts of Belyi, accompanied by constant fire from all types of infantry weapons. The Soviet air force again conducted night bombing raids against the roads being used by columns of troops and equipment of the panzer group.[108]

For the first time in Russia, soldiers of 129. Infanterie-Division's I./Infanterie-Regiment 427 spent the night in a barn, and not under the open sky. They had to observe blackout conditions, so that encircled units of the Red Army couldn't detect them. The young soldiers were all outside, because the barn didn't have enough room for all the men. Things were bad with food; only tinned fish in tomato sauce was available. The regiment itself at this time was south of Rzhev, closer to Sychevka than to Viaz'ma.

The front was not far away. The moon was bright, the breezes chilly, and there were distant sounds of explosions and crossfires. However, the first sentries hadn't yet been relieved, when at 0130 the battalion was raised on an alert and immediately sent on the march again. By 0600 it was already in Kholm-Zhirkovskii together with the rest of the regiment. On the streets of the town there were trucks abandoned by the retreating Red Army, dead horses, papers, maps and other types of property, which were also scattered about in trenches. There was a large bunker atop the hill in the beautiful city park, which had served as the Soviet command post until the city fell. There was nowhere to stop in the town and find nighttime billets, so I. Bataillon took a position in open terrain directly to the east of Kholm-Zhirkovskii, while II. Bataillon was located in woods 2 kilometers northwest of the town. However, III. Bataillon was lucky; it had reached the village of Chernovo north of Kholm.[109]

Over the preceding night, things were relatively quiet for the 107th Motorized Rifle Division, and only on the morning of 5 October did the Germans resume attacks in the sector of its 20th Reconnaissance Battalion from the direction of Aleshkovo. These attacks were also driven back by the men of the reconnaissance battalion. The reserve tank company of 8 T-26 tanks under the command of Captain Ninishvili fought heroically. Having dug in on a hill east of Nefedovo, it was able to hold out until 1600, when out of ammunition it was attacked by heavy tanks and completely destroyed. However, this delaying action gave the division an opportunity to begin a retreat and to gain separation from the enemy. The withdrawal was conducted under the direct leadership of the deputy commander of the 30th Army Major General Zhuravlev, who was located with the division.[110]

With this, the clash between these two divisions ended, and the paths of the 107th Motorized Rifle Division and 1. Panzer-Division parted forever. From this moment, the Soviet division's 25-day trek with fighting through the German rear areas began, and only on 31 October was it able to escape encirclement. However, we will still have to return to its saga, and thus we still won't say farewell to the 107th Motorized Rifle Division.

The 1. Panzer-Division also continued to advance to the east, resolving tactical situations along the way. Since the preceding day, the shock group of the division's II./Schützen-Regiment 113, reinforced with Oberleutnant Dräger's 2./Panzerjäger Abteilung 37 and II./Artillerie-Regiment 73 headed by Hauptmann Berckefelt had been defending positions on the division's left flank in the village of Medvedevo in the woods northeast of Baturino, since the Russians had been attacking there persistently throughout the night. Near sunrise a fierce battle erupted involving the 2. Panzerjäger Kompanie. Dräger managed to organize panzer support for an infantry battalion that was also defending there, as a result of which they knocked out 35 Russian tanks of the "Christie" type (apparently these were light BT tanks and/or T-26 tanks, but the number of knocked-out tanks is still disturbing).

In this action, for the first and perhaps the last time in the eastern campaign, victory was plainly on the side of the anti-tank defense provided by the 37-mm anti-tank guns. As subsequently became known, the attack was made by the Soviet 103rd Tank Division, which had recently been transferred from the Far East, and this combat with a head-on attack proved to be its first and last. However, in the process, Dräger's company alone lost all of its commanders killed or wounded up to the platoon level inclusively.

Meanwhile, Aufklärung-Abteilung 4, having gotten a rest in Baturino, once again moved out in the lead further to the east, pursuing the retreating Red Army units, while simultaneously covering the flank of Panzergruppe 3 to the north of the highway and northeast of the Dnepr River. The 1. Panzer-Division faced the task of reaching the area around Sychevka, 70 kilometers north of Viaz'ma, as soon as possible.[111]

The LVI Panzerkorps set its attack to begin at 0900, and for 10 minutes prior to its start there was a softening-up attack by 36 bombers of VIII Fliegerkorps. Three minutes before the start of its attack, LVI Panzerkorps conducted an artillery preparation with the concentrated fire of all the batteries of the Artillerie-Regiment 129 and the artillery of Panzer-Regiment 11.[112]

The XXXXI Panzerkorps on the evening before had reached the Dnepr while bypassing Spas-Demensk on two sides, in order after taking Sychevka to push on toward Torbeevo, after which temporary responsibility to control the schedule of movement to Krapivnia would be placed on its 14. Infanterie-Division (mot.), while the rest of the LVI Panzerkorps would control the road through Smetishche.

At 0845, a report arrived from XXXXI Panzerkorps at the panzer group headquarters, informing it that panzers and an infantry battalion in armored halftracks of 1. Panzer-Division had pivoted to the east, because approximately 100 Soviet tanks had been discovered in front of Romanovo [Author's note: This figure is dubious. Most likely, the pilots of VIII Fliegerkorps included both armored cars and perhaps even tractors in this total].

The corps command requested a partition of Infanterie-Division 14 (mot.), but in the headquarters of the panzer group they believed instead that the division should link up with LVI Panzerkorps, and already by the morrow be near Bor with all of its tracked equipment.

At 0930 an order arrived for 14. Infanterie-Division (mot.), together with the engineers of LVI Panzerkorps, to have all the roads leading to Zubtsov, Pochinki, Krechetskaia and Smetishche be ready by 1200. From 6 October, control over these roads would be assumed by LVI Panzerkorps. All of the road-building units for supporting movement along the route Bor – Belyi had been offered to the panzer group, and the group's quartermaster was intending on 7 October to start with the organization of traffic control posts in Belyi.

At 1005, a massed attack by Ju-87 Stuka dive bombers took place south of Kholm-Zhirkovskii, which proved to be relatively effective, after which 129. Infanterie-Division was ready to advance further. However, the possibility of such an advance didn't materialize right away, because despite the massive airstrike, the Red Army went on the attack first with infantry and tanks, which were repulsed. Three Soviet tanks were knocked out, and a lot of Red Army men were left lying where death had found them; the rest had fled. Even though their own losses proved rather painful, units of 129. Infanterie-Division went on the attack immediately following an artillery preparation.[113] Despite the concentrated fire of Russian infantry and artillery, this attack proved successful, as a result of which Infanterie-Regiment 430 by 1100 was occupying the fringe of some woods south of Kholm-Zhirkovskii, while the Infanterie-Regiment 428 around the same time took the relatively weak Russian positions in Ust'e from the march.[114]

At 1130 an order from XXXXI Panzerkorps arrived in 36. Infanterie-Division (mot.) to move out from Zheltyi and to continue an advance to the east. Hoth on his part proposed that it should attack together with 7. Panzer-Division toward Ivashkovo. Its commander Oberst Roettiger agreed with this, but expressed concern about possible strong flank attacks on the Dnepr. At the same time, the vanguard of 1. Panzer-Division from the beginning had been included in the timetable of the 36. Infanterie-Division (mot.)'s march movement.[115]

The 129. Infanterie-Division's Infanterie-Regiment 427 at this time was located in an area north of Kholm-Zhirkovskii, and from 1130 it was ready to move on. It was given a new assignment to secure the approaching panzer divisions against possible counterattacks south of the Kholm-Zhirkovskii – Tikhanovo road, since the area around Kholm-Zhirkovskii still hadn't been completely mopped up of the Red Army units that remained there. However, while I./Infanterie-Regiment 427 under the command of Hauptmann Dörr controlled the Kholm-Zhirkovskii – Tikhanovo road, constantly repelling flank attacks and suffering heavy losses as a result of them, II./Infanterie-Regiment 427, thanks to this, was hurrying to reach the line Sorokino – Fedorkino, while III. Bataillon was kept in reserve.

The tanks of Panzer-Regiment 11 were assembled within the bridgehead across the Dnepr River at Tikhanovo. To the south of the Kholm-Zhirkovskii – Tikhanovo road, waiting for the pocket to be closed, was a platoon of 88-mm anti-aircraft guns, facing southward for firing over open sights in the event of a possible tank attack from that direction. The II. and III./Infanterie-Regiment 430 were deployed in the Bolshanska area, while two battalions of the Infanterie-Regiment 428 were in the Ivanovo area.

Unaware of the potential of the Soviet artillery, the headquarters of I./Infanterie-Regiment 427 had established itself in Kholm-Zhirkovskii along both sides of the road, without any sort of overhead cover, while III. Bataillon had begun to comb through the woods north of the road in the direction of Saporkino and to the northeast toward Fedorkino.

An attack by Soviet tanks from the south wasn't long in coming. It wasn't easy to overlook one, since this was the only possible tank-vulnerable axis of concern to the defenders of Kholm-Zhirkovskii, which were now the Germans. The attack was repulsed, and all the Soviet tanks were set ablaze by the fire of the 88-mm Flak guns with the coordinated support of tank fire and artillery.[116]

However, the Soviet artillery fire didn't cease, which caused I./Infanterie-Regiment 427 to fall back a little. During the withdrawal, its headquarters together with the commander, his adjutant and other officers, radiomen and company commanders came under the concentrated fire of several Russian batteries. There were many killed and badly wounded. The battalion adjutant Leutnant Günther got caught by a direct artillery barrage, but by some miracle he came through it unscathed.

After this event, the Germans realized that Soviet artillery observers were in the church belfry in the very nearby village of Tychkovo, who were able to observe the entire plateau stretching from Kholm-Zhirkovskii to the east of the Dnepr and to the north of the Viaz'ma River, as well as all the surrounding approach routes. In order to avoid excessive losses, the division halted its head-on attack and its units went over to a tactical defense.

Meanwhile, at 1415 Infanterie-Regiment 430 also came under heavy fire from 20 Soviet tanks that were attacking it, among which were also 52-ton models (seemingly, T-35 or KV-1 tanks). The attack struck the regiment's III. Bataillon, which since that very morning had been placing strong pressure on the right flank of its adversary. However, the defenders, lacking any armor-piercing guns, were helpless against the Soviet tanks. Only grenades and demolition charges were available for use against the armor monsters. The regiment became isolated and contact with it was lost.[117]

The 6. Infanterie-Division, which arrived at the Dnepr at mid-day, immediately began to prepare for a crossing. All of the division's transport means were assembled on a gentle slope leading down to the river, while the bulk of the divisional artillery was located in nearby woods. The division command believed that immediately after constructing pontoon bridges, the division could cross to the opposite bank as rapidly as possible. Yet no one was anticipating that Soviet heavy artillery in concealed positions on the opposite bank would concentrate all of their fire here.

Here is how an eyewitness describes what happened on this day:

> Lucky is a member of a mechanized unit who also has a single slit trench available as a means of cover. Casualties from the fire are rising. The combat medics are working on the badly wounded, resulting from shells exploding among the trees. A dead man's head minus a jaw or scalp, dangling from a cable wire, is not a rare sight. Damaged guns are being hauled away under the fire. From the division's vanguard to the rear, wounded men are being transported away in halftracks, on tanks, and even in staff cars.[118]

Further on in these same documents, it is stated that the dead and mortally wounded were brought back directly to Kholm-Zhirkovskii, where a mass burial soon began. Red Army prisoners, who were also brought into the city, did the work. Among them there were also a lot of female service personnel. Yet just as the burial was taking place, there was a Soviet air attack on the site. Everything became jumbled together with the earth, including the bodies of the German soldiers and the military prisoners.

In order to silence the Soviet artillery, an airstrike with approximately 25 Stuka dive bombers was delivered against its firing positions at 1300, but this proved insufficient, and it was followed at 1600 by another airstrike delivered by 40 dive bombers. It was only after this that the artillery barrage ceased. Unfortunately, it is still unknown which Soviet artillery unit or units so thoroughly drubbed the German 6. Infanterie-Division; the archives still contain a lot of secrets.

Now, fuel starvation began to affect the 129. Infanterie-Division. The infantry, left without the support of heavy weapons and tanks, was compelled to halt. In addition, there wasn't enough time and technical equipment to do maintenance and repair work on damaged equipment. For the first order of business, it was decided to supply the division's forward combat units with fuel, and since one aircraft might deliver no more than 200 liters, then the question of keeping rear units fueled up was totally set aside for an indeterminate amount of time.

In connection with the fact that the division's attack had come to a stop on a broad front, II./Infanterie-Regiment 430 wound up on the axis most vulnerable to tanks. Its positions were located in the center of the attack sector on Hill 229.5, immediately south of Kholm-Zhirkovskii. In order to support it, 7./Infanterie-Regiment 427 had been hastily sent. Moreover, Red Army units again materialized along the road through the area of the forested tracts southeast of Kholm-Zhirkovskii, which had been combed through that morning.. The regimental scout platoon was ordered to sweep through this wooded area once again.

While Infanterie-Regiment 430 was fortifying its positions, the positions of 14./Infanterie-Regiment 427 (the regiment's anti-tank company) were attacked by 8 Soviet tanks. Now in return, Infanterie-Regiment 430 hastily dispatched a platoon of 50-mm anti-tank guns to Infanterie-Regiment 427's aid. The Soviet attack was repulsed. There were no further attacks on this axis, and the regiment remained in reserve north of Kholm-Zhirkovskii until nightfall.[119]

The 7. Panzer-Division had again been idled from mid-day due to the lack of fuel. The promised fuel was delivered aboard transport aircraft only at 1430. After refueling, in order to make up for the lost time, an attempt was made to break into Kamenets from the march, but the Soviet defense there proved to be sufficiently firm, and in order to avoid excessive losses, the Luftwaffe was called upon for help. After a powerful bombing, 6./Panzer-Regiment 5 launched an attack with the support of an infantry regiment, and already at 1500 they entered the town without encountering resistance.[120] Having seized Kamenets, Panzer-Regiment 5 moved on to the north without stopping.[121]

The 6. Panzer-Division had also come to stop, since from 1530 it had been left with only three battalions of infantry. The panzers, designated for use south of Kholm-Zhirkovskii, still hadn't arrived.

At this time V Armeekorps' 106. Infanterie-Division, repulsing strong attacks, was advancing 4 kilometers east of Skripenki; its 5. Infanterie-Division was north of Noviki, while 35. Infanterie-Division was east of the Otpisnaia – Fedino line.

In LVI Panzerkorps, 129. Infanterie-Division was slowly pushing to the south from Kholm-Zhirkovskii. In the XXXXI Panzerkorps, its 6. Infanterie-Division had entered Komary, while the 36. Infanterie-Division (mot.) had halted in Bozino since 0900. The 1. Panzer-Division with a portion of its tanks had reached the Belyi – Komary road southeast of Belyi back at 1130. Other units of the panzer corps were still locked in combat northeast of Volynovo.

In VI Armeekorps, 26. Infanterie-Division remained in reserve, and for the forthcoming isolation of Belyi, it had extended 4 kilometers to the northeast and northwest. Its 110. Infanterie-Division together with the reconnaissance battalion's bicycle squadron at 1200 was not far from the northwestern outskirts of Belyi.

At 1740 a message arrived in Panzergruppe 3 from VIII Fliegerkorps that 7. Panzer-Division was for some reason falling back rapidly, even though Kamenets was just 1 kilometer away. However, already within the hour a report arrived from the division that Kamenets had previously fallen after a tough battle, and its command was simply regrouping its units.[122]

Panzergruppe 4 by this time was already just 80 kilometers southeast of Viaz'ma. The jaws of encirclement were inexorably closing, and no one was even able to imagine the consequences of this. Just several days remained until the tragic conclusion, and the command of Panzergruppe 3 was particularly interested in the fact that its subordinate corps were now rapidly and successfully advancing to the Dnepr. For this, V Armeekorps was given II./Artillerie-Regiment 38 from LVI Panzerkorps in exchange for a 100-mm battery, while its 35. Infanterie-Division on 6 October was supposed to launch an attack with three regiments north of Fedino in order to support the 129. Infanterie-Division's own attack.[123]

Having received fuel, 7. Panzer-Division resumed its advance and by evening, in the twilight, with its first attack it broke through the Soviet field fortifications in its attack sector to their entire depth. It was anticipated that after the onset of darkness, its panzers might reach the Belyi – Viaz'ma road, approximately 55 kilometers northwest of Viaz'ma. Its Panzer-Regiment 5 had advanced as far as Volochek. Taking advantage of a pause that had arisen, the commander of 6./Panzer-Regiment 5 Schröeder decided to use the evening for refueling, bringing up rear services, and regrouping, since a further advance was expected that night. Although the infantry accompanying the tanks were extremely exhausted, there were no thoughts of rest. Fatigue would tell later, when the attacking panzer regiment came under flanking fire from all types of weapons of a rather serious and tough Soviet defense, which had been laid out in an area of lush low scrub and bushes and blocked the advance of the infantry following behind the tanks.[124]

The 129. Infanterie-Division's Infanterie-Regiment 430 earlier that day had come under an attack by heavy Soviet tanks that had left it isolated. Later it became clear that soldiers of II. Bataillon had nevertheless succeeded in destroying one such tank on Hill 229.5, in woods to the west of Ust'e. This was done by an assault detachment of infantry and combat engineers with the help of a flamethrower and demolition charges. It seems that the tank had been immobilized and was in a stationary combat position, serving as a firing point with the crew inside.

The division plainly didn't have enough strength to rescue its isolated regiment, and an order from the corps command for 6 October arrived in 35. Infanterie-Division: "After an attack by dive bombers at 0900, launch an attack from Veretino to the west and from Kasilovo to the east, with the aim of freeing Infanterie-Regiment 430."[125]

That's how this day ended for 129. Infanterie-Division. Its units captured 550 prisoners and 21 tanks. The division itself lost 2 officers and 61 junior officers and men killed; 8 officers and 270 junior officers and men wounded; and 4 junior officers and men missing-in-action. Late in the evening, its Infanterie-Regiment 428 was able to take Chemenovo and another 400 prisoners there.[126]

At 2130, 9. Armee headquarters decided what to do with 900. Lehr-Brigade (mot.), which was restricting the panzer group's freedom of action northeast of Liapkino. It was left in reserve on the army's left wing; as compensation, one panzer brigade of XXXXI Panzerkorps was transferred to the control Panzergruppe 3's headquarters.

By 2200, 7. Panzer-Division had reached the hills southeast of Nastas'ino, where the Soviet defensive positions proved to be relatively weak. Success was ensured by supporting the panzers with a motorized infantry regiment from 6. Panzer-Division, and thus the 7. Panzer-Division continued to roll forward. For its part, 6. Panzer-Division also achieved success at the southern bridgehead thanks to the strong support of field artillery, but its activity on this day along the bend in the Dnepr River toward Viaz'ma was only a preparatory attack. The main attack in this location was planned for the next day with the support of its own artillery and air support.

Intelligence information and the analysis of the situation that had arisen by this time suggested to the German command that south of Kholm-Zhirkovskii, the Soviet command had decided to reinforce its forces from the south. Its intention appeared to be to cut-off and encircle the German forces advancing out of the Dnepr bridgeheads.

In order to forestall this, V Armeekorps ordered its forward 106. Infanterie-Division, which was 7 kilometers east of Skripenki, and its 5. Infanterie-Division

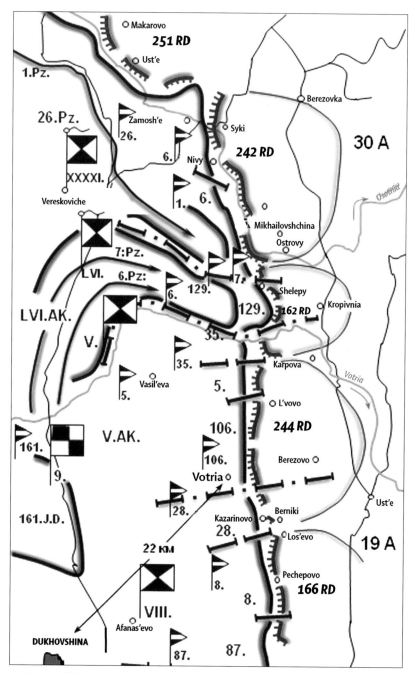

Map 1 The German 3rd Panzer Group at the boundary between the
30th and 19th armies. (Source: D.M. Glantz, *Atlas*)

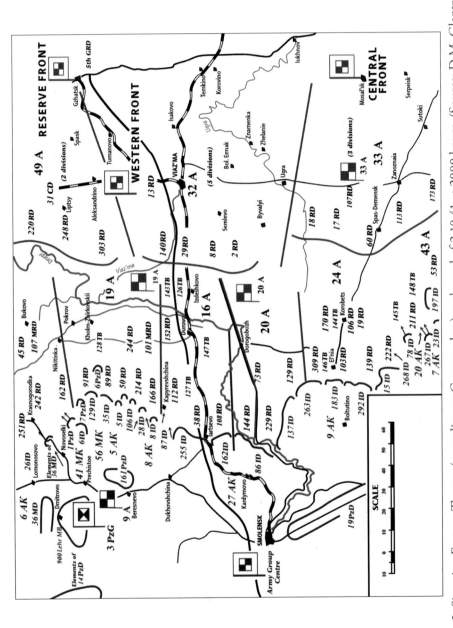

Map 2 Situation Eastern Theatre (according to German data) at the end of 2.10.41 at 2000 hours. (Source: D.M. Glantz, *Atlas*)

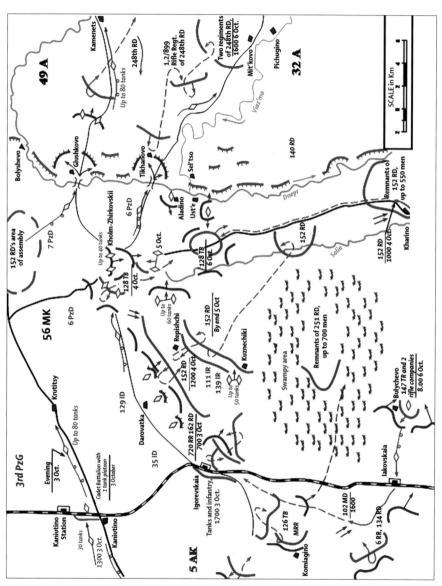

Map 3 Counter-attack by Operational Group Boldin, 3-6 October 1941.

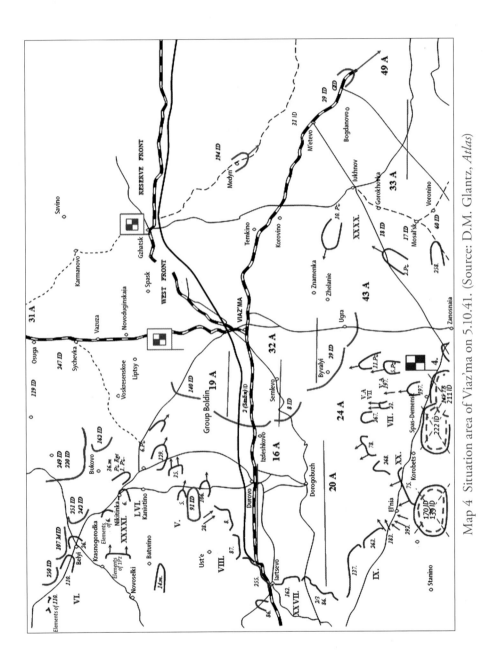

Map 4 Situation area of Viaz'ma on 5.10.41. (Source: D.M. Glantz, *Atlas*)

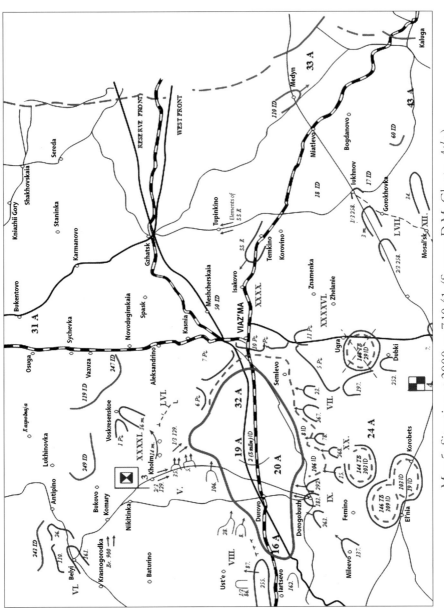

Map 5 Situation at 2000 on 7.10.41. (Source: D.M. Glantz, *Atlas*)

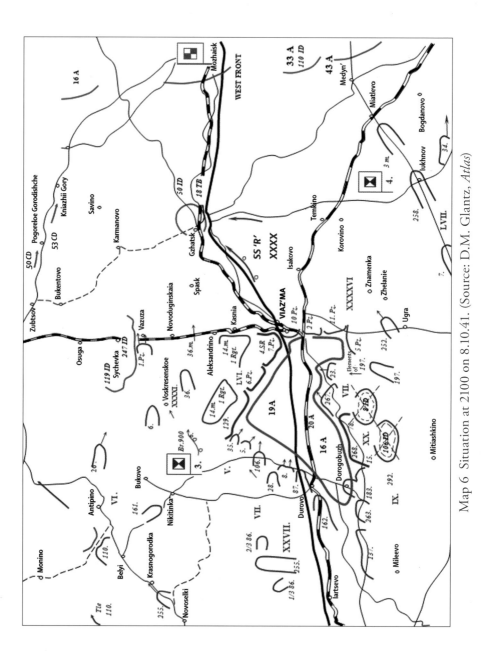

Map 6 Situation at 2100 on 8.10.41. (Source: D.M. Glantz, *Atlas*)

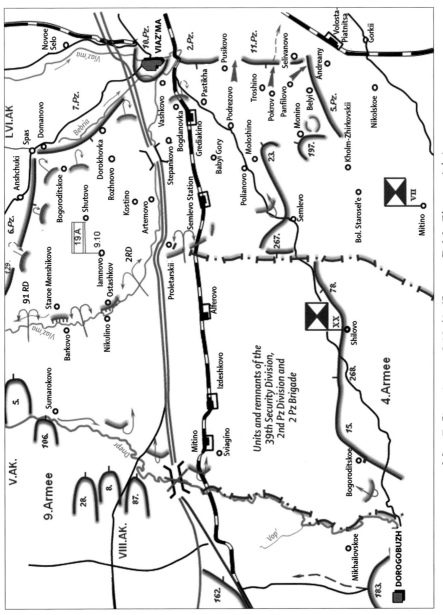

Map 7 Situation on 9.10.41. (Source: D.M. Glantz, *Atlas*)

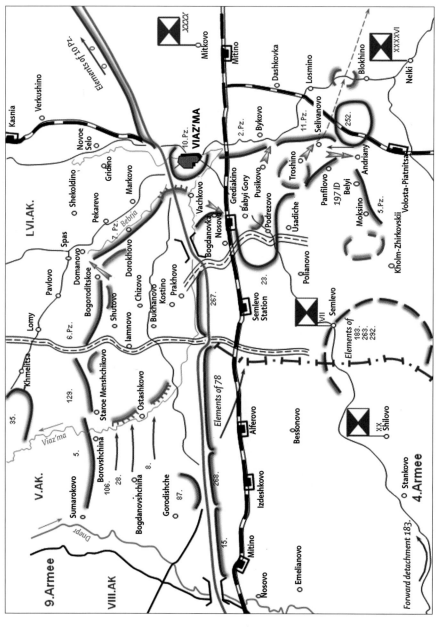

Map 8 Situation on 11.10.41. (Source: D.M. Glantz, *Atlas* – supplemented by author)

to destroy the Soviet units in the Noviki area, which were being reinforced. The 35. Infanterie-Division remained without changes.

The XXXXI Panzerkorps' 36. Infanterie-Division (mot.) was in Konakovo, while the forward units of 1. Panzer-Division were in Zheltoe, having deployed with its front to the east and having no contact with the enemy. Ol'shanka and Karavaevo had been reached. The 6. Infanterie-Division was in the area of Zheltoe and Komary. The 14. Infanterie-Division (mot.), still located in corps' reserve, had arrived on the outskirts of Shanino.

Hoth received a report from the Heeresgruppe Mitte headquarters at 2330, informing him that he must urgently take command of 17. Armee. This was so unexpected, that the question of his successor in command of Panzergruppe 3 remained undecided, so in the meantime he still commanded it. However, despite this looming command change, the plans for 6 October remained essentially unchanged. Only adjustments were made for LVI Panzerkorps, which was ordered overnight to assemble in front of the highway to the west of Viaz'ma. In addition, the command post of XXXXI Panzerkorps was shifted to Bol'shoe Shamilovo, 9 kilometers southeast of Belyi.[127]

The day of 5 October was coming to an end. The overall booty of Panzergruppe 3 amounted to 13,500 prisoners, 263 guns, 113 tanks, 41 anti-tank and anti-aircraft guns, 259 machine guns and 63 mortars.[128]

On the whole, the day had been dry, but cloudy. Toward evening rain began to fall and the conditions of the roads deteriorated significantly, especially because of the heavy wear on them. Soviet air activity had decreased somewhat.[129] True, for the first time it had been noted in the operational dispatches of the Heeresgruppe Mitte headquarters that "in front of the southern flank of 9. Armee in the area of Viaz'ma, the use by the Soviet side of aircraft of the "Hurricane" type has been established."[130]

In this same report it is again noted:

> On the 4th day of our offensive, the command of the Red Army's Western Front
> has not started the withdrawal of its main forces. Retrograde movement on sepa-
> rate sectors of the front, as well as the weak resistance in places, can be regarded
> as signs of a local weakness of the Red Army, resulting from the differing combat
> power of our formations and the variously unfolding situation.[131]

As result, a final determination was' made that the command of the Red Army intended by any means, using all possible reserves, to hold the front and to localize the breakthroughs by the German forces.[132]

In its turn, in the course of the day's combat operations, the command of Western Front had conducted a regrouping of forces, as a result of which the Reserve Front's 31st and 32nd Armies passed to the control of Western Front headquarters. At the same time, by the end of this day it had become clear that the 128th Tank Brigade of Group Boldin, after three days of fighting, had been encircled by the forces of up to an enemy infantry division.[133]

On this day, the Germans conducted their first massive air raid against Rzhev, as a result of which 52 Red Army personnel and 18 civilians were killed, and 51 Red Army men and 15 civilians wounded. The raid destroyed railroads, a portion of the Rzhev-2 Station, warehouses and residential buildings.[134]

Subsequently the situation began to develop such that on 6 October, the Western Front command was compelled to hastily move its headquarters from Kasnia Station further to the east to the village of Stolbovo.[135] By the evening of 6 October, Konev issued a command for his troops to withdraw to the prepared Viaz'ma – Rzhev defensive line. Also on this same day (5 October), at the order of Stalin, Zhukov arrived in Moscow from Leningrad.

6 October (Monday)

Group Boldin's 128th Tank Brigade, which had become encircled the day before, managed to break out with fighting in the direction of Vorontsovo. The main group, coming out of encirclement, came under the command of 19th Army and was subsequently involved in heavy fighting in the Bogoroditskoe area, 17 kilometers northwest of Viaz'ma, where the Germans were stubbornly opposing them, striving to prevent them from breaking out.[136] The fighting in the Kholm-Zhirkovskii and Tikhanovo area, which had continued on through the night, had even intensified by morning.[137]

By 0800, the 107th Motorized Rifle Division, which with the onset of darkness had managed to break contact with the enemy on the evening before, was assembled in woods 1 kilometer south of Samsonikhi, where in the course of the day it prepared to breakout of encirclement. Now, a month of roaming through the German rear areas in the woods, accompanied by fighting of local significance, confronted it.[138]

At 0815, a signals officer from the headquarters of 129. Infanterie-Division visited the commander of Infanterie-Regiment 427 Oberst Danhauser and informed him that in the division's operational sector, the Russians were showing little activity. Thus the division didn't need his regiment and it would be used for other assignments, for which it had been decided to reinforce him with III./Artillerie-Regiment 129 that had been returned from its temporary attachment with 6. Infanterie-Division.

For his part, the commander of 6. Infanterie-Division Generalmajor Landgraf was counting upon Infanterie-Regiment 427 to facilitate the division's crossing of the Dnepr River in Tikhanovo by reaching Hill 220.5 west of Petukhi with one battalion, and the line Tychkovo – Roman'kovo with a second battalion. These villages had already been taken on the first attempt by infantry units of his division, but they needed support. Simultaneously, the reconnaissance battalion of the 129. Infanterie-Division was directed to probe the area of Sel'tso.[139]

At 0845 on 6 October, a proposal arrived at the Panzergruppe 3 headquarters from 9. Armee headquarters to begin sealing the pocket in Viaz'ma, because the present positions of its units were promising for this task:

The 106. Infanterie-Division is positioned between VIII Armeekorps and the Dnepr in Sumorokovo, the 5. and 35. Infanterie-Divisionen have reached the line: Staroe Menshchikovo – north of Chupchuevo – north of LVI Panzerkorps, which is located in the Spas area 18 kilometers northwest of Viaz'ma and on its part is thoroughly covering the entire area east and north of the city. XXXXI Panzerkorps is located in the Voskresenskoe – Karavaevo – Lipitsy area, while the 6. Infanterie-Division and VI Armeekorps are already moving through Mol'nia toward Belyi.[140]

At 0950, a message arrived at the headquarters of Panzergruppe 3 from aerial reconnaissance regarding the movement of large Russian motorized columns from Viaz'ma to the north, which prompted the panzer group's command to issue an order to LVI Panzerkorps for the commander of 7. Panzer-Division General Funk to continue to push ahead.[141] Subsequently, at 1000 that division's adjutant passed an order to the commander of Schützen-Regiment 6 Oberleutnant Hasso Manteuffel to seize the Russian positions in front of him with his first attack, and having paused for a bit of rest, to exploit the offensive in the direction of the Viaz'ma River.

Having received this order, the regiment's infantry with heavy weapons boarded armored halftracks and with the support of tanks attacked the Soviet positions through the extensive area of scrub and brush, and having taken them with the first attempt, didn't linger there long. Rather, Manteuffel continued to press the offensive, having obtained the support of artillery and Schützen-Regiment 7, as well as of hunter-killers of the VIII Fliegerkorps.[142]

At 1000, a Storch aircraft that was carrying Oberleutnant Pollex of Panzergruppe 3's operations department crashed while taking off. Pollex received a light head wound and a slight concussion. This caused a perceptible interruption in the work of Panzergruppe 3's headquarters, which subsequently had a serious impact on the attacking units.

At 1120, the commander of LVI Panzerkorps reported to Hoth:

> The situation south of Kholm[-Zhirkovskii] is under control. The 35. Infanterie-Division has taken Romaniki; the 129. Infanterie-Division was already in Chernovo yesterday evening, but one of its regiments has been sent to defend the southern flank of the Dnepr bridgehead. The 7. Panzer-Division is east of Dernovo. Russians as before are in their second line of defense, but seemingly have been greatly weakened. The 6. Panzer-Division is on the southern bank of the Viaz'ma River, but without equipment, which presents a threat to its flanks in the event of a Russian counteroffensive.[143]

In order to carry out the unexpected order, 129. Infanterie-Division's Infanterie-Regiment 427 began moving out by battalion for Tikhanovo at 1200. Artillerie-Regiment 129's III. Bataillon was being towed by tracked vehicles into position west of Koshkino in order to support III./Infanterie-Regiment 427's actions. Meanwhile,

II. Bataillon would remain in reserve in Kazarinovo to the north of the bridge crossing the Dnepr, but now on its eastern bank. The regiment's headquarters was located in Koshkino, where the Viaz'ma River flows into the Dnepr. The regiment was supposed to replace the weakened German units there and continue the offensive, which was done to the letter. Afterward, I./Infanterie-Regiment 427 pushed south of the road to Kholm-Zhirkovskii through the woods and ravines. There the men discovered abandoned Soviet positions. In a damaged and abandoned staff vehicle they found a map case containing a whole series of Soviet maps that for some reason included maps of Germany's Upper Silesia area.

In Tikhanovo, there were German anti-tank and Nebelwerfer positions that extended along the valley of the Dnepr. The slope of the river's western bank was rather gentle, but the eastern bank was relatively steep, and the Soviet positions there consisted of earthworks, trenches, bunkers and barbed wire obstacles that extended both laterally and into the depth.

The forward units of Panzer-Regiment 25 had crossed the Dnepr without hindrance over the second bridge that had been taken by the Germans north of Glushkovo. A German veteran later wrote in his memoirs: "Such a mass of tanks in a restricted space was a rare sight, some sort of 'iron fist' on the eastern side of the Dnepr. The begrimed tankers were satisfied with the arrival of infantry, since lacking infantry cover they had been stopped by the meeting fire of Russian tanks."[144]

At 1200, Oberst Deister of the VIII Fliegerkorps and Oberst Eydman of Luftflotte 2 arrived at the headquarters of Panzergruppe 3 to obtain information about the current situation. They also delivered the latest intelligence from aerial reconnaissance, according to the findings of which 1. Panzer-Division was ordered to launch an offensive as quickly as possible from its current position in Gubino. The information that 6. Infanterie-Division had reached Bukovo delighted the panzer group's command, since to this point no messages had arrived from it.

At this same time, a less pleasing report arrived that 36. Infanterie-Division (mot.) had taken a wrong turn off the Komary – Ivashkovo highway and had been compelled to retrace its movement; since 1000 it was still in the process of regrouping in Bol'shoi Pot'min and was thus not yet combat-ready. In order to secure itself against possible attacks at this time, the entire space in front of its positions had been heavily mined.

In the afternoon, the command of 6. Panzer-Division also felt concerned; it had become stuck in Kholm-Zhirkovskii because of the demolished bridge across the Dnepr there, and its Aufklärung-Abteilung 57 had been unable to push further to the east. The panzer division's neighbors had long since continued ahead, and the division's flanks were exposed. At any moment, an attack might come against them, and moreover, the command had no knowledge of what forces might be lurking nearby, and what they might be capable of doing. However, Hoth calmed the 6. Panzer-Division's headquarters down, informing it that Hoepner's and Guderian's panzer groups were making splendid progress and that 7. Panzer-Division on the left was rapidly closing on Viaz'ma. In addition, aerial reconnaissance was reporting on lengthy Soviet columns, retreating to the east from Viaz'ma. This information of course inspired confidence that everything would go well, but nervousness remained, moreover because at this time the Soviet command within the forming cauldron was committing reserves from the south along both sides of the Dnepr against the entire Panzergruppe 3. Thus, its southern flank in the form of 6. Panzer-Division wound up involved in combat clashes with various disorganized units and types of Red Army forces, which had wound up in the rear of the attacking German troops, and the quantity and composition of them were still unknown.[145]

Exploiting the offensive, 7. Panzer-Division at 1250 entered Kostino with tanks, and at 1300 its reconnaissance battalion was already in Rodino.[146] There the tanks met up with the Schützen-Regiment 6, and then they moved on toward Viaz'ma with a portion of the panzer regiment and a forward platoon of infantry mounted in halftracks. The infantry commander, who was leading the column, gave the signal for full speed ahead, as far as this was possible on the Russian roads. Often, simply astonishing things took place. At one point, the Germans and Russians were moving in virtually parallel columns, but in the extremely dusty conditions apparently the Russians apparently failed to realize that the other column was German, which was striving to overtake them, and thus they made no reaction.[147]

In such situations, the forward German reconnaissance units in view of their small size sought to avoid combat with the retreating units, which were larger by many times, and attempted to find routes alternative to the main roads. However, this was no less risky, since there were still a lot of combat-capable Red Army units lurking in the forests. Strategically they were of course helpless, but on a tactical level they could still inflict serious damage. For example, in particular, a forward platoon in armored halftracks under the command of Leutnant Niklas, from the very same 7. Panzer-Division, overconfidently diverged from the road in order to follow a side track, and subsequently it was ambushed and completely destroyed before it was even able to deploy for combat.[148]

The Soviet command was still not hurrying to implement a planned withdrawal of its forces, but on the contrary was sending forward available reserves, which headed directly into the already forming pocket. For example, at an order from the 31st Army headquarters, at 1300 the 1287th Rifle Regiment of the 110th Rifle Division was sent to reinforce the 119th Rifle Division. Coming under the command of the latter division's headquarters, the arriving regiment took up a sector of defense in the area of Pokrovskoe State Farm, Ostashkov, Vyvorozh'e, Zaluch'e and Shcheberikhi. Its forward positions were situated between Lakes Seliger, Sterzh and Peno. An additional rifle company was immediately sent off to distant positions on the southern bank of Lake Seliger in the area of Usad'by. Units of the division prepared for a defense.[149]

In the afternoon, the first snow flurries fell. The 129. Infanterie-Division's Infanterie-Regiment 428 still west of the Dnepr River was conducting defensive fighting against strong attacks by Soviet forces attempting to break out from the south. In the morning, it had been quiet there, but after 1300 the Red Army resumed methodical attacks. Over the entire preceding night, Russian infantry with the support of tanks out of Erutino had repeatedly and rather fiercely attacked the positions of I./Infanterie-Regiment 428 in Chemenovo. Thus, that morning the commander of the Panzerjäger-Abteilung 129 had been sent to Chemenovo with one 88-mm Flak gun; at this time he was still en route. Two platoons of 50-mm guns of 14./Infanterie-Regiment 427 had been attached in support of him, one of which was still in its firing positions southwest of Baranovo, because it couldn't be pulled out due to the heavy fire of tanks and attacking infantry south of Hill 229.5. It wasn't clear where these Red Army forces had originated, because over the two preceding days the woods north of the Kholm-Zhirkovskii – Khanovo road had been thoroughly swept.

Twenty minutes after the start of the first Russian attack at 1300, over the radio a report arrived from I. Bataillon that "… according to the testimony of a Russian prisoner, 40 Soviet tanks are concentrated in the area of Hill 229.5 with the aim of blocking the German advance along the roads and to seize the bridgehead in Tikhanovo, and thus to hurl back the 35. Infanterie-Division."[150] In connection with this, at 1330 the command of 129. Infanterie-Division asked the chief of staff of LVI Panzerkorps about the reasons for the delay of the combat group that consisted of three 88-mm Flak guns and tanks of the 7. Panzer-Division. It turned out that at this same time they were being held up in Gordeikino by two Soviet 52-ton tanks.[151]

At 1400 6. Panzer-Division entered Mitkino, although its forward tanks had been outside the village since 1000. It had been risky to rush the attack, because according to prisoners, three intact Soviet divisions were supposedly facing the division, and this information was passed on to Panzergruppe 3 headquarters aboard a liaison aircraft. After receiving authorization to proceed with the attack, the village was taken and a reconnaissance team was sent out, which found no Red Army units in the nearby vicinity.[152]

At 1440, on the northern sector of the 31st Army, the marching columns of the 110th Rifle Division, consisting of the 1289th and 1291st Rifle Regiments and the 336th Cavalry Regiment came under aerial attack while on their way to a line of defense in the vicinity of Bol'shaia Kosha and Lipovka. As a result, before taking part in combat, the division lost 3 killed and 15 wounded. In general, throughout this day the German air force displayed activity only in the army's northern sector.[153]

At 1500, concrete steps began to be taken to form the Viaz'ma pocket. For the command of the Panzergruppe 3 it was very desirable, so that:

> VI Armeekorps also become activated in order to expand the area north of Voskresenskoe further to the east, while the army headquarters also proposed to leave 6. Infanterie-Division with XXXXI Panzerkorps. The LVI Panzerkorps was being opposed by the 13th and 18th Soviet Rifle Divisions of the Reserve Front.
>
> The XXXXI Panzerkorps is involved in heavy combat against strong positions in Nemoshchennaia. Its reinforced 36. Infanterie-Division (mot.) is developing the offensive toward Bulashovo, while one panzer regiment of 1.

Panzer-Division already at 1230 was 3 kilometers east-southeast of Kuznetsovo.
VI Armeekorps has encircled weakened Russian units in their bridgehead at
the city of Belyi from the east and north.

Preparing to close the ring, the German command was forced to acknowledge the
plain superiority of the Red Army in artillery, owing to which the expected destruction of its units south of Belyi still hadn't taken place.

By this time, 106. Infanterie-Division was located 2 kilometers west of Gorodok.
The 5. Infanterie-Division was in Bych'i, while 35. Infanterie-Division was 2.5 kilometers northeast of Fedino.

While staff officers in the headquarters were determining the contours of the future
pocket, 129. Infanterie-Division again repulsed an attack by Russian infantry with
the support of tanks out of Veretenino toward Chernovo. Moreover, aerial reconnaissance had discovered a strong mixture of various Red Army formations west of
the Dnepr, but nothing was pointing to the fact that a retreat had started there. On
the contrary, all signs indicated that the Russians were seriously planning to stop the
advance of the Panzergruppe 3.

At 1540, the headquarters of 14. Infanterie-Division (mot.) was directed to abandon
Kholm-Zhirkovskii on 7 October and pull back for rest on 8 October. Until then,
aligning with 7. Panzer-Division's northern flank, it was to continue to cover the rear
of the 6. Panzer-Division against the unceasing attacks that were striking it.[154]

By 1700, Schröeder's forward battalion of the 7. Panzer-Division's Schützen-
Regiment 6 reached the crossroads on the Viaz'ma – Moscow highway approximately
2 kilometers to the north of Viaz'ma, which came as a complete surprise not only for
the Soviet, but also for the German command. Just 15 minutes later, the entire division emerged on the highway west of Viaz'ma, but there it was forced to halt again
for the lack of fuel, since all of its remaining fuel had been given to Panzer-Regiment
25 and Schützen-Regiment 6 in order to sustain their advance. There was simply
not enough fuel for the entire panzer division. However, thanks to this decision to
allocate the remaining fuel to the two regiments, the tasks that had been set for
Panzergruppe 3 for the given day had been fulfilled.[155]

Thus, for the third time since the start of Operation Barbarossa, 7. Panzer-Division
had reached the Minsk – Smolensk – Viaz'ma – Moscow highway. The entry in its
war diary for this day briefly noted: "The Panzer-Regiment 25 together with the reinforced Schützen-Regiment 6 seized the motorway." Subsequently, panzer company
commanders Richter and Reinhardt were given a task: "Be in the burning northwestern sector of Viaz'ma this night, where the division must close the pocket". The
headquarters of Schützen-Regiment 6 reported: "Everything is developing as always.
With all means only forward!"[156]

The 129. Infanterie-Division in Chemonovo between 1300 and 1815 withstood
seven tank attacks while knocking out eight Soviet tanks. One of them had even
been able to break through the main line of defense, but it had been immobilized
by grenade bundles, and then combat engineers crept up to it and destroyed it with

explosives together with its crew. As a result of this fighting, I./Infanterie-Regiment 428 in the afternoon alone lost one officer and 23 junior officers and soldiers killed, 79 soldiers wounded, and 4 missing-in-action. In order to avoid further excessive losses, Oberst Danhauser proposed to shorten his line by withdrawing from Chemenovo, which would allow him to free up an entire company for a reserve. Having received the approval of the division headquarters, he began to implement his plan straightaway under the covering fire of the division's artillery regiment along the road leading to the south out of Kholm-Zhirkovskii. Over the preceding 24 hours, the 129. Infanterie-Division lost 38 soldiers and one officer killed, 163 soldiers and one officer wounded, and in the forward battalions of Infanterie-Regimenter 427 and 428, 12 men went missing in action.[157]

Toward evening, 6. Panzer-Division received an order from the headquarters of LVI Panzerkorps to push forward as far as possible, since it had become clear that Hoepner's Panzergruppe 4 was still 40 kilometers southeast of Viaz'ma, making the city unattainable for it on 7 October. The command of Heeresgruppe Mitte hadn't expected such a rapid advance by Panzergruppe 3 into the depth of the Soviet's Dnepr positions; it was hoping that Panzergruppe 4 nevertheless would be able to get to Viaz'ma more quickly, which would enable Panzergruppe 3, having outflanked the city to the northwest and thus having quickly completed its tasks in the operation, to pivot abruptly to the north, in order to have the possibility to take Sychevka.

An eloquent entry was made about these events in Panzergruppe 3's journal of combat operations:

> Hoth at first had concerns that the Russians might only be thrown back with a frontal attack, but these weren't confirmed, since the breakthrough of the Russian front happened so swiftly that only a small number of their scattered units were able to flee to the east. The northern wing of 9. Armee distinguished itself, and had the units of the panzer group there, or at least the XXIII Armeekorps, attacked simultaneously, then the Russians wouldn't have had time to destroy the roads and railroads so methodically and energetically. According to their plan, these shattered forces were supposed to have offered significant resistance and to have held back the German offensive toward Viaz'ma, thereby stopping a breakthrough to Moscow and Bezhetsk.[158]

At 1900, XXXXI Panzerkorps solicited Panzergruppe 3 for authorization on the next day in the course of two hours to seize a bridge across the Dnepr in the northern portion of the bridgehead with one panzer battalion supported by one battalion of infantry mounted in halftracks, in order to break through to Voskresenskoe and expand the newly-established bridgehead on the eastern bank of the Dnepr. This would facilitate the organization of the crossing of the rear services. The command gave its consent, but instructed the panzer corps to coordinate the specifics of this with V Armeekorps at 0030 of the coming day.[159]

At 2000 the Soviet 107th Motorized Rifle Division began a march toward Oskolitsa, bringing along all its weapons and motorized transport. En route the column was frequently forced to halt due to the poor road. It was necessary to lay down a corduroy road along a significant extent of it.

After the end of the fighting in Chemenovo, a forward detachment of the 129. Infanterie-Division consisting of two companies of the Kradschützen-Bataillon 6 and III./Infanterie-Regiment 427, arriving on a direct road to Viaz'ma in the twilight, reached the bridge across the Dnepr in Tychkovo.

Meanwhile, the expansion of the northern portion of the bridgehead on the Dnepr at Tikhanovo to the south of the Viaz'ma River by I./Infanterie-Regiment 427 still hadn't happened. Having endured an artillery barrage, the battalion with its forward elements only advanced a short distance to a point north of the enemy-occupied occupied Hill 220.5, where it encountered infantry units of its neighbor, which were combing through the woods. A coordinated attack was launched against Hill 220.5 and drove the defenders off of it, after which Koshkino was taken at around 2100. Subsequently, the Germans here pushed on to Sel'tso-Poressovo, where they forced a crossing of the Viaz'ma River where it enters the Dnepr River.

The II. Infanterie-Regiment 427, despite serious resistance, was nevertheless able to cross the Dnepr and reach Kazarinovo by nighttime, where the regiment's command post immediately established itself. The soldiers of the battalion settled for the night in the seized Russian system of bunkers.[160]

By 2100, VIII Fliegerkorps had been only able to deliver fuel to V Armeekorps in Kholm-Zhirkovskii, so 7. Panzer-Division on either side of the road west and east of Griaznoe was once again left without fuel. The V Armeekorps that night was obliged to share the fuel it received with LVI Panzerkorps. It was still left with sufficient fuel to ensure the fulfillment of the tasks set for 7 October, especially since the fresh Soviet 134th and 152nd Rifle Divisions from the reserve of Western Front's 19th Army had appeared in front of V Armeekorps west of the Dnepr, as had been assumed.

However, the entire 7. Panzer-Division wasn't idle. As has been mentioned, all the division's remaining fuel had been given to Panzer-Regiment 5 and Schützen-Regiment 6, and they continued to carry out the orders regarding the formation of the pocket. Here's what the commander of the division's Schützen-Regiment 7 wrote in his diary:

> Our day is going without a hitch; at the same time, Schützen-Regiment 6 under the command of Oberleutnant Manteuffel is having fantastic success breaking through the strong defenses on the Dnepr. His regiment has been on the march up until evening, and we've been astonished by the enormous columns of prisoners streaming past us. On the flipside there are previously-constructed pill-boxes and a few anti-tank ditches, which were supposed to stop us, but they weren't even used!"[161]

With the onset of darkness, in 7. Panzer-Division's sector, units of the Red Army began to make their first and relative weak attempts to escape the forming pocket, but they were blocked by Hauptmann Schröeder's already familiar 6./Panzer-Regiment 5. It seems that there, as well as at the headquarters of the Western Front as a whole, they still had no idea of the prospect awaiting them, having fallen into the pocket.[162]

To the west of the Dnepr, stubborn fighting continued only for 6. Panzer-Division; in other places, resistance was weaker. The 106. Infanterie-Division had difficulties west of Gorodok, and 5. Infanterie-Division, in assistance, swept the area northeast of the village, driving back strong attacks at Noviki and west of Otpisnaia. Between Otpisnaia and Fedino, 35. Infanterie-Division met very heavy resistance and came to a stop.

By the end of the day 6 October, XXXXI Panzerkorps had reached Nikoly Nemoshchennye with 36. Infanterie-Division (mot.), while its panzer divisions were in the areas of Sokolovo and Kuznetsovo. The fully-assembled 6. Infanterie-Division was engaged in combat on the western outskirts of Vasil'evskii. The corps command post was in the vicinity of Zheltoe.

Now, at last, it makes sense to turn to documents on the Soviet side. Most interesting to us is the axis being covered by the Reserve Front's 31st Army and all the main events involving its neighbors on the right and left. In the operational summary of the 31st Army headquarters for this day, it was written: "In the course of the day in the sector of operations of the 31st Army, which as before was part of Reserve Front, the situation was unchanged; units of the army still weren't engaged in combat operations, and the Germans in the army's sector of defense also showed no activity."[163]

In the 31st Army, over all the recent days Major General V.N. Dalmatov had been busily regrouping his units. It was only on 6 October on the basis of a directive from the *Stavka* of the Supreme High Command that the army's forces halted the process, and the army was re-subordinated to the command of Western Front. However, at the end of the day the regrouping resumed, and the 31st Army consisting of the 5th, 110th, 119th, 247th and 249th Rifle Divisions and attached means of reinforcement took up a defense on the front: Zaplav'e – Ostashkov – Selizharovo – Bol'shaia Kosha – Olenino – Valutino, as well as on the separate Svapushcha – Kokovkino, Naumovo, Vseluki and Peno sectors. The army headquarters set up in Rzhev.[164]

The 31st Army had been in the Rzhev area back in summer, tasked to create a defensive belt on the line Ostashkov – Selizharovo – Rzhev, after the army's command had been formed on 15 July 1941 in the Moscow Military District. Later, it had become subordinate to Reserve Front, which was headed by Marshal S.M. Budennyi.

With the launching of Operation Typhoon on 2 October, the army began to receive reinforcements, which continued right up until 6 October. The arriving units immediately moved into the sectors of the line that had been designated for them together with the army's existing units.

On this same day (6 October), back at 0300 the 2nd Battalion of the 43rd Horse-Artillery Regiment had unloaded in Ostashkov Station, and becoming part of the 249th Rifle Division, it immediately began moving into the strongpoint to which it had been assigned. One battery took position on the Bogoliubovskii State Farm, another 2 kilometers southwest of Zamosh'e, while the third battery set up its firing positions on Hill 222.7. The regiment's 3rd Battalion at the end of the day was still en route. The 249th Rifle Division itself, having assumed command of the 43rd Horse-Artillery Regiment and the 296th Machine-gun Battalion (minus one company) took up a defense on the previously prepared fortified line in the Zaplav'e – Bol'shaia Kosha area. In the sector of the division's 921st Rifle Regiment, scouts were immediately sent to probe out in front of the regiment.[165]

The 119th Rifle Division, minus its 365th Rifle Regiment, but with two regiments that had been given to it from the 247th Rifle Division, the 510th Howitzer Artillery Regiment from the Supreme Command Reserve, the 873rd Anti-tank Artillery Regiment and the 297th Machine-gun Battalion (minus one company) spent the day moving into the fortified belt in the area of Lipovki and Valutino.

The 5th Rifle Division was assembling in Selizharovo. There, it was being brought up to strength and putting itself in order.

On the 31st Army's right, the 27th Army was still occupying its previous lines. There was no information from its neighbor on the left, the 32nd Army. Communications in the 31st Army with the subordinate formations and along their directions were working without interruptions and being handled by radio, telegraph and liaison officers.

Also on 6 October, Major General Vitalii Sergeevich Polenov took command of a new operational group, which was given the task together with Lieutenant General Ivan Vasil'evich Boldin's group to block a German offensive toward Volokolamsk and Rzhev. Group Polenov, which consisted of the 247th Rifle Division (minus two regiments), the 365th Rifle Regiment (from the 119th Rifle Division) and the 766th Anti-tank Artillery Regiment, moved out immediately to the town of Sychevka. The Regular-army 365th Rifle Regiment had previously been sent to Sychevka from the 119th Rifle Division in order to carry out separate combat assignments; in return the 119th Rifle Division received the 920th Rifle Regiment, which had a two-battalion composition.[166]

By the end of the day, the intensive movement of Soviet military columns from Viaz'ma to Gzhatsk and Sychevka, where they loaded aboard troop trains, had been spotted by aerial reconnaissance. The command of Heeresgruppe Mitte came to the conclusion that these were withdrawing rear units, in view of the possible recognition by the Western Front command of its hopeless situation.

The Germans were continuing to press ever further to the east. However, despite their obvious success, in their operational summaries, complaints about the weather, poor road conditions and inadequate bridges that were hampering their progress began increasingly to appear. The abysmal roads required constant repair work, and the nights had become noticeably colder. October is not June.[167]

Having yielded command of Leningrad Front to his successor, on 6 October Zhukov arrived in Moscow, where he learned from Shaposhnikov that the Western and Reserve Fronts had more than 800,000 men, 782 tanks and 6,808 guns and mortars at the end of September. Already that evening he left Moscow in order to find out about the situation at the front for himself. On his way there, he was alarmed to find no troops at all; he encountered only isolated soldiers and policemen. It became clear to Zhukov that Moscow was defenseless, and in such a situation, Panzergruppe 3's offensive was putting the capital city in jeopardy.

Although the entire day was cloudy, no precipitation fell and the roads and streets were dry. The activity of the Soviet air force was significantly lower.[168]

The plans of the opposing sides remained unchanged. The Germans had the task to encircle and destroy the forces of the Western and Reserve Fronts as quickly as possible, while the Red Army command was still counting upon stopping the Germans and launching a counteroffensive.

I.S. Konev – Commander-in-Chief
of the Western Front.

I.I. Maslennikov – Commander of the
29th Army.

I.V. Boldin – Commander of
Operational Group Boldin.

V.M. Sharapov – Chief of Staff of the
29th Army.

Friedrich von Bock – Commander-in-Chief of Army Group Center.

Left: Wilhelm Keitel, chief of the OKW. Right: Hermann Hoth, Commander of Panzergruppe 3.

Georg-Hans Reinhardt – Commander of the XXXXI Panzer Corps.

Erhard Raus – Commander of the 6th Panzer Division.

Soviet riflemen.

War comes to village by-streets.

German infantry and a panzer before an attack.

German anti-tank guns and their crews could not deal with the thick armor on
Soviet tanks.

Smashed Soviet armor on a rural road.

T-34 tanks knocked out by the enemy.

A German soldier hastens to dig a foxhole in anticipation of Red Army counterattacks.

A dug-in German machine-gun crew.

The consequences of the 1941 encirclements – captured Red Army soldiers.

German officers in Viaz'ma.

4

The Defense of Sychevka

7 October (Tuesday)

The preceding night was significantly colder; it was cloudy and a biting wind was blowing. The first wet snow fell as an ominous sign of the approaching winter. The snowfall was brief, and the next several days were actually marked by heavy rains. To protect themselves from the freezing temperatures, the Germans in their overnight quarters had to light stoves, but in the absence of adequate controls, fires resulted as a consequence of the excessive heat generated by the stoves. It was precisely due to this reason that one of the huts in an unknown hamlet that was housing rear service units of Panzergruppe 3 erupted in flames; three medical officers and several of their assistants barely managed to save their things.[1]

The day proved to be cloudy, and the day's high temperature fell to 3 C. [37 F.]. On 7 October, the Germans entered Viaz'ma. The pocket began to close, and 7. Panzer-Division's Schützen-Regiment 6 with part of its forces began to construct defensive positions that faced both east and west. The regiment commander Oberleutnant Manteuffel immediately upon his arrival in Viaz'ma issued an order to all his subordinates: "Dig in!" This was necessary not only for protection against the inclement weather, but even more so as part of the defensive plan with respect to the anticipated fighting to keep the pocket sealed. Subsequent events would show how correct Manteuffel was to issue such an order.

It was believed that given the large number of encircled Red Army units, there would be locations of heavy fighting, and thus the 7. Panzer-Division command did everything possible to create defensive positions along the inner perimeter of the forming pocket. Thus, the positions facing to the east and west were fortified in every possible way. The entire burden of defense fell upon the division's motorized infantry and motorcyclists.

Schützen-Regiment 6 was positioned along the highway, with I. Bataillon oriented to the west, and II. Bataillon facing the east. Schützen-Regiment 7 was positioned north of I./Schützen-Regiment 6 with its front also facing the west. Each battalion was given a frontage of approximately 6 kilometers to defend, and thus their lines could only be in the form of infantry hedgehogs. A well-considered artillery fire plan involving Flak guns, field artillery and heavy weapons of the infantry regiments strengthened the defense. The panzer regiment was left to the division command as a reserve, in order to serve as a fire brigade in the event of extreme emergency. The artillery registered its fire. Everything was ready.[2]

In the combat messages and intelligence summaries of the Western Front's 31st Army on this day, it was noted:

> The enemy continued with his mobile formations to develop the offensive from the city of Belyi toward Rzhev and in the direction of Viaz'ma. His forward and reconnaissance units were detected already east of Belyi in the areas of Bondarevo, Bosino, Shapkovo, Lenino and Kholm-Zhirkovskii. A separate reconnaissance detachment of the enemy occupied the area of Varvarino. The Germans were striving to extend to the east primarily along roads, with small reconnaissance groups that represent no kind of threat. Separate groups of cavalrymen, motorcyclists and hooligan submachine gunners were encountered.[3]

These dry lines of the operational summary in fact spoke to the fact that the command of the Western Front still didn't fully realize what was really happening. Lulled to sleep by the standard, higher protocols that subordinate formations had to follow for recording combat dispatches, Western Front headquarters didn't immediately recognize that the encirclement of the Reserve and Western Front forces in the vicinity of Viaz'ma had taken place on 7 October. The plan of a double envelopment with the aim of destroying the forces of the Western Front, worked out in the bowels of Heeresgruppe Mitte's headquarters, was being realized in full measure; for its completion, having closed the ring of encirclement, it remained for the Germans to prevent the encircled formations from breaking out of it.

No one could still even imagine that the regular and organized units of the Red Army west of the Viaz'ma – Sychevka – Rzhev line no longer existed. Or that yesterday's fully-intact and cohesive Western and Reserve Fronts were today nothing more than isolated, disorganized units and elements, deprived of unitary command, which in small groups and solitary individual servicemen were trying by any means to escape the pocket.

Thus, the road to Moscow was open to the Germans. On top of everything else, a message flew around the headquarters of units of the Western Front like ball lightning: "Overnight, the Germans unexpectedly broke into Novodugino and took it."[4]

In this situation, at 0030 Combat Order No.070 was hastily issued by 30th Army headquarters, according to which the army's units were to withdraw to the line of villages Bol'shie Vorob'i, Zalazinka, Mol'nia, Vlasovo, Bol'shevo, Valutino and take up a firm defense there. However, until their arrival, the defense there had to be held by a composite regiment forming in Sychevka under the command of the assistant chief of the 31st Army's operations department Colonel Popov, who in the course of the coming day and night had to reorganize the separate detachments in Sychevka that had come out of encirclement, and by dawn on 8 October already be in position. The composite regiment's headquarters was located in Valutino.

The 20th Reserve Regiment was preparing to take up a defense in the Zalazniki, Vorontsovo, Mol'nia area, having set up its headquarters in Bol'shevo. Major Guliaev's 923rd Rifle Regiment of the 251st Rifle Division was preparing a defense in the Kopytovo, Savrasovo, Mikhalevo, Ol'shanets and Vasil'evka sector. Yes indeed, this is the same Major Guliaev, from whom we parted back on 2 October after the fighting in the village of Liady. He had managed back then to withdraw together with remnants of the regiment, and was able to evade encirclement. Guliaev was instructed to take command of unassigned companies of a separate anti-aircraft artillery battalion and together with the 927th Rifle Regiment take up a defense by the end of the day. The 927th Rifle Regiment took over the defense in the Vlasovo, Ryksino, Mokrishchevo, Ugriumovo, Parshino sector. Its headquarters was in Kobylino.

Control over the arrival of the units in their designated sectors and their movement into the front line was given to Colonel Busarov, whose units were supposed to prepare their own defensive sectors for the units arriving to replace them. A composite company comprised of elements of the 527th, 528th and 519th Separate Anti-aircraft Artillery Battalions, headed by a company commander of the 527th Separate Anti-aircraft Artillery Battalion, took up the defense of Andreevskoe and organized a hedgehog position there.

Taking into account that the Germans were primarily operating along roads, there was no effort to organize a continuous defensive front. Instead, the main roads were blocked with separate strongpoints with interlocking zones of fire that were also set up in the depth of the defense. Particular attention was paid to the intelligence service, observation, the organization of night patrols and nighttime operations.

Until 0700, the situation remained unchanged on the front of the 31st Army; the forces continued the regrouping in accordance with the order from the army's Military Council. There was no fresh information on the Germans. Only a single message had arrived about the accumulation of their forces in Verkhmarevo and Volodarskii.

From Major General Polenov's group, the 365th Rifle Regiment and the 766th Artillery Regiment were the first to arrive in the vicinity of Sychevka. The group's main forces were still in the stage of preparing to move out. The two regiments in Sychevka were to cover the town from the west, from the direction of Andreevskoe, and from the northwest from the direction of Karavaevo. The group was given the task jointly with units of the 30th Army to destroy the enemy grouping that was breaking through toward Sychevka.

The 5th, 119th and 249th Rifle Divisions were still in their previous positions. Communications with all the directions were functioning normally.[5]

However, the Germans weren't slumbering either. Around 0330, the recently formed 10. Kompanie led by Lieutenant Gross of the 129th Infanterie-Division's Infanterie-Regiment 427 entered the village of Romaikovo and caught Red Army servicemen who were spending the night there by surprise. Seventy prisoners, two guns and a lot of rifles and ammunition were seized without combat.[6]

Order No.70 from the headquarters of the 30th Army to defend Sychevka was handed to Polenov by two staff officers from the 31st Army headquarters, a major and a captain, who have been left unidentified in the documents, only at 0525. Just 5 minutes later, the commanders of the 365th Rifle and 766th Artillery Regiments were given a preliminary order about moving out in the direction of Andreevskoe.

However, prior to this they had spent more than an hour searching throughout the town for Polenov himself. In the process, they learned that Group Polenov had no proper headquarters, because Polenov had brought no staff officers along with him. Instead, he was doing all the work himself, which correspondingly affected the accurate and timely fulfillment of the army's order. Having located Polenov, they remained with him and sought to give him all possible help in resolving problems as they arose.[7]

At 0700 from local residents, and then again at 0730 from the commanders of the units that were arriving in Sychevka, Polenov learned that the enemy in indeterminate strength had taken Novodugino, and that German paratroopers and tankettes had landed in Chashkovo. Polenov immediately telegraphed the information to Western Front headquarters, and asked how to handle the implementation of the order to march to Andreevskoe. Simultaneously, he prudently directed a reconnaissance team and a battalion of the 365th Rifle Regiment with one 75-mm gun to make a rapid march to the Andreevskoe area. The 2nd Battalion of the 365th Rifle Regiment was concentrated in Sychevka with the 766th Artillery Regiment to defend that place.

They spent a long time searching for the commander of the Reserve Front's motorized transport battalion in order to give him an order to dispatch vehicles to Gzhatsk once the units had assembled in the Andreevskoe area. Then, with the help of a radio that was in the possession of artillerymen, at 0700 contact was established with the 31st Army headquarters, but the link wasn't satisfactory and it turned out that it was best to maintain communications through the telephone network of Rzhev's anti-air defense post, which is to say, through the Air Defense Organization's army liaison department. For this, a duty officer was posted at the telephone station in Sychevka. Also, orders from the army headquarters began to be transmitted to Group Polenov over the telephone via the 119th Rifle Division, which was positioned in Olenino.

By 0900, contact had been established with Novodugino and the Dugino State Farm, after which it became clear there were in fact no Germans in the town, the state farm or in Chashkovo for that matter. This was confirmed by the signals chief of the 220th Rifle Division, who had learned this at division headquarters. He also informed Polenov that the 220th, 48th and 18th Rifle Divisions were fighting off attacks by forward German units, and that they were still holding the Varvarino, Medvedki, Ivashkovo and Nikola-Nemoshchenka line.

Seeing such confusion, representatives of the 31st Army headquarters asked the 220th Rifle Division to send a liaison officer to Polenov and to Sychevka with a detailed picture of the situation facing their units and neighboring units, as well as information on the enemy. This was promised. After this, the 31st Army's chief of staff at 1020 was briefed on the tasks given to Polenov and the 220th Rifle Division, and on what had happened in the morning.

Then at 0900, after the situation had become more or less clear, Polenov issued an order to his units, pursuant to the order from army headquarters, to move out toward Andreevskoe. Only a single battalion of the 909th Rifle Regiment was left in Sychevka in case of an enemy breakthrough or infiltration. Two battalions of the 365th Rifle Regiment and the 766th Anti-tank Artillery Regiment had arrived in Sychevka overnight, and already by 0400 they had moved into defensive positions around the town. One battalion of the 365th Rifle Regiment and the remaining units of the 247th Rifle Division were still on the march to Sychevka, but Polenov didn't exactly know where they were located at this moment, and had sent out a party to meet them.

At dawn, three German aircraft had bombed Sychevka.[8] Then German reconnaissance elements were detected already north of Belyi in the areas of Patakhi, Prudni and Petrovo. At the same time it was learned that German formations, developing the offensive from Belyi to the east, at 0900 had in fact taken Varvarino, Medvedki, Ivashkovo and Nikola-Nemoshchenka with their forward units, which of course contradicted the previous soothing report regarding the 220th, 48th and 18th Rifle Divisions that stated they were still holding this line and repelling enemy attacks. According to unverified information that arrived in the 119th Rifle Division from the commander of the 250th Rifle Division, Belyi had been taken by the "36th, 77th and 78th Regiments of the German 28th Infantry Division".[9]

At 0900, XXXXI Panzerkorps had been ordered to break through the Red Army's field positions on both sides of Lipitsy after forcing a crossing of the Dnepr River. This would clear a path for further exploitation to the east or to the north. The VIII Armeekorps with its right wing was also crossing the Dnepr, while V Armeekorps stealthily ferried itself across to the eastern bank, even though initially the plan had been for it to take up a defense along the western bank.[10] On the right of 1. Panzer-Division, LVI Panzerkorps was advancing directly toward Viaz'ma to link up with its spearhead 7. Panzer-Division. The evening before, Kampfgruppe Kopp had been formed within 1. Panzer-Division, consisting of Panzer-Regiment 1, I./Schützen-Regiment 113, 2./Panzer-Pionier-Bataillon 37 and II./Artillerie-Regiment 73.

Having taken Grishkovo, the 7. Panzer-Division was supposed to establish a staging area on the Dnepr, and once beyond Kamenets-Volochek, it was to pivot to the north and create a bridgehead on the Dnepr west of Andreevskoe in order to facilitate the further development of 1. Panzer-Division's success. Having reached the Sikerino – Konakovo – Vladimirskoe – Zheltoe – Karavaevo – Kalinkino – Lapino line, Panzer-Regiment 1 the evening before had emerged on the Vladimirskoe – Sychevka road.[11]

At 1000, an aggregation of up to 180 German motor vehicles was spotted by Western Front's aerial reconnaissance in the area of Kholm-Zhirkovskii. Bombers struck the target and upon return reported the destruction of 5 vehicles. To say the least, this was a very effective raid.

In its turn, the Luftwaffe as if in revenge conducted three raids with bombers against Rzhev in groups of 2-5 aircraft, while in the latter half of the day it conducted a number of group missions, which subjected the areas of Belyi and Olenino to heavy bombing. By this time, German reconnaissance units had already reached the line of the Mezha River north of Belyi. The situation was in constant flux, and in order to get at least some picture of what was happening, the withdrawing Soviet units were conducting reconnaissance with the aim of clarifying the direction of the further advance of the German forces from out of the Belyi area, as well as their composition and grouping.

At this time, the headquarters of the 119th Rifle Division received a message from the commander of the 250th Rifle Division Lieutenant Colonel Stepanenko that units of his division had taken up a temporary defense, having blocked the road in the vicinity of Ivanovki with the 922nd Rifle Regiment; the 918th Rifle Regiment was in Vorot'kovo, and the 926th Rifle Regiment was in Voronino and Vasil'tsevo. The division headquarters itself was located in Khmytyli.[12]

Simultaneously, forward armored units of 129. Infanterie-Division reached Borosino around 1000 and duly dug-in there, while the headquarters of the Infanterie-Regiment 429 correspondingly shifted to Petrakovo. The regiment's I. Bataillon had been pushed forward even further to the east, between the Dnepr and Viaz'ma Rivers. Around noontime, I. and III. Bataillon were attacked by Russians out of the Dnepr River valley in strength of up to approximately an infantry battalion. With its right flank anchored on the Dnepr and Hill 220.5, I./Infanterie-Regiment 429 was able to repel the attack. However, things went badly for III./Infanterie-Regiment 429, which suffered many men killed and wounded. Two platoons of its 3. Kompanie wound up encircled, and Leutnant Eitner, all of the junior officers, 10 infantrymen and two soldiers of a machine-gun company were captured. Its 1. Zug, however, managed to stave off the attackers. Sixteen more soldiers were wounded, and several men went missing in action. However, in return approximately 100 Red Army troops were killed and another 50 were captured.

After the combat subsided, II./Infanterie-Regiment 429 was merged with the remnants of I. Bataillon, and under the command of Leutnant Bormann, it was pulled out of the front line into the close rear to serve as the regiment's "shock reserve". The composite battalion arrived at its designated place without delay and without any additional losses, but with prisoners that it had seized along the way. It turned out that having crossed the Viaz'ma River and while advancing through still contested ground it had come across a Russian captain with six soldiers, who explained that they had been waiting for the Germans for several days in order to surrender.[13] Unfortunately, I've been unable to find out any more about this story. Transcripts of the interrogation of these prisoners might cast light on this, if of course they've been preserved. At first glance there is nothing particularly unusual in this, but surprising is that fact that many more Russians ran off and surrendered to the Germans, than did those who tenaciously defended their positions. What in fact motivated these men, most likely, will be possible to learn only after the complete declassification of all the archives.

Now let's return to the bridgehead on the Dnepr east of Kholm-Zhirkovskii. For three days, units of 129. Infanterie-Division had been unable to advance a single step. You will recall that a superb observation post had been set up in the church belfry in Tychkovo, which offered Soviet artillery spotters a splendid view of the Dnepr River and all the main roads between Kholm-Zhirkovskii and the bridgehead. The Germans spotted three pairs of telephone cables that led up to the post. Both day and night, Soviet heavy artillery reacted very promptly to any movement, both within the bridgehead and around it. In order to change the situation within the bridgehead, the 14. Panzerjäger Kompanie was sent there, and on the road leading to it the tank destroyer company bumped into a Soviet group with an armored car, several trucks loaded with soldiers, and one tank. The Germans didn't hesitate, and with their first shot they struck a truck which burst into flames; the following truck ran into it and exploded. Red Army soldiers, leaping from them, simply ran away under raking fire from submachine guns.[14]

While these events were taking place, at 1000 Heeresgruppe Mitte's operations chief held a telephone discussion with the headquarters of Panzergruppe 3 regarding the question of further reinforcing the panzer group. The latter was concerned with the pressure on its northern flank from the direction of Sychevka, and wished to reinforce XXXXI Panzerkorps with one or two more panzer divisions, possibly the 19. Panzer-Division. This would enable the possibility of controlling the city of Belyi.

Feldmarschall von Bock took this under consideration, but opted to keep this option in reserve. Yet already at 1045 he informed Hoth that his panzer group was to receive 161. Infanterie-Division as a reinforcement, which would arrive in Belyi by late the next morning or in the afternoon. At the same time, the tanks and armored halftracks of 106. Infanterie-Division were directed to XXVII Armeekorps on 9. Armee's northern flank.

At 1100, the commander of 9. Armee Generaloberst Strauß himself arrived at the command post of Panzergruppe 3 and announced that he preferred instead to give the group XXVII Armeekorps, and to transfer 161. Infanterie-Division to VI Armeekorps. In this case XXVII Armeekorps would continue to advance above upwards along the Viaz'ma River, while V Armeekorps could replace LVI Panzerkorps for the further advance to the east. An hour later, the VI Armeekorps was returned to 9. Armee, while it was decided to give 14. Infanterie-Division (mot.) to LVI Panzerkorps.[15]

Around 1100 129. Infanterie-Division's Infanterie-Regiment 428 reported that it was still on the western bank of the Dnepr River south of Kholm-Zhirkovskii, and that its II. Bataillon had been attacked by 20 tanks from the directions of Ust'e and Ivan'kovo. Similar attacks were repeated that afternoon, right up until sunset. All of the attacks were driven back by one anti-tank gun of 14./Infanterie-Regiment 428, together with the division's panzerjäger battalion and light field howitzers of II./Artillerie-Regiment 129; over the day, 32 Soviet tanks were knocked out. A gunner of 1. Kompanie of the panzerjäger battalion alone knocked out 18 tanks.[16] In one attack alone around noon, 25 Russian tanks were knocked out, though it is true that the Germans also suffered significant losses.[17]

The Luftwaffe was showing increasing activity, especially in the areas of Rzhev and Sychevka and particularly with reconnaissance flights and bombers. At 1130 the Germans bombed Rzhev once again, causing destruction and casualties, both among military personnel and the civilian population.[18]

At noon, the Luftwaffe's aerial reconnaissance spotted a Russian railroad train loaded with artillery in the Sychevka – Rzhev sector, which was moving to the northeast.[19] However, the Germans still didn't understand whether this indicated a retreat or a regrouping of forces.

At 1220, a report arrived in the headquarters of Panzergruppe 3 that Panzergruppe 4's XXXX Panzerkorps had finally reached the southern outskirts of Viaz'ma at 0730 that morning. Seemingly, this time the Germans achieved success in closing the pocket simultaneously from both directions, and Panzergruppe 3 hadn't been called upon to wait long for the opposite jaw of the pincer, as had happened previously at Minsk and Smolensk.

At this same time, 106. Infanterie-Division of V Armeekorps had halted on the eastern fringe of a forest near Gorodka, while the 35. Infanterie-Division was attacking along the road west of Medvedkovo; on its right, 5. Infanterie-Division was in the process of maneuvering toward Bychki.

In the afternoon 6. Panzer-Division succeeded in breaking through the second line of Soviet defenses to Lomy, where it immediately halted to rest. However, it was ordered to head south toward Spas, where it was to link up with 7. Panzer-Division and thereby seal the pocket. The previous evening, 7. Panzer-Division had arrived on the highway together with retreating Russian columns, but once there it took no actions, since it was waiting for a new order. The 14. Infanterie-Division (mot.) was directed to get to Kholm-Zhirkovskii quickly, by 1400.

In XXXXI Panzerkorps, 36. Infanterie-Division (mot.) had stopped in Spas on the Dnepr River after taking Glushkovo and encircling remnants of the Red Army that were still offering resistance. It thereby cleared a path for the units following in its wake. The 1. Panzer-Division had arrived at Nemoshchennaia and Bakh and was continuing to drive toward the Dnepr through Riabtsevo, hoping to rest in Komary south of Belyi. The 6. Infanterie-Division had fully assembled in Bykovo, and forward units of it were already west of Mol'nia. The 900. Lehr-Brigade (mot.) was combing through the woods north of Andreikovo. As before, the corps was mercilessly employing heavy artillery against the encircled Red Army units.

That afternoon, the activity of the Soviet air force picked up again. It focused particularly on the bridges across the Dnepr and on Kholm-Zhirkovskii.

At 1300 Strauß informed Hoth that "the Russians that remained north of the city of Belyi are in full retreat, but XXIII Armeekorps was lagging for some reason." Hoth suggested detaining the retreating units, so Strauß ordered XXXXI Panzerkorps to head directly to Sychevka on its own with its available forces. Even though this was risky because of the lack of strength, Hoth nevertheless agreed and decided that he could in an extreme case support it with the single division that he had in reserve."[20]

The Red Army's 110th Rifle Division up to this day was resting in the areas of Selizharovo and Sokolovo, when at 1400 an order arrived for it to move out to its designated defensive sector.

Now it is time to discuss the 31st Army. Major General Polenov's group was given an order to defend Gzhatsk with two regiments. The 27th Army on the right continued to hold in its current positions, while again there was still no contact with the 32nd Army on the left.

However, the 247th Rifle Division received information that the Germans, having broken through 30th Army's front, were exploiting to the east and northeast, and had seized Novodugino the previous night and had made an airborne landing in Chashkovo with tankettes.[21] Apparently, by this time the headquarters of the 31st Army had received Polenov's morning report, which contained the erroneous information that he had passed on right away without checking it first.

While the headquarters of the 31st Army was looking into the reported German airborne landing with tankettes, II./Infanterie-Regiment 427 of 129. Infanterie-Division was ordered to drive the Russians out of Kuiashino and to reach the line Kolodeznaia – Hill 205.2. The battalion's vanguard 7. Kompanie, having broken the stubborn resistance in close combat, reached the Viaz'ma – Kuiashino crossroads. True, it managed to accomplish this only after employing a platoon of heavy machine guns, company mortars, and a separate mortar battery, which having carried out this task, also gave effective support to 5. Kompanie in the Trusy – Kolodeznaia area and 6. Kompanie's attack against Hill 205.2.

In the Krasnoe – Krucha area, the battalion's offensive was being supported by two artillery batteries of III./Artillerie-Regiment 129. Owing to such support, all of the objectives were gained already by 1430, while the reconnaissance battalion even arrived in the vicinity of a bridge across the Dnepr on the Mitovo – Shipulino line. Fearing it had been wired for demolition and opting not to risk crossing it, the battalion stopped on the approach to the bridge and summoned pioneers. After checking it, they found that this bridge, like many others before it, had also not been prepared for demolition.[22]

By 1500 the main forces of the 36. Infanterie-Division (mot.) had reached Voskresenskoe; its remaining elements were continuing to concentrate at uncongested crossings to the east over the Dnepr River in Riabtsevo, 5 kilometers east of Spas. In the sector of the 35. Infanterie-Division's offensive, the Red Army had initiated a rapid retreat to the southeast, which even allowed the 129. Infanterie-Division to detach one regiment in order to mop up the Viaz'ma salient east of the Dnepr.

In addition, aerial reconnaissance conducted by the VIII Fliegerkorps detected the active retreat of shattered Red Army units in the same direction to the southeast, as well as on other sectors of the front. It is odd that they didn't know that units of Panzergruppe 4 were already lying in wait for them there. Moreover, there were not any signs of Soviet forces approaching to free the encircled units. Every piece of evidence pointed to the fact that the units that had been caught in the pocket had been abandoned to their fates, while overall leadership over those who had avoided this had simply been lost.

Simultaneously, 1. Panzer-Division had succeeded in breaching the defense of the Soviet 29th Army's 220th Rifle Division on the Dnepr from the south, and having taken Baranovo and Kamenets, it reached the road hub of Volochek. From there, Gilow's panzer company from II./Panzer-Regiment 1 pivoted to the north without entering the town and supported by Körber's halftrack-equipped I./Schützen-Regiment 113, took Mal'tsevo and began to exploit toward Aleksandrovskoe. Encountering no resistance and having calmly regrouped, the kampfgruppe launched a strong attack to the northwest and seized a bridge across the Dnepr in Mostovaia, 10 kilometers southwest of Andreevskoe, having crushed the resistance of Russian infantry and field artillery there by 1520. It subsequently had to repulse several counterattacks by Christie-type tanks, knocking out a large number of them.[23] Having thereby secured a bridge for the main forces, Gilow's panzer company and Körber's halftrack battalion aimed toward Andreevskoe, having sent forward seven light tanks with the support of a company of infantry in halftracks.

Realizing that the position on the Dnepr couldn't be held, the command of the 220th Rifle Division back at 1500 initiated an organized and staged withdrawal to a new line of defense in the Valutino – Podberez'e – Mikhalevo – Alferovo area, leaving behind a covering force consisting of the 1st Rifle Company of the 909th Rifle Regiment under the command of Senior Lieutenant Efremenko and the 3rd Battery of the 774th Howitzer Artillery Regiment attached from the 31st Army. This decision to withdraw was timely and proper, since already at 1530 the covering force was engaged in combat with the forward detachment of Gilow's panzers and Körber's infantry.

In the initial attack, the Germans lost two tanks and took casualties in personnel, after which frontal attacks were halted. The Russian positions were then subjected to methodical tank and small-arms fire. Our artillery ceased responding, and thus with the onset of darkness, the surviving defenders retreated from the village, having lost 10 killed, 25 wounded and two men missing-in-action. Senior Lieutenant Efremenko and the company's political leader were both killed.[24]

Subsequently from the evening report of the acting chief of staff of the 31st Army's artillery Captain Khasin, it became known in the army headquarters that in the area of the village, the retreating defenders had stumbled across an abandoned 152-mm howitzer and tractor of the 3rd Battery of the 774th Howitzer Artillery Regiment.[25] No one could explain when, and on what basis, the howitzer battery had pulled out of its positions during the battle, and where it might be located now.

With the taking of Andreevskoe, 1. Panzer-Division secured itself against possible repeated counterattacks from the north by leaving Gilow's panzers there. Meanwhile, Körber, having pushed on, halted his battalion at Dugino, just short of the Vazuza River.[26]

Covered by the company in the Andreevskoe area, the 220th Rifle Division was able to withdraw and take up a defense on the line Valutino, Lenino, Vasil'evo and the Nemoshchenka River, having the 119th Rifle Division on its right. The boundary between the two divisions in Valutino was being secured by the 9th Company of the 119th Rifle Division's 365th Rifle Regiment, which that morning at the order of the 29th Army headquarters had been withdrawn to the rear, into the army reserve.[27] The rest of the 119th Rifle Division was at full readiness in their former combat positions, but still had no contact with the Germans.[28]

In fact, forward German reconnaissance detachments appeared after mid-day only in the sector of Major B.A. Atamanov's 634th Rifle Regiment in the vicinity of Olenino District's village of Dudkino. The regiment's positions were extremely well-chosen. Both flanks were secured by swampy forests. Thus, they could not be outflanked, and in the given case, the Germans had no choice but to launch frontal attacks.

Opposite a rifle battalion that had taken up a defense in the village itself, the Germans had assembled units of the 6. and 26. Infanterie-Divisionen, a portion of the 110. Infanterie-Division, and six batteries of artillery, which they threw into battle in successive waves. In the course of the day, the Germans launched 11 attacks, several of them human wave assaults. Many attacking companies were totally destroyed in these attacks. An anti-tank ditch in this sector was completely filled with the corpses of their soldiers and officers. Even so, having an advantage in numbers of 5-6 times that of the defenders, the Germans were able to overcome this ditch and to seize the villages of Dudkino and Aksenino, thereby threatening to fragment the division's combat formations. The battalion commander Captain Ivanov, having rallied all his remaining forces led them into a counterattack and drove the Germans out of Dudkino. Twice-wounded in the attack, he continued to direct the fighting, but in the following attack he died as a hero.

With the subsequent introduction of reserve forces, the Germans managed to push our units back and create a 4-kilometer penetration into the depth of the fortified area, having taken Tishino and other villages in Olenino District. The dispersal of the 119th Rifle Division's strength across a broad front, the lack of a sufficient quantity of motorized transport, and the possibility of the enemy's appearance on other sectors of the defense didn't allow the rapid assembly of the necessary forces in order to launch a general counterattack against the German penetration. Taking every measure to sustain stubborn resistance on the left flank of the fortified area, the 1st and 2nd Rifle Battalions of the 634th Rifle Regiment repeatedly launched local counterattacks, the majority of which reached the point of hand-to-hand combat. Several times, they drove the Germans out of the villages that they were occupying, but lacked the adequate strength to destroy the enemy.

At the order of the commander of the 119th Rifle Division Major General A.D. Berezin, the 920th Rifle Regiment and two rifle battalions of the 421st Rifle Division moved up to assist the 634th Rifle Regiment. After conducting a 30-kilometer march, they went straight into battle and threw back the Germans, but for operational reasons they were halted and went over to a defense of the ground that had been gained.[29]

Having suffered a serious setback here, the Germans fell back and the Soviet side lost contact with them. Just before sunset, wagons of the rear services of the retreating 30th Army, the headquarters of which was in the Dneprova area, appeared on the left flank of the 634th Rifle Regiment.[30] This threatened the intermingling of the rear echelons of the two armies, but fortunately there was heavy cloud clover and the Luftwaffe was inactive.

At 1800 at an order from the headquarters of Heeresgruppe Mitte, 161. Infanterie-Division moved out of Belyi and went on the march southward to Kholm-Zhirkovskii, where after crossing the Dnepr River it was supposed to replace the motorized units holding the inner ring of encirclement. This was done because there were doubts in 9. Armee headquarters that there was enough strength under their command to prevent a breakout by encircled Russian units. Thus, VI Armeekorps had been ordered when possible to move to Pokrov. The maneuver of the 161. Infanterie-Division was prefer-able for Panzergruppe 3, since the infantry division wouldn't be crossing its lines of supply. The developing situation prompted a reminder of the option involving 19. Panzer-Division, as had been previously discussed.

Everything was still going according to plan in the neighboring V Armeekorps; its 5. and 35. Infanterie-Divisionen had reached the Dnepr with no opposition. There, it began preparations to begin a crossing once the sun set.[31]

Before twilight, 1. Panzer-Division, moving in the vanguard of XXXXI Panzerkorps, arrived at the Vazuza River, having taken Tiukhovo. However, in the absence of bridges, it was unable to cross the river from the march. In order not to slacken the pace of the advance, all efforts were committed to the construction of a full-value bridge overnight. Major Wolf's 1. Panzer-Kompanie, in the role of a forward detachment of the division, continued pushing to the north, scouting and reconnoitering. Without meeting any resistance, it managed to find a suitable place for a river crossing, after which Wolf decided to advance directly to the Novodugino railroad station, which he took after a short, sharp battle. The Russians there savagely defended the station, even with the help of air support, which inflicted significant losses to the Germans.[32]

Had the defenders known that that they were facing just a single panzer company, which had become widely separated from the main forces, then the fate of Wolf and his soldiers would have been different. However, with the onset of darkness, the defenders opted to slip away. Most likely, the panicky rumors about a German airborne landing with tankettes that had been circulating since morning, the lack of intelligence about the enemy, and the Western Front's loss of command and control over its forces all played a role in this decision to retreat. Why aerial reconnaissance wasn't used also isn't clear, or perhaps for some reason they just didn't trust the pilots. In sum, the Germans were simply enjoying the devil's own luck; not halting in Novodugino, Wolf's panzer company kept pushing on, and reached Syrokoren'e, south of Sychevka, by the end of the day without any hindrance. However, by this point the entire 1. Panzer-Division was experiencing a shortage of fuel, and Kampfgruppe von Hey was brought to a stop because of the lack of fuel in its Panzer-Regiment 1.[33]

In the afternoon of 7 October, a long railroad train was spotted by German aerial reconnaissance on a sidetrack in Makherovo, west of Rzhev, and already at 1800 it was attacked by 11 German bombers and completely destroyed. It had been carrying ammunition for the 30th Army, which was falling back to new defensive positions. Bombers also struck the nearby Olenino and Chertolino Stations, causing large destruction of property and human casualties.[34] Not a single German bomber was shot down. It is surprising that such a train hadn't been unloaded for some reason, and had no serious anti-aircraft cover or any sort of aerial protection at all. At the very least, it is impossible to exonerate this absence of anti-aircraft weapons and fighter aviation, because in the Moscow zone, the Air Defense organization had plenty of both. The reason for this, from all appearances, and for other such incidents, must be found at the level of command no lower than the Western Front. Alas, all of the *Stavka* directives to the *fronts* are still classified. As a result of this German success, the 30th Army that was falling back to a new line of defense was left without a strategic reserve of ammunition, which naturally told on subsequent events.

At 2045, an order arrived in Panzergruppe 3 from the headquarters of Heeresgruppe Mitte: "According to intelligence information, attempts to break out from the west to the east by large forces of encircled Russians are expected tonight in the sector of 7. Panzer-Division. Do not allow a rupture in the line of encirclement, and bear in mind that according to aerial reconnaissance, the Russians are retreating beyond the Dnepr to the southeast in complete disarray."[35] Other elements of LVI Panzerkorps were hastily sent to the sector of the anticipated breakout in support of the panzer division.

In the course of the day, troops of the Western Front had continued to conduct stubborn fighting with the attacking enemy while withdrawing to the east. However, in the northern sector of the front, where the 31st Army was located, the Germans throughout the day again showed no activity. Its army headquarters was in an information vacuum. It had no information about the situation on the fronts of the neighboring 22nd and 29th Armies because of the absence of communications with them. No information or orders were coming from Western Front headquarters either. So the forces of the 31st Army continued their partial regrouping, and by 2100, were still in movement or continuing to fortify the line they occupied:

> 110th Rifle Division with one regiment was positioned on the defense between Zaplav'e and Ostashkov;
>
> 247th Rifle Division as part of Group Polenov was continuing to march toward Sychevka;
>
> 119th Rifle Division consisting of the 365th Rifle Regiment and an artillery regiment had moved out of the Sychevka area in order to take up a defense in the Gzhatsk area.[36]

Communications with all the subordinate units was continuing to operate without interruption.[37]

At the end of the day, Hoth agreed upon a new plan of cooperation and aerial reconnaissance with the commander of VIII Fliegerkorps, explaining that now the immediate objectives of his panzer group were Rzhev and Kalinin. Hoepner's Panzergruppe 4 had the ultimate objective of the northern portion of Moscow, while Guderian's Panzergruppe 2 had been directed to an area south of Moscow.[38]

At 2130, the commander of 9. Armee Adolf Strauß issued directives, which contained an order from Heeresgruppe Mitte, according to which the forces of Panzergruppe 3, which had previously been allocated around the pocket's eastern and northern faces, were by the end of the next day to regroup to the Gzhatsk – south of Sychevka line in order to start an advance toward Kalinin through Rzhev.

The 161. Infanterie-Division had been withdrawn from the command of Panzergruppe 3 to the Vladimirskoe area for rest and refitting and was under the immediate command of Heeresgruppe Mitte. Its units were moving only at night, in order not to disrupt the movement of supplies to Panzergruppe 3. The 19. Panzer-Division remained at the disposal of LVI Panzerkorps. There were no other additional reserves for the panzer group.

The 7. and 10. Panzer-Divisionen were on the verge of linking up within Viaz'ma, and their forward patrols were on the alert for friendly contact. After the bitter counterattacks southeast of Lomy had been repulsed, 6. Panzer-Division by the end of the day had reached Pavlovo west of Spas, and was heading to meet up with the 7. and 10. Panzer-Divisionen in Viaz'ma. Thus, the first major pocket in the center of Western Front had been closed. After 7. Panzer-Division's Schützen-Regiment 4 captured the intelligence chief of Lieutenant General M.F. Lukin's 19th Army in Lomy, it became clear that units of Western Front's 19th, 20th, 24th and 32nd Armies were trapped inside the pocket. In addition, under interrogation he indicated that the 19th Army headquarters had been located in Lomy from the outset of Operation Typhoon right up into 7 October itself.[39]

After the closing of the pocket, the Russians made great exertions to break out of it to the east while avoiding the main Smolensk – Moscow highway. They exploited the vast and dense wilderness to the north of the highway that was quite amenable for this purpose, which placed the main burden of the defensive fighting on Schützen-Regiment 7 and Kradschützen-Bataillon 7. These competently-conducted breakout attempts didn't allow the German troops' rest, while the numerous Russian riflemen lurking in the woods made the delivery of food and ammunition difficult throughout the day.[40]

Without slackening the pace of advance, 129. Infanterie-Division was attacking with Infanterie-Regiment 427 alone. By evening, the regiment's I. Bataillon had entered the village of Troinia, southeast of Kholm-Zhirkovskii, and had stopped there for the night. Its II. Bataillon further to the southeast had reached the line Kniazhino – Trusy – Kolodeznaia and had also come to a stop there.

It is baffling, but repeatedly the Germans noted that the local population on the territory they had conquered greeted them in a friendly fashion and were offering all sorts of cooperation to arrange night quarters for them. In Troinia, soldiers of the I.

Bataillon were even treated to an evening tea from a samovar.[41] How must the local authorities have treated the local population, if people were greeting the German aggressors in this way?

Over the five days of the offensive, 129. Infanterie-Division had captured 41 heavy guns, 4 anti-aircraft guns and 4 anti-tank guns; 95 tanks; 138 machine guns; 4 mortars; 5 tractors and 60 trucks; and 4 radios. In addition, 3,635 prisoners had been taken. The division in return had lost 181 men killed, of which 6 were officers; 826 wounded, 20 of them officers; and 32 missing-in-action, of which one was an officer.[42]

The Western Front command no longer had any reserves. Konev's troops were the last defenders in front of Moscow, and the capital was essentially defenseless. Assessing the situation that had developed, General der Panzertruppen Georg-Hans Reinhardt, the commander of XXXXI Panzerkorps, who had been recommended by Hoth to take command of Panzergruppe 3, proposed to 9. Armee command to reach the line Gzhatsk – south of Sychevka with the forces of Panzergruppe 3, and subsequently to advance in the direction of Kalinin or Rzhev in order to guard the Viaz'ma pocket from the north. Then, with the northern wing of 9. Armee and the southern wing of 16. Armee, he proposed to destroy the Red Army formations north of Belyi and Ostashkov, thereby breaking ground communications between Moscow and Leningrad. Once this task was completed, he would send the freed-up forces directly toward Moscow. However, the commander of Heeresgruppe Mitte von Bock categorically opposed this idea, since he believed that the main bulk of his armored forces, having moved so far to the north, wouldn't have strength then for a direct lunge toward Moscow. He was concerned that the promised reserves still hadn't arrived, while the new Russian line of defense still hadn't been breached.[43] However, of course, had he listened to Reinhardt at this moment, history might have taken a different course. Fortunately, Madame Fate doesn't hold much truck with the subjunctive mood and perhaps thanks to the rapidly changing circumstances, before making his final decision von Bock still hadn't received the evening combat reports, other than one that stated: "Reconnaissance of 7. Panzer-Division to the northwest has established that the bridges are intact and Red Army units are completely absent to a depth of up to 25 kilometers, although to the east along the highway in the sector of its operations, Russian field artillery is conducting intense fire, while on the Dnepr in front of XXXXI Panzerkorps, resistance had weakened already by the afternoon and the shaken enemy was retreating in shock."[44]

However, on the other hand it is also difficult to accuse von Bock of poor judgment, since the situation at the front at the moment he made his decision was quite complex. For example, according to the obligatory combat reports that arrived at Panzergruppe 3 headquarters by 2100:

> The 106. Infanterie-Division of V Armeekorps was compelled to repulse a regiment of Russian tanks that attacked its positions out of the woods around Gorodok, although in turn the 5. and 35. Infanterie-Divisionen were able to

crush their adversary in the process of pursuing him beyond the Dnepr west of
Boiarkov and south of the oxbow on the Viaz'ma River.

In LVI Panzerkorps, 14. Infanterie-Division (mot.) with a composite regiment advanced from the southeast toward Kamenets under the cover of a panzer
battalion. The 129. Infanterie-Division with two regiments is west of Kholm-
Zhirkovskii, with one regiment east of the Dnepr.

In the XXXXI Panzerkorps, 36th Infanterie-Division (mot.) and 1. Panzer-
Division are in defensive positions along the Dnepr, while 6. Infanterie-Division
still hasn't arrived at Mol'nia by the scheduled time.[45]

However, the vacillations of the Heeresgruppe Mitte command when making strategic decisions didn't prevent units of Panzergruppe 3 from taking the area between
Gzhatsk and Sychevka and thereby closing the front of encirclement from the northeast. Thanks to this, all of Panzergruppe 3's uncommitted forces were concentrated
there for the planned offensive toward Kalinin and Rzhev.[46]

At 2310 it was announced in the units of Panzergruppe 3 that Generaloberst Hoth
earlier that day had appointed General der Panzertruppe Georg-Hans Reinhardt as
his successor, who had previously been commanding XXXXI Panzerkorps.[47]

At the headquarters of the Western Front, they were also tabulating the day's
results:

Units of the 30th Army were conducting stubborn fighting to withdraw from
encirclement in the northeast and east directions.

The entire 251st Rifle Division by the end of the day was still fighting to
break out in the area of Shatkovo. The situation of the neighboring 162nd Rifle
Division remains unknown, although its headquarters is outside the pocket in
the village of Barkovo, in the dispositions of the 19th Army's units.

The 152nd Rifle Division, after stubborn fighting managed to break into
Igorevskoe with one battalion and to seize a significant amount of booty there,
but they were driven back out of the village by arriving German reserves in
strength of up to two battalions.

Nothing is known about the situation of the majority of units of Group
Boldin.

The 220th and 18th Rifle Divisions of the 32nd Army were cut off from the
rest of the army by attacks from the direction of Kholm-Zhirkovskii, but not
for long. Coming out of encirclement, the 220th Rifle Division retreated to
Sychevka, where it was re-subordinated to the commander of the 31st Army,
while the 18th Rifle Division retreated in the direction of Gzhatsk and became
part of the 16th Army.[48]

After analyzing the situation as it stood that evening, the Western Front command
made the decision to transfer the remaining units of the 30th Army to the 31st and
49th Armies, and to withdraw the 250th Rifle Division, consisting of the 918th,

922nd and 926th Rifle Regiments, the 790th Artillery Regiment and the 1st Battalion of the Horse-Artillery Regiment to a new sector of defense in the area of Vorob'ia and Zalazenka.

Radio communications were constantly maintained with many of the encircled units, and the Western Front command was kept informed of what was happening with them:

> The 107th Motorized Rifle Division consisting of the 120th and 237th Motorized Rifle Regiments, the 143rd Tank Regiment and the 118th Artillery Regiment wound up encircled a couple of days ago in the area of Samsonikha, continued a fighting withdrawal, and at 2300 arrived in the area of Chicherinka and Sikerino, having the primary task to withdraw to the line of Zalazenki and Mol'nia. The division has suffered heavy losses not only in manpower, but also in materiel.[49]
>
> Considering that a withdrawal from encirclement through areas occupied by the enemy lays ahead, and also in view of the absence of roads and the lack of fuel, the division command made the decision to destroy the motorized transport and artillery, having first fired off all of its remaining shells at the foe in the areas of Bykovo and Turchino, and to conduct the breakout on foot.[50]
>
> The 242nd Rifle Division consisting of the 900th, 897th and 903rd Rifle Regiments, the 769th Artillery Regiment and the 2nd and 3rd Battalions of the 992nd Horse-Artillery Regiment wound up encircled in Mikhino, but as a result of an organized withdrawal, came out of it and took up a front in the area of Mol'nia and Boloshevo, having also suffered heavy losses in men and materiel. Separate elements of it consisting of the signals battalion and approximately 500 soldiers from various units of the division, having come out of encirclement, have assembled in Sychevka.
>
> The 51st Separate Pontoon Battalion also came out of encirclement, numbering 308 men and 8 vehicles, and has assembled in the area west of Viazovets.[51]

Winter was showing its impatience. A strong wind blew all day, and its heavy gusts were ready to sweep away everything in its path. It became much colder and snow fell, though in truth by evening it had melted away, as a consequence of which the roads dissolved away and now only indicated the direction of movement, while the vehicles were bogging down up to their axles and even higher in the impassable conditions. It was necessary to use tanks as prime movers, which weakened the German offensive impetus.[52]

8 October (Wednesday)

The night was still cloudy, and a mixture of rain and snow fell. The morning was also gloomy, but there was no precipitation and the winds subsided; only in the afternoon did a drizzle again begin to fall. The muck of the worn-out roads prevented the movement of equipment for both the attacking Wehrmacht and the retreating Red Army. The weather wasn't making things easy for either side.

At 0200, the 5. and 35. Infanterie-Divisionen began to cross the Dnepr River. At the same time, the commander of 9. Armee Adolf Strauß announced that the routes of advance for the units of the Panzergruppe 3 for the ensuing capture of Sychevka would be determined once VI Armeekorps had reached the area of Pokrov. Next there followed concrete directives for the forward units of LVI Panzerkorps to begin moving out to the Gzhatsk – Tesovo line at 0900.

The XXXXI Panzerkorps continued the process of breaking through the positions of the Red Army's second line of defense at Lipitsy in order to arrive on the line: Tesovo – fork of the roads – south of Sychevka. The 1. Panzer-Division by 0350 reached the point where the Vazuza River runs through Lipitsy. The 36. Infanterie-Division (mot.) was on the highway south of Voskresenskoe, while its 5. Radfahr Schwadron [Bicycle Squadron] was approaching the railroad. It was proposed to keep the 129. and 6. Infanterie-Divisionen with Panzergruppe 3.

According to plan, the LVI Panzerkorps with units of 14. Infanterie-Division (mot.) was already to be in Torbeevo by this day. Reconnaissance elements of LVI Panzerkorps had managed to make their way to the Sychevka – Tesovo road. Based on the unfolding situation, 9. Armee headquarters decided quickly to replace the units of LVI Panzerkorps that were still sealing the Viaz'ma pocket with an infantry division, in order to free up the panzer corps for an offensive toward Gzhatsk.[53]

The evening before, 129. Infanterie-Division had fully managed to break through the Soviet positions on the Dnepr, and later that night made contact with forward units of 7. Panzer-Division approaching from the north and of 10. Panzer-Division arriving from the south. On this morning, 129. Infanterie-Division was left with only its Infanterie-Regiment 427 and III./Artillerie-Regiment 129 attached from 6. Infanterie-Division. The regiment's III. Bataillon was continuing to hold its positions in the area of Khaniutino, and overnight, it was planned to replace it with I. and II. Battalions of the same regiment, Kradschützen-Bataillon 6, and a portion of Schützen-Regiment 114. After this, the defense of the northern perimeter of the pocket to the west of the Dnepr and in the area of Viaz'ma would be entrusted to Infanterie-Regimenter 427 and 428, Schützen-Regiment 114, and other motorized units of 6. Panzer-Division. Infanterie-Regiment 430 was directed to arrive in the Mitkovo – Pigulino – Gavrikov area.

The situation of the units of 129. Infanterie-Division east of the Dnepr was complicated by the fact that not only were the positions of Infanterie-Regimenter 427 and 428 kept under machine-gun and mortar fire from the south and southwest throughout the day, but in addition Soviet artillery was constantly shelling the traffic routes of 6. Panzer-Division and 129. Infanterie-Division to the north of the Viaz'ma River. The I./Infanterie-Regiment 427 had been directed to advance from the area of Troinia to the northwest as far as the Viaz'ma River and to wait there for the arrival of the regiment's II. Bataillon as a "shock reserve". There was only a small, narrow and rickety bridge there, which was completely under Russian observation and vulnerable to artillery fire from the hills of their Dnepr position. During one artillery barrage, the bridge was destroyed in front of the eyes of everyone there by the second shell, together with a group of infantry from Leutnant Bormann's company and one horse-drawn cart. Bormann immediately decided to ford the river approximately 80 meters to the north of the demolished bridge with the remaining units of his company. Their boots had to be held above their heads, because the water was up to their knees. Icy wind was blowing and snow flurries were falling. Having clambered up the opposite bank, the soldiers found themselves in Gridino on the northern bank of the river, where they came across only recently abandoned Russian artillery positions. As soon as the company joined back up with its battalion, the soldiers with their wet legs and feet were sent to a road southeast of the Petrakovo – Mitkovo – Borisovo line. From their right, the Russian artillery was continuing to conduct a constant harassing fire. Only after passing through the zone of fire was it possible for the soldiers to stop and to warm up and dry out with the help of metal buckets filled with smoldering coal.[54]

Ever since 3 October, forward units of the German 26. Infanterie-Division had been opposite the left flank of the defensive sector of the 29th Army's 119th Rifle Division, but they hadn't undertaken any active operations over all these days. Only on this day, 8 October, at dawn did German infantry with the support of armored halftracks attack positions of the 1st Battalion of the division's 634th Infantry Regiment on a front of only 3-4 kilometers after a heavy artillery and mortar preparation. However, the attackers were met with concentrated artillery and mortar fire and heavy machine-gun fire, and they retreated. Having launched three more fruitless attacks, the Germans quietened down and showed no further activity for the rest of the day.[55]

The 119th Rifle Division, remaining it its positions, conducted a regrouping: the 920th Rifle Regiment, as the division's reserve response grouping, assembled in the areas of Grishino, Mostishchevo and Osinki, while its 2nd Battalion, left behind in its positions in the area of Razboinia, was transferred to the operational control of the 634th Rifle Regiment.

While the Germans remained inactive, retreating units of Western Front's 29th and 30th Armies were streaming past both flanks of the 119th Rifle Division, exploiting gaps in the German line. Units of the 29th Army were retreating toward Olenino, north of the railroad, while units of the 30th Army were falling back to Sychevka and partially to Olenino as well.[56] As the front receded, the 119th Rifle Division of the Reserve Front's 31st Army, which had been holding a position in the rear of the 29th and 30th Armies, wound up on the front line.

By this time German intelligence had already determined that not only Western Front's 19th and 20th Armies and Group Boldin were caught in the forming pocket west and northwest of Viaz'ma, but also Reserve Front's 24th and 32nd Armies. There was no longer any doubt that the Red Army on this direction had ceased being an intact organism since the day before. Apparently realizing this, in his daily summary of the situation on the Eastern Front for 8 October, the 4th Oberquartermeister of Germany's OKH reported "The impression is beginning to form that the enemy no longer has any major forces at his disposal with which to halt the advance of German forces east of Viaz'ma."[57]

Did they realize this in the headquarters of the Western Front and in higher headquarters? Apparently not; otherwise, how is it possible to explain the situation when information from aerial reconnaissance obtained at 0930 that morning, which revealed that a German train had begun to unload at Kaniutino Station in the 31st Army's sector of defense, became known in the headquarters of 31st Army only late in the evening; that increased movement of armor, motorized transport and motorcyclists had begun along the roads to the east of the railroad station; and that concentrations of them had been spotted in Mal'tsevo, Parshino and Kamenets? Fortunately, at this time, the German command had other concerns and important questions, so the offensive on this axis hadn't yet started, although German preparations for it were obvious.

By 1000, 1. Panzer-Division had reached the railroad east of Lipitsy. However, just as it was approaching Dugino Station, an order arrived from XXXXI Panzerkorps to move instead to the area northeast of the Tesovo – Sychevka highway, having crossed the Dezha River at a ford in Ostolopovo. The 36. Infanterie-Division (mot.) of the same panzer corps was pushing forward south of Glebovo with a crossing of the Kasnia River at Kosarevo.

Aerial reconnaissance of VIII Fliegerkorps had detected the movement of encircled Red Army units out of the pocket to the east. In connection with this, the command of Heeresgruppe Mitte demanded that Panzergruppe 3 increase the pressure toward Rzhev.

The V Armeekorps was hurrying to catch up with the panzer corps. The 106. Infanterie-Division of V Armeekorps marched through Zholia at 1000. The corps' 5. and 35. Infanterie-Divisionen east of the Dnepr encountered light opposition, and having broken it from the march, 5. Infanterie-Division continued moving toward Matchino, while 35. Infanterie-Division advanced toward Samykino. The V Armeekorps command believed that it would be able to reach Viaz'ma before nightfall. VIII Armeekorps was keeping pace with 106. Infanterie-Division.

The 7. Panzer-Division, moving to link up with 10. Panzer-Division, reached the main highway into Viaz'ma with the forces of its Schützen-Regiment 1. The highway was jammed with motley units of the Red Army that were in headlong flight to the east. Having received this information, 9. Armee headquarters urgently passed it along to Heeresgruppe Mitte, the headquarters of which in turn obliged Reinhardt to prepare a special report on this same day that would guarantee that the link-up between 10. Panzer-Division and the 7. Panzer-Division would take place on this same highway; this he did. The German command made every effort to prevent any possibility of escape by the encircle Red Army forces, although Heeresgruppe Mitte headquarters was already confident that the pocket was tightly sealed and that a breakout of the encircled forces would not be permitted.[58]

The front was continuing to roll away to the east and irresistibly approaching Sychevka. Already, its defenders and citizens were beginning to sense its fiery breath.

The stream of disorganized combat units that were coming out of the encirclement and heading into the city for reforming and replenishing the ranks of its future defenders was the first sign of this. The closer the front approached, the tenser became the situation in headquarters. This was a consequence of the lack of information about the real situation of affairs, which naturally led to the incorrect assessment of the situation and affected the decisions that were made.

Yet even in such a complex situation, only thanks to the experience and professionalism of the chief of staff of the 31st Army Colonel Nikolai Pavlovich Anisimov, the work of the headquarters of the army's subordinate units was being recorded literally down to the minute, and already at 1200, the headquarters of the 247th Rifle Division issued Combat Order No.5, according to which the primary defensive preparations should be completed already by 0800 the next morning. According to this order, the defense of Sychevka was planned so that the heroic 909th Rifle Regiment together with the 1st and 2nd Companies of a separate engineering battalion were assigned to take up a sector of defense in the Krasnoe, Kobzevo, Sokolovo area and on the western outskirts of the town. The regiment was given an artillery support group, consisting of two batteries of the 778th Artillery Regiment, the 1st and 2nd Battalions of the 392nd Horse-Artillery Regiment and the 3rd Battalion of the 774th Howitzer Artillery Regiment. The commander of the 778th Artillery Regiment was placed in command of the support group. The 3rd Rifle Battalion of the 930th Rifle Regiment, minus one rifle company, was assigned to occupy a defense in the area of Zhuchki, Zelenaia Roshcha, Nikolaevka and the Mal'tsevo State Farm with the attached 3rd Company of the combat engineer battalion.

Of the division's inherent artillery, there remained the rest of the 778th Artillery Regiment and the 392nd Horse-Artillery Regiment, three batteries of the 774th Howitzer Artillery Regiment, and two batteries of the 783rd Anti-tank Artillery Regiment. A 76-mm battery of the 18th Leningrad People's Militia Division, which had come out of encirclement, was also attached to the division. However, soon the 3rd Battery of the 774th Howitzer Artillery Regiment and the 2nd Battery of the 778th Artillery Regiment were ordered to be ready to meet the enemy already by 1600 that day, while the 392nd Horse-Artillery Regiment was instructed to complete its movement into firing positions by 0500 the next morning.

The division's medical battalion was located in Maloe Petrakovo. The division's command post had been set up on the grounds of the railroad station on the western outskirts of the town, but after 2000 it shifted to Pyzino.[59]

The ink of General Polenov's signature beneath the order still hadn't had time to dry, when at 1205 the movement of a German column consisting of 20 covered trucks and armored vehicles was spotted by Soviet pilots on the road leading from Vladimirskoe to Rudakovo. However, once again, the transmission of reconnaissance reports was impermissibly slow, and the headquarters of the 31st Army learned about this information only later that evening.[60] In this situation, just imagine trying to take timely and correct decisions, especially when the wave of the German offensive was rolling forward irresistibly, and each minute is precious.

By 1600, 106. Infanterie-Division had reached the Dnepr River northwest of Oshurkino, while V Armeekorps with all three of its divisions at the given time was crossing the Dnepr over the pontoon bridges that had been constructed. The 5. Infanterie-Division was in combat west of Borovoe. The 35. Infanterie-Division as before was in Samykino. The 129. Infanterie-Division was fully on the eastern bank of the Dnepr and had linked up with 6. Panzer-Division as a result of its breakthrough between Samykino and Avdeevo. On the front of 7. Panzer-Division, attempts by encircled Soviet units to break out were broken up by long-range artillery fire. The 14. Infanterie-Division (mot.) had reached the Dnepr with two regiments in the Nastas'ino – Kostino – Zhilino – Torbeevo – Pobochevo area.

The XXXXI Panzerkorps, overrunning light local resistance, was rapidly pushing to the east. Its 36. Infanterie-Division (mot.) was approaching the Vazuza River northwest of Soroch'e and its 5. Radfahr Schwadron was expected to arrive in Tesovo quite soon. The 1. Panzer-Division was 2 kilometers east of Novodugino Station. The 6. Infanterie-Division as before was continuing unhindered movement toward Mol'nia and Bolshevo. The 900. Lehr-Brigade (mot.) was in the vicinity of Bulashevo; it had been given the task to take Spas.

East of Kholm-Zhirkovskii, there was no way to accelerate passage across the Dnepr River. The bridges and bad roads were jammed with vehicles.[61]

In the afternoon, the Luftwaffe increased its reconnaissance and bombing activities. It struck railroads, station buildings and populated places with impunity in groups and solitary aircraft, as a result of which movement by rail in the 31st Army's defensive sector became totally paralyzed by 1700. It had become obvious that the Germans' main effort was directed toward Sychevka and Rzhev. Unexpectedly, an order arrived from the headquarters of the Western Front about transferring the 110th Rifle Division to the Mozhaisk area, and about the removal of the 119th and 5th Rifle Divisions from the army's control to be placed at the disposal of the Front headquarters.

The fate of Sychevka lay in the hands of the 247th Rifle Division and the composite units that had come out of encirclement, which were under the command of Major General Polenov. As we've already stated, since the previous day a continuous front no longer existed. However, the 220th Rifle Division, with its headquarters in Kliuchiki, was continuing to hold its line in the areas of Pustysh', Lipka, Koroblevo and Shiriaevo, with the 27th Army on its right. There had been no contact with the neighbors on the left for a long time, and in reality no one could say anything knowledgable about what had happened there.

In addition to all this, at the army level, for the first time wire communications had ceased to function. Command of the troops had to be conducted only by radio.[62]

All of the units entering the area of the Sychevka defenses, including those coming out of encirclement, were being unified under the command of General Polenov and being added to the 247th Rifle Division, with the task to defend Sychevka stubbornly and to prevent a German breakthrough to Rzhev.[63]

At 1830 on 8 October, Adolf Strauß asked Reinhardt over the telephone to do everything necessary to prevent a breakout from the pocket to the main Smolensk – Moscow highway or to Spas. The latter responded that with the onset of night, he had no concerns, because units of the 14. Infanterie-Division (mot.) were now backing the 6. and 7. Panzer-Divisionen and ready to move out at any moment. Reassured by this information, the headquarters of the LVI Panzerkorps sent an order to 6. Panzer-Division with the following content: "Since the SS *Reich* Division has already reached Gzhatsk, 6. Panzer-Division should push on to the east as soon as possible."[64]

At 1910, Panzergruppe 3's transmitted the next day's requests for air support and cover of the defensive front against attacks from the east, as well aerial hounding of the columns trying to break out of the pocket, to the headquarters of VIII Fliegerkorps. The accident involving Oberleutnant Pollex that had taken place on 6 October had adversely effected the situation regarding the internal organization of rear support and supply for the entire panzer group. Pollex would spend the next 2-3 days in a hospital, while his deputy Major Mendrzyk had been hospitalized long before. The ordinary supply officer Hauptmann Hagen, who had assumed his duties, had no practical experience in the given work. Considering the situation that had arisen, the panzer group headquarters asked the quartermaster of the XXXXI Panzerkorps Major Lindner to serve as Panzergruppe 3's acting quartermaster as well, until Pollex's return to active duty.

To further complicate matters, the supply of Panzergruppe 3 had decreased by approximately 25% due to mechanical breakdowns and crashes involving the supply trucks. Interruptions in fuel deliveries arose. Because of the deteriorating weather conditions, the motorized transport's expenditure of fuel and lubricants had doubled. With the aim of excluding a total collapse in the movement of supplies, the corps commanders subordinate to Panzergruppe 3 were compelled to offer their own transport means as an auxiliary possibility to keep the troops' transport operations moving.

However, despite the difficulties that had arisen with logistics, the command of Heeresgruppe Mitte issued an optimistic order for 9. Armee; after the liquidation of the Viaz'ma pocket, it was to head toward Moscow with its right flank, while Panzergruppe 3 was to attack through Rzhev directly toward Kalinin.

In order to hasten the execution of the given order, 9. Armee headquarters decided that any breakouts by encircled units could be prevented by infantry alone and the defensive strength of the inner ring of encirclement was now adequate to stop breakout attempts. Thus, in order to develop the offensive further, first 6. Panzer-Division would be released from its defensive duties. However, 7. Panzer-Division's release was still being delayed because once again the panzer group headquarters had informed 9. Armee headquarters that it was unable to exploit its successful advance from Kamenets to Viaz'ma due to the strong pressure being offered by the encircled Red Army units.[65]

In addition, 10. Panzer-Division to the south of 7. Panzer-Division was also left in place, since the encircled divisions of the Red Army west of Viaz'ma were still fighting, and it was necessary to prevent any possibility of their breakout from the pocket to the east, as well as any attempts to free them.[66]

At 2000 the 31st Army's artillery was still carrying out the regrouping that it had initiated that morning in accordance with the order from the army's Military Council. The artillery of the 249th Rifle Division was still occupying its former positions in readiness to transfer to the control of 22nd Army. In connection with the departure of the 110th Rifle Division, the 336th Horse-Artillery Regiment remained on the line of defense between Bol'shaia Kosha and Lipovka, but until the arrival of the 22nd Army's units in the position, it remained operationally subordinate to the commander of the 249th Rifle Division. The 510th Howitzer Artillery Regiment of the Supreme Command Reserve was given an order to pull out of its positions in the 119th Rifle Division's defensive sector and to march to the Ligostaevo – Dubrovka area, where it would be placed at the disposal of the 31st Army commander.

Retreating artillery units of the 30th Army throughout the day continued to arrive in Sychevka, where they were merged with the 31st Army's artillery units. Thus, in particular, the 392nd Horse-Artillery Regiment with 10 M1937 152-mm howitzers received the order by 10 October to come under the command of the 247th Rifle Division for the defense of Sychevka. The 542nd Horse Artillery, equipped with 7 M1937 152-mm howitzers, was ordered to assemble in the area of Maksimovo by 0600 on 11 October, where it would receive its next assignment from the 31st Army's artillery headquarters. The 3rd Battery of the 774th Howitzer Artillery Regiment, with 11 M1938 152-mm howitzers, joined the 909th Rifle Regiment's infantry covering group in the Pyzino, Stepankovo, Karavaevo areas.

In the course of 8 October, German bombers bombed Sychevka three times, as a result of which three buildings were destroyed. In addition, three men were killed and three wounded. Among the wounded were two soldiers of the 909th Rifle Regiment and the commander of the 6th Rifle Company Lieutenant Shtan'ko.

Units of the 247th Rifle Division were occupying the sectors and areas of defense in accordance with the previously mentioned Order No.5 and were ready to meet the enemy. Constant reconnaissance patrols were being conducted in the areas of Kozitsino, Andreevskoe, Oparikha and Perchikha.

Units and elements that were coming out of the pocket continued to stream into Sychevka in an uninterrupted procession. Remnants of the 251st Rifle Division's 923rd and 927th Rifle Regiments and the 528th Separate Anti-aircraft Battalion were transferred to the command of the 247th Rifle Division and assigned to the 920th Rifle Regiment's 3rd Battalion, where they were given separate areas of defense.

The neighboring 220th Rifle Division on the right had fallen back to the Bezymianka – Krucha line that evening. Just as before, there was still no word from the neighbors on the left, nor any information about what was happening there.

Over the preceding 48 hours in the fighting and bombings, 3 commanders, 3 junior commanders and 13 privates of the 247th Rifle Division had been killed, and another 3 commanders, 6 junior commanders and 23 privates wounded. Two soldiers went missing in action. Communications with the units and their elements were conducted over the radio and by telephone; in addition, messengers on horseback and motorcycles were used.

The 247th Rifle Division's 778th Artillery Regiment was in support of the 909th Rifle Regiment. Its 1st Battery was positioned in Volkovo, the 3rd Battery in Stepankovo, while the 6th Battery had set up its firing positions 1 kilometer to the south of Pyzino; together with the attached 3rd Battery of the 774th Artillery Regiment, they comprised the 909th Rifle Regiment's artillery support group. The 2nd Battery of the 778th Artillery Regiment was occupying a nameless hill 2 kilometers south of Podozer'e, while the 4th and 5th Batteries had deployed on the southwestern outskirts of Sychevka.

The 2nd and 5th Batteries of the 873rd Anti-tank Artillery Regiment were prepared to meet the German tanks in the area of the villages of Bol'shoe Krasnoe and Karavaevo.[67] In general, the leaders of Sychevka's defense possessed ample artillery, in addition to personnel that were constantly arriving from the units that were coming out of encirclement.

Units of V Armeekorps that had managed to cross the Dnepr at 2145 northwest of Borovyi and south of Samykino encountered well-equipped Soviet positions, but in the darkness opted not to attack them. Instead, they called upon their artillery to suppress them. However, the German artillery was struck by powerful counterbattery fire in response, and the Germans made no further progress until morning.

The VIII Armeekorps' 28. Infanterie-Division had stopped for the night in the village of Pogoreloe on the Dnepr. The 35. Infanterie-Division was marching to the north in order to replace the 6. Panzer-Division and in support of 7. Panzer-Division.

The 129. Infanterie-Division was also preparing to replace 6. Panzer-Division, which to a certain extent and in a certain way would have supported the offensive of the V and VIII Armeekorps, but its progress was being strongly hampered by the lack of serviceable transport. Its command was forced to have a conversation with 35. Infanterie-Division, requesting transport support whenever the latter could render it.[68]

The Viaz'ma pocket was very similar to the previous Minsk and Smolensk pockets, because just as in those situations, there was relatively little counteractivity by the encircled units. In Panzergruppe 3's war diary, this was directly noted: "The Russians situated in the cauldron as before are rather passive and accordingly they will be destroyed in good time by the second echelons of the front, attacking from the west."[69]

Really, what were those caught in the pocket waiting for? Did their commanders really not understand that the longer they waited the less chance they had to break out, especially since there are few who can endure three or four October days in our forests and swamps, given such inclement weather? It is possible only to assume that they were waiting for promised help from outside the pocket, but it seems not only that no one was hurrying to free them, but apparently there were no intentions to do so at all. Unfortunately, any sort of documents of the units that managed to break out of the cauldron are totally absent in the Podol'sk archive. Apparently, there was a reason why all of their documents were destroyed after coming out of the pocket, while the units themselves were disbanded.

5

The Front Continues to Roll to the East

In places opposite the XXXXI Panzerkorps, the hasty retreat of Red Army units began. By evening 5. Infanterie-Division had reached the Dnepr River east of Kholm-Zhirkovskii, 5. Radfahr Schwadron of the 36. Infanterie-Division (mot.) was 5 kilometers southeast of Kniazh'ino, forward units of 1. Panzer-Division were in Syrokoren'e itself, and 6 kilometers southeast of there, 6. Infanterie-Division was fortifying its bridgehead across the Dnepr in Bolshevo.

On 9 October, V Armeekorps continued to advance to the southeast in order to support the LVI Panzerkorps with its infantry. XXXXI Panzerkorps faced the task of reaching the Tesovo – south of Sychevka line, and given favorable conditions, it was thought it had enough fuel to reach Sychevka itself.

With the approach of nightfall on 8 October, the combat activity of the two sides subsided; results were being compiled and orders issued for the next day. As a result of the fighting since 2 October, Panzergruppe 3 had seized 19,554 prisoners, 359 guns, 222 tanks, 62 anti-tank and anti-aircraft guns, and 337 machine guns.[1]

In Sychevka itself, by the end of the day for the first time since the start of the German offensive, they began to realize the full seriousness of the developing situation. War, which before yesterday was still distant, today was in fact approaching the town.

The 247th Rifle Division consisting of the 909th Rifle Regiment; the 3rd Battalion of the 920th Rifle Regiment; the 778th Artillery and 392nd Horse-Artillery Regiments; the 3rd Battery of the 774th Howitzer Artillery Regiment; and the 2nd Battalion of the 783rd Rifle Regiment; reinforced with anti-tank support and one 76-mm battery of the 18th Leningrad People's Militia Division was occupying a defense with its front line extending from Krasnoe through Kobzevo and Zelenaia Roshcha to Nikolaevka, with the task of preventing a German breakthrough to Rzhev. The division's outpost line ran through the northern outskirts of Bol'shoe Krasnoe and Kotovka; the southwestern outskirts of Mukovesovo, Piskovo, Slesarevo and Bubnovo; over Hill 195.0; and ended in Netertovka.[2]

The day of 8 October had passed relatively quietly for the defenders of Sychevka. Units of the 247th Rifle Division maintained constant reconnaissance out in front of them, but no approaching Germans were detected. Patrols established that there were no Germans in the areas of Leokshino, Kozitsino, Orel, Diatlikha, Klikunikha, Svistaevo or Oparikha either, as had been previously assumed.

However this was only an apparent calm; in reality the Germans were preparing to take Sychevka. At the end of the day, Heeresgruppe Mitte headquarters ordered Panzergruppe 3 together with VI Armeekorps to take the town on 9 October.[3]

In the course of the day, the Germans had continued bombing the areas of Rzhev, Zubtsov and Sychevka, as well as sectors of the Rzhev – Sychevka railroad. Three missions were flown against Rzhev by groups of 8-15 aircraft, and damage was caused. Indeed, in general Luftwaffe activity on the Rzhev – Sychevka axis increased noticeably, while the Soviet air force's own activity significantly declined.

On the northern sector of the 31st Army's front, the situation remained unchanged, but on the southern sector, the Germans were continuing to advance in the general direction of Sychevka and Rzhev. The army's headquarters received information that a German infantry division had begun to assemble in the Bukovo area.

The situation was demanding the activization of reconnaissance with the task to reveal the enemy forces that were attacking from Belyi toward Olenino and Sychevka, and it was necessary to check the reliability of the information about the enemy's presence in the Bukovo area and to monitor the approach of new units from the depth of the German rear. Only toward the end of the day did the first reconnaissance reports arrive, and it turned out that already at 1400, the Germans in strength of up to one infantry regiment with the support of 20 tanks and two artillery batteries had taken the villages of Vasil'evo, Pokrov and Shizderevo, while intelligence arrived from the 30th Army headquarters that confirmed the aggregation of up to 5,000 enemy infantry with wagons and anti-aircraft machine guns in the area of Bukovo.[4]

Everything pointed to the fact that the Germans were seriously preparing to storm the town. Indeed, owing to the opening of the archives in 1991, from German captured documents it became known that the German command was viewing Sychevka as the key to Rzhev, without the capture of which the overall German offensive toward Moscow would bog down.

At first glance, there is seemingly nothing new or unusual in this, but the question asks itself: What exactly was the higher command of the Red Army doing at this time, when it was receiving intelligence reports about an aggregation of German forces on these directions? There are no answers to this question, and indeed many others, and apparently there won't be as long as many more documents in the archives remain classified.

Well, while it waited for the German attack, there remained nothing else for Sychevka's garrison to do with its available forces and means, but to continue to fortify its defenses, while reinforcing itself via the shattered remnants of Red Army formations and units that were coming out of encirclement and with people's militia units arriving from Moscow. By the end of the day, after three days of fighting, the

128th Tank Brigade from Group Boldin emerged from encirclement.[5] It was also on 8 October opposite the 26. Infanterie-Division in the area of Lipitsy south of Sychevka that German reconnaissance first detected people's militia units arriving from Moscow, which according to prisoner interrogation and the documents found on them turned out to be the 18th and 54th Rifle Regiments of People's Militia.[6]

In their combat messages, the Germans separately observed that "soldiers of the people's militia, who remained alive after the very first combat encounter, more often than others immediately surrender, and moreover, in groups of up to 60 men."[7] According to information obtained from prisoners, German analysts came to the conclusion that "in the units of the Red Army that wound up encircled after 2 October, signs of demoralization and disintegration are beginning to appear. Not only militiamen, but also even those regular units of the Red Army located in encirclement are beginning to surrender in groups. In the area of Viaz'ma, an entire artillery battery together with its guns and crews even surrendered."

However, at the same time German intelligence still recognized that in particular opposite V Armeekorps, units of the Red Army had maintained overall command and control, and were making an orderly withdrawal to the line of the Viaz'ma River; in places they were even offering rather stubborn resistance. Opposite XXXXI Panzerkorps, the resistance of the Red Army had even increased, especially opposite the bridgeheads occupied by the Germans on the Kasnia and Shchesna Rivers.

Separately, German records noted the fierce resistance of Soviet units, which had taken up a firm defense based on concrete pillboxes that were embedded within an elaborate network of field fortifications for covering infantry south of Sychevka. Which particular defensive line this was, and who was standing there to their deaths even at a time when the front had already moved on to the east, is unknown. The Germans were able to overcome this line only after several days of tough combat.[8] This information only appears in German summary account documents, and unfortunately, without any supplementary details. In our own records, kept in the Central Archives of the Russian Ministry of Defense, there is absolutely no information whatsoever on this matter. Plainly this subject still awaits research. Only one thing is clear: These unknown heroes didn't retreat, and with their lives they gave the Sychevka garrison valuable extra days to prepare for a defense. Unfortunately, on the strategic level this no longer played any role whatsoever, because the Red Army's higher command made no use at all of such cases of self-sacrifice, not even tactically.

9 October (Thursday)

The arriving morning was just as cloudy; at times, the clouds were spitting a cold drizzle, which periodically changed over to wet snow. This worsened the condition of the roads, which even without this precipitation were deteriorating from the heavy traffic and soldiers' boots of the retreating side, followed by those of the attacking side. Progress by the German army was made more difficult by the washed-out roads and enemy minefields, which affected the timetable of carrying out the tasks that had been assigned by higher command.[9]

During the preceding night, I./Infanterie-Regiment 427 of the 129. Infanterie-Division had reached Khmelity, where it set up its command post. There, a large and lengthy anti-tank ditch was also discovered that was part of the Soviet second line of defense backing the Dnepr River. Infanterie-Regiment 430 Infantry Regiment over-night hadn't moved from its positions on the Mitkovo – Pigulino – Gavrilkovo line.[10]

Forward units of the LVI Panzerkorps' 36. Infanterie-Division (mot.) had seized Tesovo on the night of 8/9 October. However, the remaining units of the panzer corps came under very heavy fire from Soviet artillery and were even compelled to fall back a bit.

By the morning of 9 October, it was already fair to say that the German opera-tion to complete the double envelopment of the Western Front's forces was already entering its culminating phase. Western Front's final agonies were approaching.[11]

At a nighttime conference in the headquarters of Panzergruppe 3, priority was given to keeping contained the remnants of the Red Army's encircled units west of Viaz'ma. In connection with this, Panzergruppe 3 could not detach any units and prepare for a new onslaught to the east. The panzer group's further offensive was thus suspended until the final liquidation of the pocket.

The V Armeekorps was continuing to advance to the southeast. VIII Armeekorps was digging in between the Dnepr and the main highway, in order to replace LVI Panzerkorps. However, this was to take place only after the front had been pushed beyond the Gzhatsk – Tesovo line to enable a further advance to the northeast. The XXXXI Panzerkorps was given a position south of Sychevka and in the Tesovo area. Despite their assignments to press the offensive to the east and northeast, both of these panzer corps simultaneously had to remain ready to counter attempts to break out of the pocket.[12]

Now it is time to discuss the Sychevka garrison. Its day began at 0300, when a blocking detachment of the 634th Rifle Regiment that was deployed in Shivarevo joined battle with forward German units. The first German attack was driven back. After a short lull in the fighting, at 0800 up to a company of infantry supported by 20 tanks, following a preparatory mortar barrage, overran this detachment and quickly reached the southern outskirts of the village of Zhuchki (just several kilometers south of Sychevka), with the aim of taking possession of Sychevka from the march. From Zhuchki, the Germans could already see conflagrations on the southern outskirts of their objective.

Units of the 31st Army were still in their former positions, continuing to conduct a regrouping of their forces. The army headquarters still had no information about the situation of the 247th Rifle Division, although its 909th Rifle Regiment had already been attacked at 0830 by ten German tanks.[13] This attack was repulsed, but one of the regiment's 45-mm anti-tank guns was disabled, and the assistant artillery chief of staff of the 247th Rifle Division Captain Mil'kovsky was wounded. The division's reconnaissance battalion lost up to a third of its personnel. After this action, the

778th Artillery Regiment had only one combat load of ammunition left, while the 3rd Battery of the 744th Horse-Artillery Regiment had just 10 shells left per gun. In the meantime, the Germans were closing on Sychevka from the south as well.[14]

At 0900, Generaloberst Hoth visited Panzergruppe 3 again and held a conference with its headquarters staff. His trip was connected with the replacement of XV Armeekorps' commander. Hoth's panzer group had become renowned previously in Eastern and Western Europe and its opponents had begun to fear it, because all of the major victories were connected with his name. Hoth wanted to protect his reputation.

After his arrival, the group headquarters received an order from 9. Armee headquarters to squeeze the Viaz'ma pocket through actions of the LVI Panzerkorps to the southwest and west. Artillery control over the highway from the north had been secured prior to this. It became known from prisoners and turncoats that there were still motorized formations of the Red Army in their former defensive positions within the pocket. Even though they were now not so strong, since they had become broken up, their threat of a breakout from the cauldron hadn't lessened.

Simultaneously, a request from XXXXI Panzerkorps about the need to increase the norm of fuel expenditures in connection with the damp weather conditions came under discussion at the conference. Two options were considered: "Increase the norms starting 12 October for the vehicles of each corps and each of their infantry divisions, or introduce an outright ban on any increase prior to 14 October."[15] However, the discussants were unable to reach a concrete decision and the given question was set aside, since the panzer group's command was more concerned with the matter of how to allocate its forces more rapidly and in the best way in order to control a larger area, because the encircled units still hadn't surrendered and were for the most part continuing to defend stubbornly. In particular, after 6. Panzer-Division announced that it could be freed up no sooner than 10 October, the decision was reached that the process of relieving units of LVI Panzerkorps and 14. Infanterie-Division (mot.) would begin on 12 October. In addition it was assumed that 129. Infanterie-Division would first relieve those units that were unengaged or could be spared from the task of keeping the pocket sealed. At 1200, the new commander of Panzergruppe 3 General der Panzertruppe Reinhardt arrived and assumed command.[16]

The day was again cloudy, with periods of rain. Everyone in motion was struggling with the roads that had become mired from the rain. Of course, the Germans were fortunate that they had closed the ring of encirclement before the onset of the worsening weather, since immediately the replacement of losses and supplies slowed down, and now everything depended solely on the efficiency of the road services.

At noontime, Adolf Strauß announced the new plans of Heeresgruppe Mitte to 9. Armee, according to which:

> Panzergruppe 3 orients itself primarily in the northern direction in order to join up with the northern wing of 9. Armee and the southern wing of 16. Armee to destroy the enemy between Belyi and Ostashkov.
> VI Armeekorps marches to Rzhev.

It will be better if XXXXI Panzerkorps gets moving already tomorrow. The army wants 6. Infanterie-Division and 900. Lehr-Brigade (mot.) to be attached temporarily to VI Armeekorps in the event that XXXXI Panzerkorps is unable to move out on 10 October.[17]

Indeed, already by 1300, an order followed from Panzergruppe 3 to the XXXXI Panzerkorps: "It is necessary to take Rzhev and Zubtsov as soon as possible, but with your own forces. You must use available reserves in case of extreme necessity."[18]

After the arrival of the order from Strauß, Reinhardt expressed his disagreement with some of its provisions, stating: "It [the order] views his 161. Infanterie-Division on the newly created northeastern direction, while Heeresgruppe Mitte is directing it to the southeast, because it is under the latter's operational control, even though it forms a part of the panzer group." After a series of consultations with 9. Armee headquarters, the decision was made that for a start, the 161. Infanterie-Division should "destroy the Russian tank group in the Komary area, which according to prisoners has no fuel. It is assumed that 20 to 30 tanks are there, under the command of some general. Apparently this is the remnants of the two Russian tank divisions that linked up south of the city of Belyi."[19]

It was also decided that:

LVI Panzerkorps tomorrow with Aufklärung-Abteilung 5 from the 14. Infanterie-Division (mot.) continues movement toward Spas and Baskakovo, while on 11 October it should assemble a separate brigade out of separate units of the 6. Panzer-Division and send it from Gzhatsk – Bulchevo to an area north of Shakhovskaia Station. The 14. Infanterie-Division (mot.), keeping pace with the corps, should move from Samuilovo to Krasnyi Kholm, while 129. Infanterie-Division [advances] between them to the north. It is necessary to send XXXXI Panzerkorps in the Zlatoustovo – Karmanovo direction, so that in an extreme situation it will be easier for LVI Panzerkorps to retain possession of the route through Bulchevo.[20]

A report arrived in Panzergruppe 3 headquarters at 1230 that the SS *Reich* Division of Panzergruppe 4 had just seized Gzhatsk.

In the positions of 129. Infanterie-Division's Infanterie-Regiment 427, a heavy cannonade had been audible to the southwest ever since the morning. The sound of battle spoke to the fact that 35. Infanterie-Division on the Dnepr River had gone on an offensive to the east. At 1300, however, the positions of the regiment's I. Bataillon were attacked from the southwest by approximate 15 Soviet tanks, which intended to create a breach in the ring of encirclement toward Reutovo and Spas-Demensk, through which the following infantry was to surge. However, since the regiment's artillery had done a good job registering targets ahead of time, these tanks were destroyed by its fire at the very outset of their attack. After the battle, a combat dispatch reported:

The Russians are taking incalculable losses; they have been scattered in groups of up to a battalion, but with the support of tanks they are still trying to break out of the pocket. There are a lot of prisoners and deserters. Infanterie-Regiment 427 has collected approximately 1,000 prisoners in a church in Khmelita. It has become known that the Russians are trying to penetrate the boundary between the 6. and 7. Panzer-Divisionen in the direction to the north.[21]

In order to cover this boundary more securely, 6. Panzer-Division's Schützen-Regiment 114 was sent there with the aim of blocking any and all attempts to breakout of the pocket.[22]

The Luftwaffe in the course of the day flew aerial reconnaissance and bombing missions over the areas of Rzhev, Zubtsov, Sychevka, and sections of the Rzhev – Sychevka railroad. Their aircraft ruled the skies with impunity, until gunners of the 257th Separate Anti-aircraft Artillery Battalion of the 119th Rifle Division at 1400 managed to down one Ju-88 bomber. Only after this did the Germans begin to show caution.

At this same time (1400), the headquarters of the 644th Cavalry Regiment emerged from encirclement in the Glinovka area together with the regiment's rear elements.[23] However, many plans of the Soviet command were fated never to be realized. The Germans had repeatedly demonstrated the ability to attack at a point where they were least expected. The troops of the 31st Army, which had yet to finish their regrouping, met the enemy in Shizderevo, Vasil'evo, Berezka-2 and 2.5 kilometers south of Sychevka.

The 247th Rifle Division entered the fighting at 1500 in the area of Zhuchki and Zelenaia Roshcha. The 916th and 920th Rifle Regiments were hastily directed to there for support. However, they didn't arrive at the designated time and seemingly vanished – their whereabouts were still unknown even at 2000. Until they were located, the division's training battalion was sent in their place, but moving on foot, it had only passed through Podmoshchitsa by 2000.

The 250th Rifle Division, which had previously received the task to march to Olenino Station to load aboard trains bound for Sychevka, was compelled to join battle in the vicinity of Berezka-2. The 119th and 120th Rifle Divisions remained on their lines, although a separate blocking detachment of the 119th Rifle Division had already joined battle in the Pokrov area.

Separate, fragmentary groups of the 30th Army were hastily re-subordinated to the 31st Army. The 29th Army positioned on the 31st Army's right began a planned withdrawal to a previously prepared line of defense. As before, there was no information coming from the left, where the 24th Army was holding the front.[24]

At 1530, a telephoned directive arrived in 6. Panzer-Division from the panzer corps' operations department: "Prepare a forward group so that tomorrow 14. Infanterie-Division (mot.) will be north of Gzhatsk." The given group was to be formed out of Schützen-Regiment 4 (which had been transferred from 7. Panzer-Division); Panzer-Regiment 1's I Panzer-Abteilung (minus one panzer company);

and IV./Artillerie-Regiment 76. All of this created confusion, and the division commander Generalmajor Raus was unhappy, concerned that with his remaining forces, he wouldn't be able to stop the next attempt to break out of the pocket.[25]

However, despite his disagreement, by 1600 the panzer group command had set the immediate objectives for its units: "LVI Panzerkorps: specifically for 14. Infanterie-Division (mot.) – Krasnyi Kholm, and for 129. Infanterie-Division – Nikulino Gorodishche. XXXXI Panzerkorps – Zubtsov and Staritsa."[26] Next Reinhardt personally requested from the commander of VIII Fliegerkorps to deliver 100 cubic meters of fuel to Dugino in the course of 10 October, for which a landing strip suitable for Junker transport aircraft had already been prepared by units of XXXXI Panzerkorps.

At 1630, information arrived in the Heeresgruppe Mitte headquarters: "The previously-occupied Russian positions on the eastern bank of the Dnepr River opposite the north wing of V Armeekorps have been rolled up after their abandonmnent of Viaz'ma."

Attempts by the Red Army's encircled units to break out of the pocket became more frequent. Their savage attacks toward Avdeevo and Shipulino were driven back with serious losses for both sides. Only in the sector held by units of 7. Panzer-Division were the breakout attempts rather weak, but the Russian artillery fire out of an area south of Golovlevo was very disturbing. The 6. Infanterie-Division was countering breakout attempts on the eastern side of the Dnepr north of Demidovo.

In the area of XXXXI Panzerkorps' operations, according to intelligence information, increased resistance of the Russians at the bridgeheads across the Kasnia River in Tesovo and Borisoglebskoe was being anticipated, as well as on the Shchesna River southwest of Gol'nevo.[27]

Progress by Kampfgruppe von Hey of 1. Panzer-Division toward Sychevka from the south had been stopped since the evening before. It was being blocked by strongly fortified field positions with concrete pillboxes, with both artillery and infantry cover. It didn't seem possible to break through these positions until the arrival of the panzer division's main forces.[28] However, despite this, the panzer division command was hoping that the day would still end successfully, because motorcyclists of I. Bataillon, with the support of IV/Artillerie-Regiment 73, under the command of Oberleutnant Wendt, had taken an important road hub in Podsosen'e, 3 kilometers south of Sychevka, by 1930 with an outflanking maneuver. However, this group's Forward Detachment "Wie" was unable to make any further progress by day's end.[29]

In order to secure support, at 1800 V Armeekorps had moved out of Vladimirskoe toward Kholm-Zhirkovskii, and it was expected to arrive there by morning. To avoid unanticipated obstacles, supplementary transport that had been offered by 9. Armee command to Panzergruppe 3 was ensuring uninterrupted movement of reinforcements along the Belyi – Kholm-Zhirkovskii highway to the units already located in their positions at Kholm-Zhirkovskii.[30]

The headquarters of the 31st Army as before was located in Rzhev, where the headquarters of the 29th Army also arrived at 1800. Since all the divisions of the 31st

Army had been already transferred to other armies and there was nothing left for its headquarters to command, it began to assist the 29th Army headquarters with the organization of a defense, but now in the Rzhev area.

The 251st Rifle Division of the 30th Army, now with no more than 500 men on its roster, was assembling in the Aleksandrovka area, 16 kilometers northwest of Sychevka, and on the night of 9-10 October, it was to arrive in the area of the town's defenses. The 250th Rifle Division together with remnants of the 242nd Rifle Division was assembling in the Gusevo area, with its rear support units in Olenino, from whence it was also preparing to march with approximately 500 men to Sychevka to assist in the town's defense.

The 31st Army had left only the 247th Rifle Division, with its two rifle regiments defending the town together with composite units.[31] The 126th Rifle Division had just arrived in Rzhev; the question of whether it should be sent on to Sychevka had yet to be decided.[32]

Another day was coming to end. Both sides were summing up its results and planning measures for the next day.

At 2210, Reinhardt proposed to XXXXI Panzerkorps to spend the night developing land routes that would bypass Sychevka on its eastern side, since attempts to assault the fortified belts of defenses directly from the south would lead to excessive losses.

Encircled Red Army units were offering strong resistance to V Armeekorps only in isolated places. In 7. Panzer-Division's sector of defense, the number of Red Army men coming across the lines and surrendering had grown, as a result of which the entire area beyond the Shchesna River turned out to be clear. North of Bolshevo, 6. Infanterie-Division drove back two attacks out of the pocket.

Units of 106. Infanterie-Division were located between the Dnepr and the Viaz'ma Rivers, and with the freezing weather, they were planning to pivot to the south. The 5. Infanterie-Division as before was in Ivanniki. The 35. Infanterie-Division was to arrive in Samykino to the northeast of Viaz'ma in order to reinforce the forward detachments of the 129. Infanterie-Division's western wing.

Based upon the day's achievements, for the coming day it was planned to push the XXXXI Panzerkorps and separate units of the LVI Panzerkorps to the north, in order to reach the Krasnyi – Zubtsov line, and for Aufklärung-Abteilung 5 to take Zubtsov with a *coup de main*. In order to realize this plan, it was agreed with 9. Armee headquarters that starting at 0830 the next morning, Junkers of the VIII Fliegerkorps would deliver 25 cubic meters of fuel to Dugino every three hours. However, it turned out that the transport aviation's capabilities were rather limited, and not more than 100 cubic meters would be delivered by four aircraft.[33]

The approach of winter became ever more noticeable. At night the temperatures fell well below freezing; the mud on the roads hardened and it became easier to move.[34] To a great extent thanks to this, despite the increasing opposition of the Red Army, XXXXI Panzerkorps had managed to make a significant advance to the east and north.

Meanwhile, south of Sychevka, the unknown units of the Red Army that had been abandoned to fate, which had taken up a stiff defense in concrete pillboxes and the field positions around them, were continuing to hold out, thereby slowing the progress made by 1. Panzer-Division.

The final document that recorded the events of the receding day was Summary No.116 of the 4th Oberquartermeister of the Wehrmacht OKH regarding the situation on the Eastern Front: "The Briansk cauldron has been sealed. Opposite the left flank of the Army Group [Center], the enemy is falling back behind fortified positions."[35]

It was also being reported that according to prisoner testimony, the Red Army command had only NKVD and militia units in the Moscow area, no artillery, and few heavy weapons. However, at the same time the German command recognized that pressure was beginning to build from the southwest on the units of Panzergruppe 3 that were south and southwest of Sychevka, and that disorganized Red Army groups were continuing to hold out opposite the 26. Infanterie-Division. In the sector of XXIII Armeekorps, contact with retreating units of the Red Army had been lost in the difficult terrain conditions.[36]

Despite the isolated cases of heroism and tenacity on the part of Soviet units and elements, the German army was still not meeting organized resistance. The Red Army's front, in general, from the very start of the German offensive consisted of isolated strongpoints with no connections between them, which the Germans didn't assault, but simply bypassed, and their garrisons, left without supplies and support, were doomed to death or imprisonment, which was simply a matter of time.

For example, the Germans themselves recorded the defense of an unknown Red Army combat element with a small quantity of artillery at Boloshevo, 15-20 kilometers southwest of Sychevka, where it was able to hold out until evening, at which point it was partially destroyed and the survivors taken prisoner.[37]

6

The Fall of Sychevka

10 October (Friday)

The night of 9-10 October was cloudless; the winds were calm and the moon was bright. By morning, the temperature had fallen to - 40 C. [- 40 F.]. The roads had frozen up and were in good condition. Later that morning, clouds moved in and a heavy snow began to fall, but the skies cleared once again that afternoon, the sun re-emerged, and the roads immediately thawed.[1]

Bypassing the heavily fortified position with pillboxes south of Sychevka, forward detachments of the 1. Panzer-Division on the preceding night had reached a railroad crossing 4 kilometers south of Sychevka. This put them effectively behind the troublesome Soviet positions.[2]

After its lengthy absence over the battlefield, the Soviet air force became active again. This particularly affected XXXXI Panzerkorps, the positions of which were bombed repeatedly throughout the night. In addition to this, problems other than with fuel became revealed, since it turned out that in the sub-zero temperatures, engines wouldn't start, and the fluid in the radiators, having frozen, put the vehicles temporarily out of action. It had been impossible to drain the fluid from the radiators simply because of there weren't enough containers for such a large number of vehicles; in the absence of suitable containers there was nowhere to drain the fluid other than onto the ground. However, even had there been enough containers, the fluid in them still would have frozen overnight, and in combat conditions, no one would have given permission to light fires in order to thaw them out. Thus once the offensive resumed, all of the panzer group's transport vehicles lagged behind, but largely this involved those vehicles that were not directly necessary for conducting combat operations.[3]

However, the Luftwaffe didn't remain idle, and all through the preceding night it displayed significant activity over Rzhev, bombing the city between 0120 and 0300 with only short intervals between attacks. Buildings near the main structure housing the 31st Army headquarters were demolished, and there were casualties among the personnel of the army headquarters' field command post. All forms of communication, other than radio, with the divisions and the city were interrupted during the bombings. However, already at 0530, contact with the units and neighbors was re-established through the Central Rzhev Telegraph Exchange.[4] Meanwhile, at this time V Armeekorps began squeezing the Viaz'ma pocket from the east.[5]

By 0600, there had been no changes in the position of the 31st Army's units and neighbors. The 119th Rifle Division was conducting reconnaissance in the area of Bolevo and Aksenino with the elements of the 634th Rifle Regiment. The headquarters of the 220th Rifle Division was in the village of Stepanki. According to intelligence arriving at the 31st Army headquarters from there, up to two enemy artillery regiments, numbering 60 pieces of artillery were deployed in the area of Bol'shie and Malye Vorob'ia, and up to 120 tanks were in the area of Zabolot'e.[6]

The 31st Army command over the preceding days had been screening the Sychevka area from the west and southwest with a portion of the 247th Rifle Division. It had concentrated the rest of its units in the town itself.

A counterattack launched by the 247th Rifle Division's 909th Rifle Regiment (minus one rifle battalion) on this morning in the direction of Zhuchki and Syrokopen'e against 1. Panzer-Division had no success, and so the regiment went over to the defense on the southern outskirts of Sychevka, with its front extending on the line Krasnoe – Zhuravlevo – Podsosen'e – Ivashkovo.

Having lost contact with its 916th and 920th Rifle Regiments on the evening before, the 247th Rifle Division today was awaiting the arrival of batteries of the 18th People's Militia Rifle Division, 10 152-mm howitzers of the 392nd Horse-Artillery Regiment, 7 152-mm howitzers of the 542nd Horse-Artillery Regiment and 11 152-mm howitzers of the 3rd Battery of the 777th Howitzer Artillery Regiment, which were still on their way to the Sychevka area in order to reinforce the 909th Rifle Regiment there.

At 1030 1. Panzer-Division launched its first direct attack toward Sychevka in the Kruglitsa – Zhuravlevo – Podsosen'e sector with 45 tanks supported by motorized infantry. This attack was driven back by soldiers of the 247th Rifle Division's 921st Rifle Regiment.[7] Having suffered a check in this frontal attack, the Germans fell back and contact with them was lost. At 1100, the headquarters of Panzergruppe 3 received a request from the 7. Panzer-Division: "Use the dive bombers, which have been sent directly to the [VIII] Fliegerkorps, against the encircled Russian grouping in Griaznoe. Oberst Meister considers that this assistance is necessary."[8]

From 1200 V Armeekorps was again placed at the disposal of 9. Armee commander and was carrying out the order for a double encirclement. The LVI Panzerkorps was already securing the initial encirclement, and its command was awaiting word that the 6. and 7. Panzer-Divisionen had linked up, which would significantly ease the overall situation. But until this occurred, Reinhardt issued an order to LVI Panzerkorps to use some of its panzers to bolster the defense, which of course wasn't the best option. However, since this order was obligatory for all of the units of the first line of the enveloping ring, the decision was made to use only non-operational tanks that would be dug into the ground.[9]

At this time the Germans again attacked Sychevka, but this time from the west, from the direction of Nikitino. As a result, a portion of their tanks broke through in the direction of Zabelino, and having cut the highway to Rzhev, began to push to the northeast in the direction of Zubtsov.[10]

At 1230 the commander of Luftflotte 2 called the headquarters of Panzergruppe 3 with the good news that rather greater prospects of supplying it with fuel had appeared, and requested that it not hesitate with requests. This of course could not but gladden Reinhardt, because his motorized and panzer units were now east and north of Sychevka, and their constant advance was putting strain on the available fuel supplies. However, on the other hand thanks to this, a reconnaissance battalion and two battalions of 36 Infanterie-Division (mot.) had already been moved out in the direction of Karmanovo in order to protect his eastern flank.

Kampfgruppe von Hey of 1. Panzer-Division bypassed Sychevka on its eastern side and at 1300 its vanguard, under the command of Major Eckinger, seized a road bridge 3 kilometers northeast of the town intact. This allowed a further advance to the north to continue unhindered, until the column of a reinforced battalion of 1. Panzer-Division's Schützen-Regiment 113 was detained for several hours in the woods west of Nikol'skoe, at a point where the road narrowed, by accurate sniper and rifle fire. Only after combing through the woods with infantry was Leutnant Gayen's company of II./Schützen-Regiment 113, supported by Viesler's panzer platoon from III./Panzer-Regiment 1 and other panzers of Panzer-Regiment 1, able to continue advancing toward the Upper Volga in the direction of Rzhev.[11]

At 1400, the next attack was launched from out of the pocket against the boundary between 6. and 7. Panzer-Divisionen. The outcome at first hung in the balance, but with their own forces, the panzer divisions were able to restore the situation before counterattacking, as a result of which Bogoroditskoe was taken, where 80 men were taken prisoner.[12] Even before the attack, during the night observers had noticed several occasions when Soviet aircraft flew into the pocket in this area, but they always returned to their bases before dawn. These were undoubtedly Po-2 aircraft. One of these aircraft was shot down, and later under interrogation its pilot explained that those who had tried to break out had retreated, and the regular army 114th Rifle Division, which consisted of well-trained soldiers with two years of combat experience, was attempting to escape.[13]

At 1430, 36. Infanterie-Division (mot.) with a portion of its forces moved out from the bridgehead at Gol'nevo in the direction of Karmanovo. The activity by the Soviet air force was insignificant, and it was unable to render any restraining influence.

Yet 1. Panzer-Division was now scattered. Its forward elements were already at Khlepen', 18 kilometers northeast of Sychevka, after having driven Red Army units out of the village after stubborn fighting. Other units of the division were now on the northeastern outskirts of Sychevka. There were also those that were still locked in combat in the area of concrete fortifications south of Sychevka, where the unknown heroes were continuing to fight to the last man.

Simultaneously with 1. Panzer-Division, elements of 6. Infanterie-Division had entered Sychevka from the west, although the rest of the division was tied up in tough fighting with encircled Red Army units. They didn't encounter the anticipated organized defense of the city, except for a few pockets of resistance from Red Army elements that hadn't had time to escape the town. While eliminating these pockets, the Germans noticed that disorganized elements and units of the regular Red Army were opposing them, but primarily they consisted of garrison troops who lacked combat experience.[14] In contrast, at this same time, in the sector of the front in the Olenino area, units of the attacking 9. Armee had bumped into a tough defense by the Red Army in well-fortified positions, the withdrawal from which was being implemented gradually and in stages.[15]

At 1530, the commander of V Armeekorps was informed by Panzergruppe 3 that at 9. Armee's orders, its 5. and 35. Infanterie-Divisionen were to begin the process of replacing the 6. and 7. Panzer-Divisionen respectively in their defensive positions along the perimeter of the pocket. At 1630, Generalfeldmarschall Kesselring again assured Reinhardt over the telephone that fuel would be delivered by air without interruption.

In one of Reinhardt's reports to 9. Armee headquarters, the views with respect to the situation with fuel looked as follows:

> The resolution of the problem with fuel supplies demands the decoration of all chiefs, if of course their service in this is not under doubt. The highway leading to Kholm-Zhirkovskii still isn't open. Its quickest possible clearance is a necessary condition for the rapid organization of the supply with fuel. The panzer group has created intermediary places for the layover of vehicles and the temporary housing of headquarters. Luftflotte 2 is guaranteeing the further delivery of fuel at the expense of its own interests. For the panzer group it can supply everything necessary by air, even if this will tell on its own capabilities of direct action against the enemy, and believes that this is more important than support of the ground troops from the air. Hounding the retreating enemy from the air is considered a lower priority.

On the afternoon of 10 October, the 6. and 7. Panzer-Divisionen were formally relieved in their positions along the eastern and northeastern perimeter of the pocket by the infantry of V Armeekorps and pulled back into reserve. There, they began preparations for a further offensive to the east. The command of LVI Panzerkorps was also keeping two divisions in its reserve. Its 129. Infanterie-Division, after being replaced, marched in full-strength to the area south of Zhilino.

Having analyzed the developing situation, Reinhardt believed that it was more advantageous to take Kalinin as soon as possible, rather than Torzhok. There, the Volga might be used as a natural screen. The headquarters of 9. Armee agreed with this conclusion and directed VI and XXIII Armeekorps to alter their directions of advance from the northeast more to the east. However, they were to be careful not to interfere with the panzer group's movement. Even so, 9. Armee commaander Adolf Strauß personally preferred for VI Armeekorps to head directly toward Rzhev.[16]

In accordance with the plan, Hauptmann Schulenburg's III./Panzer-Regiment 1 of 1. Panzer-Division successfully took the strongpoint of Sharikov by evening. In the assault, a lot of anti-tank guns in armored turrets and a lot of vehicles were destroyed, and more than 1,200 prisoners were taken.[17] Simultaneously, the area of concrete fortifications 6 kilometers south of Sychevka was finally taken, which had been holding up elements of 1. Panzer-Division for almost three full days.[18]

Upon its arrival in the 31st Army, the recently arrived 126th Rifle Division was immediately directed to make a march with its full complement to the area of Baranovo and Chupiatino. However, it wasn't fated to take up a defense there; instead from the march it had to go into battle piecemeal against the motorized units of 1. Panzer-Division that had broken through. Even though by 1700 it had managed to stop the enemy and was holding on the Karasi – Tsybino line, the commander of the 31st Army ordered it to make a fighting withdrawal to Zubtsov because of the lack of shells for the artillery. As a consequence of this, by 1700 separate German tanks were freely approaching Khlepen'.[19]

At 1800, at the request of Heeresgruppe Mitte, Reinhardt summarized the results that had been achieved over the first day of his command:

> LVI Panzerkorps still hasn't reported.
>
> The reconnaissance battalion of the 14. Infanterie-Division (mot.) is at Baskakovo, XXXXI Panzerkorps with its reconnaissance battalion and two battalions of the 36. Infanterie-Division (mot.) is in Karmanovo, and with one regiment and I./Schützen-Regiment 113 is beyond Sychevka and moving toward Zubtsov from the east. The 6. Infanterie-Division is west of Sychevka and moving from the southeast toward Rzhev.
>
> In order to begin the realization of the plans for 11 October, 129. Infanterie-Division and 14. Infanterie-Division (mot.) will move in the direction of Krasnyi Kholm; it is anticipated that Aufklärung-Abteilung 5 of 6. Panzer-Division will shortly move out toward Shakhovskaia Station.
>
> In the course of the day, VIII Fliegerkorps delivered 65 cubic meters of fuel to XXXXI Panzerkorps, and tomorrow guarantees the delivery of an additional 60 cubic meters. Further progress will depend on the availability of fuel.
>
> The reconnaissance battalion of 14. Infanterie-Division (mot.) in Baskakovo is setting up a bridgehead on the Shchesna River.
>
> Units of 36. Infanterie-Division (mot.) encountered a column of Russian tanks moving to the south in Zlatoustovo, and stopped it with anti-tank artillery; it has begun to establish a staging area beyond Gzhatsk.[20]

Before the onset of darkness, 1. Panzer-Division's Aufklärung-Abteilung 4 on the division's southern flank seized the abandoned airfield in Novodugino without opposition, and Leutnant Stern's engineers of the reinforced 3. Kradschützen-Kompanie immediately set to work to make it operational again. Simultaneously, the division's intelligence department identified the hasty retreat of Russians out of Khlepen' (seemingly this was the 126th Rifle Division), and the division command believed that it would face no obstacles in crossing the Gzhat' River on the next day.[21]

Things were going less well for the Wehrmacht's 6. Infanterie-Division west of Sychevka. There, bypassed Red Army units were still offering fierce resistance, and although situated in deep encirclement, they had maintained command and control and were conducting stubborn, organized attacks with the aim of breaking out to the east.

By 1830, units of 1. Panzer-Division that had entered Sychevka back at 1430 had driven the last of the town's defenders out of it after stubborn fighting. Without a pause, and meeting no further resistance, they moved on toward Zubtsov, but night-fall forced them to stop 3 kilometers to the northeast of Sychevka. Of the number of defenders of the town, 1,151 became prisoners. In the surrounding forests, there were piles of abandoned Red Army gear and equipment.[22]

Thus, Sychevka fell at 1830 on 10 October

The town, which had been preparing for a defense in the course of a week, was supposed to be defended by the full-strength 247th Rifle Division, reinforced with composite units and a full complement of anti-aircraft, anti-tank and heavy howitzer artillery, under the leadership of a full major-general. But in fact it held out for less than a day, having been yielded practically without combat to some motorized infantry regiment and 60 panzers, and the 10-15 aircraft that were supporting them.[23] However, no evidence has yet been found in the archives as to when, under what conditions and in what manner the city had been abandoned by the organizers and leaders of its defense. Possibly, light will be cast on this by the transcripts of interrogations of our military prisoners, which should still be preserved in Germany's Bundesarkhiv or in the US National Archive. However, this is a matter of further research.

Altogether in the battle for Sychevka, the Germans took 2,000 prisoners, destroyed 40 guns, and seized 20 empty railroad wagons and 4 warehouses with aircraft engines and spare parts for them.[24] In the city, the roads and pontoon bridges across the Vazuza River had been destroyed. The railroad bridge across the river had been partially demolished, but infantry could still use it.[25]

On this day, the remaining forces of the Western and Reserve Fronts were merged into a new Western Front under the command of General of the Army G.K. Zhukov, while Colonel General I.S. Konev was left as his deputy on the Kalinin axis. N.A. Bulganin, I.S. Khokhlov and I.A. Serov were appointed as members of the Western Front's Military Council. Lieutenant General V.D. Sokolovsky remained as its chief of staff.

Night fell, and another freeze struck. All of the vehicles left abandoned on roads for the night were found the next morning frozen in the mud up to their axles. It was impossible to drag them out of it without the causing of a lot of damage to them, so there was nothing left to do but wait until the day warmed up, when it would become possible to free them.[26]

11 October (Saturday)

The night was frigid, but by morning the temperature had risen a bit above freezing. The roads again began to thaw, and once again vehicles were struggling forward, wallowing in the muck.[27]

Struggling along such roads, just like everyone else, 129. Infanterie-Division reached the city of Gzhatsk, which had fallen the evening before, only after midnight, and there its troops settled in for the night. It was possible to spend a restful night only in the villages along the main roads, because the surrounding territory for the most part was still occupied by encircled units of the Red Army. The division's headquarters deployed in Gornovo. Here, too, the local population proved to be rather friendly. The Germans were able to sleep in homes and buildings, but on the floor. Their greatcoats didn't protect them from the cold, and the home's residents warmheartedly showed kind consideration and obtained thatch for everyone, which allowed the Germans to spend the night in relatively comfortable conditions.[28] I cannot even conceive how to explain such conduct. I can only repeat the question: How must the local authorities have treated the population, so that the people greeted the aggressors with joy?

After 1. Panzer-Division's ten days of intense combats with a serious adversary and in difficult terrain, the breakthrough's successes had become obvious. Already at 0510 on 11 October, Kampfgruppe von Hey consisting of II./Schützen-Regiment 113 and Strippel's panzer platoon of III./Panzer-Regiment 1 reached Zubtsov, and an armored column of Panzer-Regiment 1 rolled into Ivashkovo by noontime.

Entering the southern districts of Zubtsov, Kampfgruppe von Hey's panzers and halftracks together with Leutnant Gayen's 2. Kompanie as the first matter of priority seized an intact bridge across the Vazuza River. Other bridges across the Volga in the nearby area had been blown up.[29]

From the morning of 11 October, the encircled Red Army units became active. They increasingly reminded the Germans of their presence, striving to break out of the ring of encirclement and reach friendly lines. However, they of course didn't know that having broken through the first ring they would have immediately encountered a second, now with practically no strength to breach it. The principle of a double ring of encirclement was working without reproach. For example, some still unidentified Red Army units that were retreating from the west during the preceding night had managed to advance with combat far to the east, and by 0700 on 11 October, having crossed the Gzhat' River, they had assembled in the Nikol'skoe area, 14 kilometers northeast of Gzhatsk. There, they fought their last battle, having bumped into the outer ring of encirclement.

By 0730, the Red Army units in front of XXXXI Panzerkorps had retreated to Zlatoustovo, 36 kilometers southeast of Sychevka; later, they moved to the area 8 kilometers south of Karmanovo. There were still some units located in encirclement southwest of Sychevka, but their attempts to break out of the pocket on each occasion became weaker and weaker. Northeast of Sychevka, prisoners were taken from the

107th Motorized Rifle Division and the 126th and 251st Rifle Divisions. According to prisoner testimony, the Germans learned that the 242nd and 247th Rifle Divisions were in the pocket southwest of Sychevka, while 6. Infanterie-Division faced the truncated 220th Rifle Division, which had been cut off from its own 137th and 563rd Rifle Regiments.[30]

Here we again have returned to the 107th Motorized Rifle Division, which we left behind in the narrative. Obviously, it had persistently continued to fight its way out of encirclement and its example is enlightening, so it is worth digressing from the chronology and discussing it in more detail. It is fortunate that its war diary has been preserved.

Back on the night of 7-8 October, the division on foot moved out from Okolitsy in the direction of Gorodnia. The division marched primarily at nighttime and spent the daylight hours resting, in order to avoid a direct encounter with the Germans. Having stopped for its next period of rest on 10 October, no one in the division could imagine that the Germans were fully aware of this Soviet division that was trying to break out of the pocket, and its movement route, as far as possible, was under their control, even though it ran through dense woods, bypassing any populated places. During the daytime, the Germans periodically swept the general area of the division's position with machine-gun fire, showing that they were aware of its approximate location. The men received no rest, and the division command sent out a reconnaissance team toward the Vladimirskoe – Belyi highway. Even though it revealed that the highway was being covered by rather strong detachments, the command made the determination to break out across it. It was decided to launch the attempt at 0500 on 11 October, and by this time, the division's units had taken up their jumping-off positions. On the highway, there was the active traffic of German cavalry and supply wagons. Through observation, camouflaged artillery guns, machine-gun nests and even two tanks were spotted among the roadside buildings.

The 20th Reconnaissance Battalion was given an order – to jump off first and to cover the other units with fire as they crossed the road. The breakout began with the reconnaissance troops' attack, which came as a surprise to the Germans; with some delay they opened a scattered fire at the attackers. But it was too late; the reconnaissance men, having tossed grenades into the firing positions and tanks, dashed forward with bayonets at the ready. Hand-to-hand combat between desperate men began, in which there were only two ways out – death or victory. The sanguinary struggle still hadn't ended, when the division's main forces began to cross the highway, firing and tossing grenades at the Germans. The division attacked in two separate columns, one of which was led by the division commander himself, Colonel Chanchibadze, and the other by the division's chief of staff, Major Iagodkin.

In this battle the Germans lost 17 vehicles, two tanks and two artillery guns, 6 machine-gun nests, and approximately a company of soldiers. The 107th Motorized Rifle Division, exploiting the surprise attack, lost 3 men killed and 17 wounded.

While crossing the highway, one group of officers and soldiers, numbering up to 300 men, became separated from the rest of the division. Subsequently splitting into small groups, they separately tried to make their way out of encirclement. Some managed to do so, but the fate of the majority of these men remains unknown. Evidently, it was from among this group that the Germans took prisoners on this day northeast of Sychevka, which is mentioned in their combat reports. No one else of the 107th Motorized Rifle Division was in that area.

After breaking out, the division kept moving almost until nightfall, and halted for the night at 1800, only having reached a wooded area southeast of Bugovo. Now the division was forced to keep moving in the daylight hours, since the presence of such a large combat formation in their rear prompted the Germans to begin a pursuit and to deploy blocking detachments, redoubling their efforts to re-establish the division's movements.

In this manner, separating from the pursuers and knocking aside the blocking detachments, the division kept pushing to the east, until on 31 October it linked up with regular units of the Red Army. Thus, its odyssey of escape from encirclement, which lasted for 25 days, came to an end. On this we could wrap up the discussion. However, some mention must be made of the incomprehensible behavior of the civilian population of the majority of villages and towns of Smolensk Oblast, which for the most part viewed the Red Army with hostility and offered no assistance; on the contrary, the 107th Motorized Rifle Division's war diary states that they refused to serve as guides, failed to give places of rest and shelter, and refused to offer food. Instead, they all too often simply informed the Germans of the Red Army soldiers and officers that were trying to make their way out of encirclement.[31]

Now let's return to the morning of 11 October. At 1030, LVI Panzerkorps reported to Panzergruppe 3 headquarters: "Renewal of the attacks on the part of the encircled units was only toward the highway, and according to prisoner interrogation, three Russian divisisions are squeezed into a restricted space west of Bogorodskoe and are out of fuel. The [VIII] Fliegerkorps has been requested to drop leaflets there."[32]

At 1045, 1. Panzer-Division's reconnaissance battalion reached a railroad crossing lying 2 kilometers southwest of Zubtsov without having seen any sign of Red Army forces. All around, it was silent and there was not a single person. The reconnaissance troops apparently still didn't know that the southern portion of the town had been in the hands of Kampfgruppe von Hey from their division since early that morning.[33] At 1200, 7. Panzer-Division was re-subordinated to V Armeekorps, while LVI Panzerkorps returned again to Panzergruppe 3.[34]

Units of the 31st Army from the morning had been conducting stubborn fighting in the areas north and west of Sychevka while falling back to the line of the Osuga River. As has been established, at noon the morning combat dispatches and reports from the units had arrived in the army headquarters and were being analyzed:

> 126th Rifle Division minus the 210th Rifle Regiment, falling back to the northeast behind the Osuga River, was fighting in encirclement northeast of Sychevka on the Vazuza River. Nothing was known about the situation of the 210th Rifle Regiment.

247th Rifle Division with one rifle regiment was making a fighting withdrawal to the northeast in front of the enemy that has broken through northeast of Sychevka. The situation with its 916th and 920th Rifle Regiments is also unknown.

220th Rifle Division with its main forces had reached the line: Pribytki – Viazovka – Loshaki this morning while its 675th Rifle Regiment has assembled in the Osuga area.[35]

There were a lot of similar reports. Even if in places they still weren't giving a clear picture of what was happening, in the headquarters of the Western Front they should have realized what was going on. However, while the incoming messages were being processed, discussed and pass on to higher levels of command, the Germans kept moving. By the time the Red Army's higher command reached any sort of decision, the operational situation had changed, and often fundamentally so.

Thus no one knew that the Germans had taken Bol'shaia Antonovshchina by noon, while in the area of Drozdovo, they had launched an attack out of Gorki in strength of up to a battalion. No one knew that they had launched an attack toward Peno, and an attempt had been made out of Torg toward Podgliad'e, 10 kilometers north of Peno. All of these attacks were ultimately driven back, and combat reports generated in the units, the information of which would only arrive at Western Front headquarters at the end of the day. Thus, having no accurate information about what had happened or about the real situation of the units at this time, Western Front's headquarters made the decision to shift these units to the Rzhev area.

However, the Germans weren't slumbering, and out of the area of Ivanovka and the woods northeast of Bogoroditskoe, they committed large groups of submachine gunners, with the support of mortar crews and 50 tanks, and with a single blow they isolated the first echelon of the new Western Front, contact with which was lost immediately.[36]

At 1215, the full complement of the 1. Panzer-Division rolled into Zubtsov and began spreading throughout the entire city. This had happened so quickly owing to the fact that its Kampfgruppe von Hey before sunrise had seized the intact bridge across the Vazuza River and kept possession of it this entire time. The departure of the Red Army units from the town happened so rapidly, that to the delight of the 1. Panzer-Division command, approximately 600 cubic meters of fuel was discovered on the grounds of some industrial enterprise, which even so was still short of the needs of both the panzers and the division's transport.[37]

The offensive of Panzergruppe 3's units was proceeding so rapidly that Reinhardt issued an order to them not to stop, but to keep going as long as they had the fuel to do so. Meanwhile, VIII Fliegerkorps that afternoon sent three Junkers with fuel to an undamaged airfield found 3 kilometers south of Zubtsov.

By this time, 6. Infanterie-Division had also broken through the Soviet defenses north of Sychevka on the line of the Pakitnia River, and without stopping it continued its advance to the east. Everything that had happened that morning was rather surprising, and plainly unexpected to both sides. The following unequivocal entry was made in Panzergruppe 3's journal of combat operations: "The Russians are seemingly shocked by the advance of Panzergruppe 3 to the north. In Rzhev and northeast of it, a large amount of traffic is being observed. Thus, given a necessity, the panzer group will accelerate its drive to Kalinin, which will depend on the depth of the Russian operational positions."[38] Just a short time later, a reconnaissance plane of VIII Fliegerkorps spotted approximately 500 transport vehicles with tanks and armored cars on the Rzhev – Staritsa highway.[39]

The Western Front command was taking hasty measures to defend Rzhev. This had been prompted by a report from the 31st Army's intelligence chief, to the effect that "a group of tanks in unestablished number has broken through at Zubtsov and is threatening Rzhev."[40]

Had the Red Army command known that the Wehrmacht from the very outset of 22 June 1941 was experiencing a chronic deficit of fuel, the decisions that it made might have been of a completely different nature. The failure in this matter can be attributed to the intelligence service exclusively, and to a great extent to its highest leadership. If such information was arriving, then why was it being ignored, and if not, then why was intelligence failing to gather such information? But the chronic fuel shortages were in fact influencing the decisions of the German command: At 1423 Reinhardt advised the commander of XXXXI Panzerkorps "to refrain from making a premature attack toward Rzhev, since it can do so only after it comes into possession of fuel somewhere. It is better to push forward to Koledino on the remnants of fuel and stop the Russian units that are attacking northeast of Rzhev."[41]

That afternoon, the command of 1. Panzer-Division's Schützen-Regiment 1, having learned that its Kradschützen-Bataillon 1 had linked up with I. Panzer-Abteilung, decided to implement its available alternative option of an advance to the north, in which the motorcyclists would provide infantry cover for the panzers. Oberleutnant Feig's III./Schützen-Regiment 113 was fortifying itself on the northwestern heights beyond the Volga and establishing firing positions there. Thus, for the first time in the war, German soldiers were viewing the great Russian river.[42]

At 1500, 36. Infanterie-Division (mot.) reached Pogoreloe Gorodishche Station, but it was unable to take it from the march and fell back after its initial attack was repulsed. The rest of the division launched an attack with its main forces to the south. Not even a half hour after its start, the neighboring 14. Infanterie-Division (mot.)'s Aufklärung-Abteilung 5 reached Prechistoe, and after a short battle, it seized a bridge there that the defenders of it had failed to destroy before retreating. Having crossed the river, the reconnaissance battalion, without waiting for the arrival of the main forces, began a pursuit of the retreating Russians, sending forward a special kampf-gruppe for this purpose.

Having launched its attack, 36. Infanterie-Division (mot.) had run into stiff resistance and came to a stop. Its command, having learned that Prechistoe had been taken, requested support from there in order get its attack to the south going. However, Aufklärung-Abteilung 5 was not in a condition to do this, since when capturing the bridge it had lost 14 men killed alone, and those who had been sent in pursuit had not yet returned. The attack launched by 36. Infanterie-Division (mot.) sputtered to a halt, and Reinhardt himself drove there to find out what was going on. Simultaneously, he also visited the neighboring 6. Infanterie-Division.

Having returned to his headquarters, he urgently called for a conference, in which it was noted that thanks to the freezing weather, the condition of the roads had improved markedly, but once again the problem with fuel was growing acute, and he gave those who had gathered for the meeting a directive: "It is necessary when interrogating prisoners to obtain detailed information from them about the possible location of fuel. An analogous telegram has been sent to the individual corps."[43]

Well, why then wasn't the given situation being taking into account by the higher Red Army command? There isn't a single piece of evidence in the available archives that when planning operations the Red Army gave consideration to the Wehrmacht's thirst for fuel.

At 1745, the reconnaissance battalion of the 36. Infanterie-Division (mot.) after a short combat managed to seize Pogoreloe Gorodishche itself.[44] Yet another railroad station on the path to Moscow was now in German hands. With each new station in its possession, the supply of its subordinate troops became easier for the German command. It is strange, but a fact is a fact: In the German documents of these days, there is not a single mention of the destruction of railroads or railroad infrastructure by the retreating Red Army. Moreover, the Germans sought to spare the use of the Luftwaffe against the defenders of these railroad stations, and for the most part seized them with infantry units, striving to preserve everything with minimal damage, so that they could immediately be put to use by their own forces.

Toward evening, the long-awaited Pollex arrived back in the panzer group, and everyone immediately sensed the impact of his return. The supply of the troops with food and ammunition changed for the better. In particular, the supplementary delivery of bread for 7. Panzer-Division was organized. Initially, fuel for the corps' motorized divisions had been set at 150 cubic meters for each 50 kilometers, but then its delivery to Kholm-Zhirkovskii was arranged, where mobile refueling points began to be organized directly along the highway. Panzergruppe 3's war diary notes:

> Pollex made every effort in order in the course of two days to supply the troops with all the fuel they needed so that they could continue the offensive. Moreover, it was being expected that the situation with supplies would ease even more, once the deliveries could go to Viaz'ma, and from there along the railroad to Sychevka; thus the panzer group would receive adequate supplies from there.[45]

Thus it was not in vain that the Germans had placed great hopes on the rapid capture of Sychevka, and they weren't betrayed in their expectations. The town had fallen into their hands like an overripe fruit.

At 1930, reconnaissance by VIII Fliegerkorps reported that 1. Panzer-Division's movement toward Staritsa had halted. In response to the panzer group headquarters' bewildered question about what was happening, the division command explained that the enemy still held Rzhev out in front of it and that there was concern about its left flank. As a result of this prompting from higher command, the division command at its own initiative decided to push on to Rzhev, so that after taking it, its panzers would have free movement across the Volga toward Staritsa. The panzer group's war diary notes: "Reinhardt did not agree with this and believed that it would be better for the division to advance directly to the east, and in the event that it became clear that the Russians were retreating from Rzhev to Staritsa, simply to bypass Rzhev."[46]

By 2100, the daily reports began to arrive in the panzer group's headquarters:

From VIII Fliegercorps, confirmation arrived about the delivery of fuel on 12 October by 27 aircraft in the area 3 kilometers south of Zubtsov. Then General Baron von Richtofen personally called the Panzerkorps commander and reported that an airstrike was being prepared at the request of 1. Panzer-Division, because it had again come to a stop and was fighting off Russian aircraft only with rifles and machine guns.

XXXXI Panzerkorps announced that it was possible to reach Kalinin from the east and from the bridgehead simultaneously, since no Russians were expected east of the Panzerkorps because a Russian captain taken prisoner in Sychevka had said under interrogation that his division was the final reserve, 2/3 of which had been in Sychevka, 1/3 of which was in Rzhev. The units of the division in Sychevka had been crushed, and his men had been resisting to the end. It seems that the Russians no longer actually had any combat reserves.

It had been proposed for LVI Panzerkorps to deploy at the front as many motorcycle battalions as possible, since they were more economical in the expenditure of fuel; this had become even more vital before the lengthy dash to Kalinin. The 14. Infanterie-Division (mot.)'s Aufklärung-Abteilung 5 had been detached to advance as far as possible forward.

Again, the activity of Russian aircraft was rising in the XXXXI Panzerkorps' sector of operations. The strongest Russian attacks from out of the pocket were being conducted against 7. Panzer-Division. The 35. Infanterie-Division is on the defensive and is being used in order to organize a main command post.[47]

After analyzing the arriving documents, not only had the prospects for the coming day become clear to Reinhardt, but also those for the next several days:

The 129. Infanterie-Division should be in the north in the area northeast of Gzhatsk; Aufklärung-Abteilung 5 and the reinforced regimental group of the 14. Infanterie-Division (mot.) should arrive in Prechistoe along the route through Savino, Krasnyi Kholm, Ul'ianovskoe, Nikulino, Gorodetskoe and further to Kalinin.

The 1. Panzer-Division of the XXXXI Panzerkorps should advance from Zubtsov through Pogoreloe Gorodishche, Vlas'evo and Staritsa to Kalinin.

Units of the 36. Infanterie-Division (mot.) located in Pogoreloe Gorodishche are capable of doing this. The 6. Infanterie-Division extends the line of security to the north and southwest from Rzhev.

From Kalinin, the panzer group, as has been planned, advances to the northwest to Torzhok and Vyshnyi Volochek.[48]

An interesting incident happened late in the evening with a staff officer of 7. Panzer-Division Hauptmann Liese and the division's chief of material-technical supply. He wrote about this in his report: "Returning to division headquarters, in the darkness we came upon a group of Russians in the woods. Both sides were moving a short distance apart and giving no notice of the other. We recognized the Russians by their steel helmets, which prompted us to retreat hastily."[49] Not even this Liese could imagine how much trouble and problems this Russiaan group would bring to them. However, we'll return to this matter in a bit.

With this, the day came to an end. The command post of Panzergruppe 3 was located in Voskresenskoe.[50] The headquarters of the 31st Army that was opposing it was located as before in Rzhev.[51]

The day had proved to be clear and sunny, but cold. The temperature was freezing in the mornings. Even though the road conditions improved because of this, they were still overcongested, which resulted in traffic jams that told on the pace of the movement of forces. Thus, with the aim of establishing more precise control over troop movements, with the onset of the new day, 9. Armee command directed that all non-motorized units in the sector of its offensive would move only between the hours of 1800 and 0500, while the rested motorized units would have sole use of the roads between 0500 and 1800 and get rest again at night.[52]

12 October (Sunday)

Overnight, attempts by the encircled units of the Red Army to break free of the pocket increased and continued throughout this day and following days, but this was already the agony of the doomed. Here are a few examples, taken from German combat reports:

The II./Panzer-Regiment 3 of 2. Panzer-Division in heavy fighting repulsed a Russian attempt to break out from Batishchevo. Thousands of prisoners and hundreds of captured trucks. There are many Russian corpses in front of the battalion's positions.[53]

In 7. Panzer-Division's sector of defense, at 0300 Russians that were attempting to break out materialized and the artillery observers that had been posted out in front in the artillery's sector were compelled to defend themselves against hand grenades and rifle fire. The Russians were moving between the firing positions of the German artillery batteries and were being supported by their artillery with great effect. Led by some energetic officer, they were divided into groups of 30-100 men each, and attacking, broke through our firing positions and our rear and transport communications and disappeared. Those who failed to break out were either killed or taken prisoner by a counterattack. The location of those who broke out and their number is unknown.[54]

Our documents, naturally and unfortunately, were not preserved, and from the German documents, of course, we can't find out who organized and led this breakout, as well as who organized and led many of the other attempts. How many of you unknown heroes are still lying throughout the forests, unburied and forgotten? That's how your heroism and dedication to the Motherland were valued by those, thanks to whom you in fact wound up in encirclement.

In the German archives, I came across an account by Leutnant Jäger, a platoon commander with 7. Panzer-Division's Schützen-Regiment 7, who gave a description of the following episode in the actions of their Sturmgruppe Lungershausen. Today this area of the cited village along the Dnepr River is in the Novodugino region of Smolensk Oblast. It is painful to read this document, so I have decided to offer it without any accompanying commentary. Let this be a requiem to all those warriors who were killed in the fighting:

On Sunday, the Russians struck our positions with a powerful artillery barrage, interspersed with occasional salvoes from Soviet rocket launchers firing from Pekarevo. This unrestrained barrage of our rear areas continued until noon.

Then, at 1500 the Russians attacked in large forces and having broken through to Zhegulino at the boundary of our right flank Knorr's platoon, linked up there with forces just as large. At the order of our company commander, without firing a single shot we closed with them and unexpectedly opened fire with our rifles.

A disorganized wave of men in Red Army uniforms were now advancing with their forward units toward the river channel. The enemy was ready to rush us with infantry, cavalry and tanks with the aim of breaking out. They opened fire suddenly. The attackers, in uncounted thousands, were using every weapon available to them. This initial fire attack caused us large losses in personnel and equipment. It seems that this fire would continue, so that they could move all the columns, artillery, horse-drawn wagons and trucks, without breaking apart into pieces, directly toward us and into the broad forest beyond Zhegulino. They were presenting a target for our forward artillery, and one after another the shells were mercilessly falling on this mass. Nearly unimaginable destruction was beginning.

Meanwhile, Russians in hundreds were approaching our 3. Kompanie. Its soldiers were killing as many of the enemy as they were able, but were not able to stop this mass of men, which was many times superior to us in strength. Leutnant Knorr maintained contact with the attached assault guns and was pointing out the most vulnerable targets for them. The energetic intervention by the assault guns was connected with the fact that only they were able to retain their position without an increase in losses.

Russian tanks approached the river channel in order to support their attack, but to our good fortune they became bogged down there. This threat was detected and within 20 minutes all of them had been destroyed by the artillery platoon of 10. Kompanie and mainly by the assault guns. Eleven tanks were knocked out by us; two turned back toward Zhegulino, but en route they were knocked out by the fire of the assault guns. The attack against our right flank was driven back, but the Russians were still in a large mass in front of our positions. One could even say, in an enormous mass.

I. Bataillon had a weak line of defense and it was unable to withstand the next attack. Soon these masses were moving in the northeast direction, so the situation seemed in our favor. Around 1700, a fruitful panzer counterattack from north to south was undertaken by us. The Russians were hurling everything possible in front of our tanks in order to save their lives. Hundreds of them had gathered like a herd in the river channel and apparently thought they were safe there. As a result, hundreds of vehicles, horses with carts, tractors and so forth had collected there; thus, a second application of artillery and panzers was necessary in order to destroy them.

Unprecedented destruction was taking place in front of our eyes. Now Leutnant Knorr together with the assault guns launched a counterattack from our position against the smashed Russians. This led to a heavy close combat, which prompted concern, since the 3. Zug was almost without ammunition. Nevertheless, it proved able to destroy a large number of Russians and to take around 150 prisoners. Thus, Leutnant Knorr was able to hold his position. The Russians were using the river channel for their defense and did this until twilight, after which they attacked again. They managed to seize Hill 286.5 and the forward positions in front of Docharovka. This became dangerous for 1. and 2. Zug. In a large superiority in numbers they were closing upon our rear areas. Our machine guns were firing incessantly and inflicting heavy casualties upon them. The platoon had deployed them particularly advantageously on the flanks. It seemed that the attack had been driven back. However, at 1800 a report arrived that 2. Zug had been attacked by superior numbers of infantry, and its central positions had been breached. Even a counterattack led by Feldwebel Teissen couldn't regain the position, because the Russians were many times superior to us in numbers. The company commander Oberfeldwebel Biech received an order to prevent a breakthrough to the south with the remnants of 2. Zug.

Recognizing the danger, Oberleutnant Enckevort personally arrived with several panzers, which in the afternoon went on the counterattack. Meanwhile, Biech had managed to rally the remnants of 2. Zug and sent them on motorcycles to cover the left flank. Almost at this same time, the Russians in overwhelming numbers attacked the company's positions in the center with shouts of "Ura!" The most threatening situation was in the 1. Zug; it seemed threatened with complete destruction. The company was firing from all types of weapons in order to stop the swiftly running masses of men. Hauptfeldwebel Echrat himself lay down behind a machine gun and was firing, but the Russians had already broken into the position. One machine-gun team in a farm field, just like Echrat's machine-gun squad, fell back somewhat, while continuing to fight back. A machine-gun platoon, a battery of heavy mortars and anti-tank guns were firing at the attacking Russians. Our soldiers, faithful to their oath, preferred death before giving up their positions.

Fortunately, just at this critical moment, Oberleutnant Enckevort arrived with the panzers and went on the counterattack. However, full squads of Russians were already intermingled in the positions with our soldiers and were firing heavily from their rifles. Enckevort himself was firing a Soviet rifle, standing behind a panzer, and from there he was issuing orders to the platoon commanders that the position had to be held at any cost. However, here he was killed by a close shot to the head.

Thanks to the employment of every man, especially in 1. Zug, these attacks were still being repulsed. The soldiers had very little ammunition left, but under extreme pressure they held their positions sometimes even intermingled with Russians as they waited for the attacks to end.

Around 1900-2000, approximately 80 Russians made an attempt to break out from the south in the direction of Leonovo at the boundary with 2. Zug. This attack was repulsed by Biech's group. At the time, there was still no threat to the company. At an order from the battalion commander, now the remnants of 2. Zug headed by Leutnant Jäger were assembled together with four panzers in order to return to their old positions as quickly as possible. Some time later, around 2130, Echrat reported an attack on his right flank. With the shout "Ura!", the Russians began to assault 1. Zug's most vulnerable point on its right flank. Indeed, in this close combat several of our soldiers were killed. Seeing the danger, Biech covered the rear with four or five drivers.

No sooner had they changed their position when 70-80 attacking Russians again appeared in front of them with cries of "Ura!". Obergefreitor Sösemann and Obergefrietor Klingel with three motorcyclists were defending the building containing the wounded. When Russians began to hurl grenades into this building, the most recently wounded man was already clambering through the window. Then, medic Unteroffizier Weber took off and dragged out Obergefreitor Reich, who was lying on a stretcher. But almost immediately he was shot by the Russians from approximately four meters away, even though he was wearing a Red Cross armlet. The motorcyclists who took part in this battle consider him to be a hero.

Meanwhile, Sösemann from a panzer set fire to several nearby structures, in order to see where to fire. These buildings and front yards were in the possession of a group of Russians, numbering up to 40 men, and all around heavy gunfire was going on. Soon another three of our panzers arrived, and a front of defense in the rear was formed out of artillery spotters and all available soldiers. They were firing at everything that moved. However, meanwhile some of the Russians located in Leont'evo again attempted to break through our forward line. With a powerful "Ura!" they rushed out of their buildings and gardens and attacked our soldiers from the rear. Everyone who was still able to do so along the front and in the rear immediately opened fire. Several of the arriving panzers headed to this place, in order somehow to overcome this menacing situation, which might have become fatal for the company. Approximately 40 Russians remained lying dead and approximately 40 men, including the most seriously wounded, were taken prisoner. A lot of Russians were still continuing to roam around the village, in order to make their way out of the pocket during the night. Precious little ammunition remained and it had to be scrupulously spared. Biech radioed the battalion commander about the dangerous situation in the company, after which two panzers brought up ammunition, and Biech sent them directly to the machine-gun positions.

Russians twice our size in number with the cry of "Ura!" again attempted to attack the badly weakened 1. Zug, but our soldiers held their positions, carrying out the order of their fallen commander. It became a little quieter in the center of the company's positions. The 3. Zug and the machine-gun platoon didn't have any communications between each other. Leutnant Knorr headed directly to the signals battalion, in order to inform the command in person about the situation in 3. Zug. He reported that the platoon was holding its positions, although 8. Kompanie had withdrawn its left flank about 400 meters from the western outskirts of Pekarevo, which had created a significant gap. The day of 13 October arrived and only at 0300 did a platoon of motorcyclists arrive in support, with which it became possible to close the gap partially.

Around 0600, the Russians in enormous number struck the boundary of 1. Zug again. As a result, they had to abandon their positions on the right flank, because there were very few soldiers holding them. Fortunately, the Russians didn't venture further and were content to hold the seized positions.

The remaining platoons continued to hold their positions and were firing ineffectively at the right flank of the Russians that had broken through; the forward positions were continuing to be occupied by them. With the next counterattack by the remaining platoons, they were partially regained. Under fire, Obergefreitor Knoll voluntarily, with hand grenades, bounded forward in rushes and blew up a bunker full of Russians. By some miracle he came back under the same heavy fire. Now we were advancing behind two panzers, in order to destroy the remaining Russians.

The platoon was compelled to defend its position with only one machine gun and one mortar. Understanding the danger, at dawn Leutnant Knorr arrived with his platoon and machine-gun squad and headed to the western outskirts of Pekarevo in order to support 8. Kompanie that had fallen back from there.

As soon as it was able to regain the abandoned positions, the Russians again attacked them with superior numbers. Thanks to the excellent cooperation of the assault guns and the well-directed fire of the machine-gun squad, this attack too was repelled.

From this moment, the Russian artillery was for the most part firing upon our rear areas. Attacks were continuing, but for the first time such a large mass of Russians were digging into the river valley in front of our positions. No reinforcements were expected and the company's situation was quite serious. Would it be able to withstand fresh enemy attacks? This question alarmed us over and over again. At the order of the battalion commander, two platoons were to be left with Leutnant Jäger, while Oberfeldwebel Biech, who to this point had only been receiving and passing along orders, assumed command of the company. The battalion commander was constantly receiving information over the radio about the situation in the company. Now we had time to bring up ammunition for the machine-gunners. The Russians were still out in front of us.

From the battalion they informed us over the radio of the impending relief of the infantry. Around 1800, the group of artillery spotters returned from the river channel. Thus, the next night of 13/14 October was approaching, and our soldiers with extreme nervous tension were waiting for the Russian "Ura!", which they had grown to hate. However, fortunately, it never came. At approximately 0100 in the morning, the command implemented the infantry's replacement in the line, and everyone gave a sigh of relief. Around 0200 the company headed to the rear to their vehicles. One heavily overloaded car was moving with it. It was carrying the bodies of the dead, including that of Oberleutnant Enckevort.[55]

*   *   *

As a result of this October offensive, in the course of eight days the German forces succeeded in breaking through the center and left flank of the Western Front's defenses, resulting in the encirclement of the forces of the 16th, 19th, and 20th Armies and Group Boldin, as well as the 107th Motorized Rifle Division and the 241st and 252nd Rifle Divisions of the 30th Army. In that time span, the Germans advanced 230 to 250 kilometers to the east (between Iartsevo and Dorokhovo), at an average pace of 8-10 kilometers a day.[56]

The Wehrmacht forces, having broken through the Red Army's defensive front to its entire operational depth, destroyed the bulk of the Western and Reserve Fronts, and having approached the Mozhaisk line of defense with a delay of eight days, created the conditions for a lunge toward Moscow. *Eight days, a total of only eight days, but how the enemy would miss them two months later,* when some of its troops were already viewing our capital through binoculars, rubbing their hands with desire in the euphoria of victory. However, the Germans wouldn't have those eight days, and they would have to make a retreat over a similar distance even faster.

True, the price of these eight days was horrifying. According to the latest confirmed data, it amounted to 688,000 human lives, and for the most part this sacrifice was totally unjustified.

Eight days, just eight days, but how much ignorance, conjecture and often outright fabrication swirls around them. However, the work of the retired Soviet army officer L.N. Lopukhovsky can be considered one of the most authoritative domestic studies of the course and details of the 1941 Viaz'ma operation at the present time. In the course of forty years, he gathered documentary evidence about this tragic period of the Great Patriotic War, trying to learn the details of the death of his father, Colonel Nikolai Il'ich Lopukhovsky, who was recorded as missing-in-action on 30 November 1941. The result of his exhaustive search is his book *1941. Viazemskaia katastrofa*, which came out in 2007. Many of his conclusions fundamentally refute the official point of view of these events that held sway for decades. In fact, the given research is merely an addendum to his labors.

I promised at the beginning of the book not to offer any personal conclusions; thus, keeping my word, I allow the reader the possibility to draw their own conclusions regarding these tragic events.

The Red Army would return to Sychevka only a year later. In its ranks would be some of those who in October 1941 had impeded the enemy that was keen to take the capital, but only a an extremely few remained who could let the entire country know about what took place here, while naturally it wasn't advantageous to those who were responsible for this tragedy to flaunt the details of their ignomy. Thus only the names of places on the maps and in the combat reports were a reminder of what had taken place, as well as the former defensive lines of the Red Army that had been converted by the Wehrmacht to serve its own needs – and they still had to be overcome. However, this is a subject for my next book. This will be the "accidentally" forgotten Operation Mars, about which palace historians fortuitously "failed to remember" prior to 1991 and only now is the curtain over this tragedy starting to be opened. It would have it its own heroes and correspondingly pseudo-heroes and anti-heroes!

But in the meantime the Wehrmacht was continuing to plunder the Russian land!

Notes

Preface

1   A recent exception to this, as well as an effort to consider where the Rzhev-Viaz'ma battles fit within the context of the Battle of Moscow, is Svetlana Gerasimova's doctoral study, which was later translated and published into English in 2013 by Helion under the title *The Rzhev Slaughterhouse; The Red Army's Forgotten 15-month Campaign against Heeresgruppe Mitte, 1942-1943*.

Chapter 1

1   TsAMO RF, F. 208, op.2511, d. 216, p.7.
2   "Combat path of the 923rd Rifle Regiment", TsAMO RF, o. 391427, d. 1, s. 7.
3   TsAMO RF, F.208, op.2511, d.216, pp.5-7 (Data in the table are from pages 5-6)
4   Brigade Commander was the military rank of the Red Army's high command staff between 22.09.1935 and 7.05.1940.
5   "Account of Panzergruppe 3's combat operations over the period 02.10 – 20.10.1941", TsAMO RF, F.500, op.12462, d.231, pp. 85-99.
6   Ibid.
7   Ibid.
8   Ibid.
9   Ibid.
10   Ibid.
11   Ibid.
12   Ibid.

Chapter 2

1   Kriegstagebuch der 3 Pz Gr. 9 Army AG "Center". 25.09.41 (National Archives Microcopy No. T-313, USA, Washington D.C.). Henceforth, this source will be given as "Kriegstagebuch der 3 Pz Gr." with the date of the entry following it.
2   Boucsein Heinrich. *Halten oder Sterben. Die hessisch-thüringishche 129 Infanterie-Division im Rußlandfelzug und Ostpreußen 1941-1945*. Berg am See: Kurt Vowinckel Verlag KG, 1999, p. 60.
3   Kriegstagebuch der 3 Pz Gr. 25.09.1941.
4   Paul Wolfgang. *Brennpunkte*. Hentges-Verlag: Krefeld, 1977, p. 139
5   Heeresgruppe Mitte/Artillery Staff Offleer. War Journal with appendices. 25.09.1941 (Heeresgruppe Mitte/Stoart. Kriegstagebuch mit Anlagen).
6   Manteuffel Hosso von (Ed.). *Die 7 Panzer-Division im Zweiten Weltkrieg*. Traditionsverband ehem 7 Panzer-Division-Kameradenhilfe E.V.: Krefeld, 1965, p. 187.
7   Kriegstagebuch der 3 Pz Gr. 26.09.1941.
8   Ibid.
9   Wolfgang, Op. cit., p. 140.
10   Kriegstagebuch der 3 Pz Gr. 26.09.1941.
11   Heeresgruppe Mitte/Artillery Staff Officer. War journal with appendices. 26.09.1941 (Heeresgruppe Mitte/Stoart. Kriegstagebuch mit Anlagen).
12   Kriegstagebuch der 3 Pz Gr. 27.09.1941
13   Wolfgang, *Brennpunkte*, p. 140.

14   Kriegstagebuch der 3 Pz Gr. 27.09.1941.
15   Ibid.
16   Ibid.
17   Heeresgruppe Mitte/Artillery Staff Officer. War journal with appendices 27.09.1941 (Heeresgruppe Mitte/Stoart. Kriegstagebuch mit Anglangen).
18   Kriegstagebuch der 3 Pz Gr. 28.09.1941
19   Wolfgang, op. cit., p. 140.
20   Kriegstagebuch der 3 Pz Gr. 28.09.1941.
21   Ibid.
22   Wolfgang, op. cit., p. 140.
23   Kriegstagebuch der 3 Pz Gr. 29.09.1941.
24   Boucsein, op. cit., p. 61.
25   Kriegstagebuch der 3 Pz Gp. 29.09.1941.
26   Ibid.
27   Ibid.
28   Ibid.
29   Ibid.
30   Ibid.
31   Ibid.
32   Wolfgang, op. cit., p. 141.
33   Heeresgruppe Mitte/Artillery Staff Officer. War journal with appendices 30.09.41.
34   Kriegstagebuch der 3 Pz Gr. 30.09.1941.

Chapter 3

1   Wolfgang, op. cit., p. 142.
2   Kriegstagebuch der 3 Pz Gr. 01.10.1941.
3   Wolfgang, op. cit., p. 142.
4   The Nebelwerfer was the German towed rocket launcher. Because of the characteristic sound made by its rockets in flight, the Soviet soldiers nicknamed it "Ishak" [donkey]. It was initially designed to launch smoke shells, however, primarily the rockets carried high-explosive fragmentation warheads, or more rarely, incendiary. On the Wehrmacht's tables of organization and equipment, it was listed under the name "rocket cannon". It had six 150-mm tubes and fired 39-kilogram shells to a range of 6.8 kilometers. Its relatively low range was compensated by its powerful shells and its use as a tactical cover.
5   Kriegstagebuch der 3 Pz Gr. 01.10.1941.
6   Kriegstagebuch der 3 Pz Gr. 02.10.1941.
7   Boucsein, op. cit., p. 62.
8   "Historical logbook of the 119th Rifle Division", TsAMO RF, F.1083, op.1, d.1, pp. 60-84.
9   Heeresgruppe Mitte/Artillery Staff Offleer. War journal with appendices. 02.10.1941.
10   Boucsein, op. cit., p. 63.
11   Ibid.
12   Manteuffel, op. cit., p. 188.
13   Stoves Rolf, 1 Panzer Division 1935-1945. Verlag Hans-Henning Podzun: Bad Nauheim, 1961, p. 251.
14   Wolfgang, op. cit., p. 143.
15   Kriegstagebuch der 3 Pz Gr. 02.10.1941.
16   Ibid.
17   Ibid.
18   Boucsein, op. cit., p. 63.
19   Ibid.
20   Kriegstagebuch der 3 Pz Gr. 02.10.1941
21   Ibid.
22   Wolfgang, op. cit., p. 142.
23   Ibid.

24 Kriegstagebuch der 3 Pz Gr. 02.10.1941.
25 Ibid. Hiwi, a contraction of the German *Hilfswilliger* [those desiring assistance] were Wehrmacht "volunteer assistants", gathered (including through compulsory mobilizations) from the local population on the occupied territories and from among prisoners of war. Initially they served in auxiliary units as drivers, medics, sappers, cooks and so forth. Later the Hiwi began to be used directly in combat actions, operations against partisans, and for punitive acts.
26 Boucsein, op. cit., p. 64.
27 Kriegstagebuch der 3 Pz Gr. 02.10.1941
28 Boucsein, op. cit., p. 65
29 Kriegstagebuch der 3 Pz Gr. 02.10.1941
30 Boucsein, op. cit., p. 64.
31 Stoves, op. cit., p. 252.
32 "Operational summaries of the 119th Rifle Division's headquarters", TsAMO RF, op.8583, d.50, pp. 120-127.
33 Boucsein, op. cit., p. 65.
34 Ibid.
35 Wolfgang, op. cit., p. 143.
36 Kriegstagebuch der 3 Pz Gr. 02.10.1941.
37 Ibid.
38 Boucsein, op. cit., p. 66.
39 "Combat path of the 251st Rifle Division", TsAMO RF, F.1538, op.1, d.43, pp. 23-42.
40 Kriegstagebuch der 3 Pz Gr. 02.10.41.
41 "Combat path of the 923rd Rifle Regiment", TsAMO RF, op.391427, d.1, p. 7.
42 Kriegstagebuch der 3 Pz Gr. 02.10.1941.
43 "Combat path of the 923rd Rifle Regiment", TsAMO RF, op.391427, d.1, p. 7.
44 Boucsein, op. cit., p. 66.
45 Kriegstagebuch der 3 Pz Gr. 02.10.1941
46 Ibid.
47 Ibid.
48 Manteuffel, op. cit., p. 188.
49 Kriegstagebuch der 3 Pz Gr. 02.10.41.
50 Boucsein, op. cit., p. 66.
51 Kriegstagebuch der 3 Pz Gr. 02.10.1941.
52 Ibid.
53 Ibid.
54 TsAMO RF, F.208, op.2511, d.216, p. 5.
55 "Operational reports and summaries of the headquarters of Heeresgruppe Mitte", TsAMO RF, F.500, op.12462, d.757, p. 148.
56 Kriegstagebuch der 3 Pz Gr. 02.10.1941.
57 Kriegstagebuch der 3 Pz Gr. 03.10.1941.
58 Boucsein, op. cit., p. 66.
59 Kriegstagebuch der 3 Pz Gr. 03.10.1941.
60 Boucsein, op. cit., p. 67.
61 Kriegstagebuch der 3 Pz Gr. 03/10.1941.
62 Stoves, op. cit., p. 252.
63 Kriegstagebuch der 3 Pz Gr. 03.10.1941.
64 Wolfgang, op. cit., p. 143.
65 Kriegstagebuch der 3 Pz Gr. 03.10.1941.
66 Boucsein, op. cit., p. 69.
67 On these days, the 107th Tank Division had been reformed into the 107th Motorized Rifle Division, and thus it is worth calling it a motorized rifle unit. Apparently, the Germans found documents on prisoners that indicated it was a tank division, and naturally they couldn't know about its renaming.
68 TsAMO RF, F.1158, op.1, d.11a (file of the 49th Guards Rifle Division, 03.10.1941).

69   Kriegstagebuch der 3 Pz Gr. 03.10.1941.
70   Ibid.
71   Wolfgang, op. cit., p. 143.
72   Kriegstagebuch der 3 Pz Gr. 03/10.1941.
73   Boucsein, op. cit., p. 141.
74   Ibid., p. 143.
75   Manteuffel, op. cit., p. 188.
76   Stoves, op. cit., p. 252.
77   Boucsein, op. cit., p. 69.
78   Kriegstagebuch der 3 Pz Gr. 03.10.1941.
79   Boucsein, op. cit., p. 69.
80   Stoves, op. cit., p. 252.
81   Kriegstagebuch der 3 Pz Gr. 03.10.1941.
82   Wolfgang, op. cit., p. 143.
83   Kriegstagebuch der 3 Pz Gr. 03.10.1941.
84   Ibid., 04.10.1941.
85   TsAMO RF, F.1158, op.1, d.11a (files of the 49th Guards Rifle Division), 04.10.1941.
86   Stove, op. cit., p. 253.
87   Boucsein, op. cit., p. 70.
88   Ibid.
89   Kriegstagebuch der 3 Pz Gr. 04.10.1941.
90   Boucsein, op. cit., p. 68.
91   Kriegstagebuch der 3 Pz Gr. 04.10.1941.
92   Manteuffel, op. cit., p. 189.
93   Boucsein, op. cit., p. 68.
94   Kriegstagebuch der 3 Pz Gr. 04.10.1941.
95   Wolfgang, op. cit., p. 145.
96   Kriegstagebuch der 3 Pz Gr. 04.10.1941.
97   TsAMO RF, F.1158, op.1, d.11a (files of the 49th Guards Rifle Division). 04.10.1941.
98   Boucsein, op. cit., p. 69.
99   Kriegstagebuch der 3 Pz Gr. 04.10.1941.
100 Stoves, op. cit., p. 254.
101 Boucsein, op. cit., p. 70.
102 Kriegstagebuch der 3 Pz Gr. 04.10.1941.
103 "Account of Panzergruppe 3 on the combat actions over the period 02.10.1941 and 20.10.1941",
     TsAMO RF, F.500, op.12462, d.231, pp. 85-99.
104 "Operational dispatches and summaries of the headquarters of Heeresgruppe Mitte", TsAMO
     RF, F.500, op.12462, d.757, pp. 148-236.
105 Kriegstagebuch der 3 Pz Gr. 04.10.1941.
106 "Account of the headquarters of Panzergruppe 3 on the combat actions over the period from
     02.10.1941 to 20.10.1941", F.500, op.12462, d.231, pp. 85-99.
107 Manteuffel, op. cit., p. 191.
108 Kriegstagebuch der 3 Pz Gr. 05.10.1941.
109 Boucsein, op. cit., p. 70.
110 TsAMO RF, F.1158, op.1, d.11a (files of the 49th Guards Rifle Division). 05.10.1941.
111 Stoves, op. cit., p. 254.
112 Boucsein, op. cit., p. 70.
113 Kriegstagebuch der 3 Pz Gr. 05.10.1941.
114 Boucsein, op. cit., p. 70.
115 Kriegstagebuch der 3 Pz Gr. 05.10.1941.
116 Our documents weren't preserved, but in the German documents the number of attacking tanks
     wasn't indicated.
117 Boucsein, op. cit., p. 70.
118 Ibid., p. 71.

119 Boucsein, op. cit., p. 72.
120 Kriegstagebuch der 3 Pz Gr. 05.10.1941.
121 Manteuffel, op. cit., p. 191.
122 Kriegstagebuch der 3 Pz Gr. 05.10.1941.
123 Ibid.
124 Manteuffel, op. cit., p. 191.
125 Boucsein, op. cit., p. 72.
126 Ibid.
127 Kriegstagebuch der 3 Pz Gr. 05.10.1941.
128 Ibid.
129 Ibid.
130 "Operational dispatches and summaries of the headquarters of Heeresgruppe Mitte", TsAMO RF, F.500, op.12462, d.757, pp. 148-236. This information is totally surprising, since according to the official Soviet history, the supply of these aircraft from Great Britain to the USSR was begun only in October 1941, and at that, only to Murmansk in order to protect naval convoys; however, it turns out that these fighters were already being used in combat on the Western Front. Of course, the decision had to be made, and then an agreement had to be worked out between Great Britain and the USSR about their delivery and the conditions of it. Then time was necessary to ship the Hurricanes, to translate and study the technical documentation regarding them, and finally, to complete the training of the pilots for them. The well-warranted question arises – when in fact did their first deliveries begin?
131 Ibid.
132 Ibid.
133 TsAMO RF, F.208, op.2511, d.216, p. 42.
134 "Operational summaries of the 31st Army headquarters", TsAMO RF, op.8583, d.47, pp. 97-103.
135 TsAMO RF, F.208, op.2511, d.216, p. 37.
136 Ibid., p. 42.
137 Kriegstagebuch der 3 Pz Gr. 06.10.1941.
138 TsAMO RF, F.1158, op.1, d.11a (files of the 49th Guards Rifle Division).
139 Boucsein, op. cit., p. 72.
140 Kriegstagebuch der 3 Pz Gr. 06.10.1941.
141 Ibid.
142 Manteuffel, op. cit., p. 192.
143 Kriegstagebuch der 3 Pz Gr. 06.10.1941.
144 Boucsein, op. cit., p. 73.
145 Wolfgang, op. cit., p. 146.
146 Kriegstagebuch der 3 Pz Gr. 06.10.1941.
147 Manteuffel, op. cit., p. 193.
148 Ibid.
149 "Historical log book of the 920th Rifle Regiment", TsAMO RF, op.481005, d.1, pp. 1-5.
150 Boucsein, op. cit., p. 74.
151 Ibid., p. 75.
152 Kriegstagebuch der 3 Pz Gr. 06.10.1941.
153 "Operational summaries of the headquarters of the 31st Army", TsAMO RF, op.8583, d.47, pp. 97-103.
154 Ibid.
155 Manteuffel, op. cit., p. 193.
156 Ibid.
157 Boucsein, op. cit., p. 175.
158 Kriegstagebuch der 3 Pz Gr. 06.10.1941.
159 Ibid.
160 Boucsein, op. cit., p. 74.
161 Manteuffel, op. cit., p. 195.
162 Ibid.

163 "Operational summaries of the headquarters of the 31st Army", TsAMO RF, op.8583, d.47, pp. 97-103.
164 Ibid.
165 Ibid.
166 "Historical log book of the 920th Rifle Regiment", TsAMO RF, op.481005, d.1, pp. 1-3.
167 "Operational summaries and dispatches of the headquarters of Heeresgruppe Mitte", TsAMO RF, F.500, op.12462, d.757, pp. 148-236.
168 Kriegstagebuch der 3 Pz G. 06.10.1941.

Chapter 4
1   Kriegstagebuch der 3 Pz G. 06.10.1941.
2   Manteuffel, op. cit., p. 195.
3   "Combat dispatches and summaries of the headquarters of the 31st Army", TsAMO RF, op.8583, op.
4   TsAMO RF, F.386, op.8583, d.63, pp. 46-47.
5   "Combat dispatches and summaries of the headquarters of the 31st Army", TsAMO RF, op.8583, d.46, pp. 24-44.
6   Boucsein, op. cit., p. 75.
7   "Combat dispatches and summaries of the 31st Army", TsAMO RF, op.8583, d.46, pp. 24-44.
8   Ibid.
9   "Historical log book of the 920th Rifle Regiment", TsAMO RF, op. 481005, d.1, pp. 1-3.
10 Kriegstagebuch der 3 Pz Gr. 07.10.1941.
11 Stoves, op. cit., p. 255.
12 "Operational summaries of the 119th Rifle Division headquarters (29th Army)", TsAMO RF, op.8583, d.50, pp. 120-127.
13 Boucsein, op. cit., p. 76.
14 Ibid.
15 Kriegstagebuch der 3 Pz Gr. 07.10.1941.
16 Boucsein, op. cit., p. 76.
17 Kriegstagebuch der 3 Pz Gr. 07.10.1941.
18 "Operational summaries of the headquarters of the 31st Army", TsAMO RF, op.8583, d.47, pp.97-103.
19 "Intelligence summaries of Heeresgruppe Mitte headquarters", TsAMO RF, F.500, op.12462, d.623(vol.2), pp. 4-49.
20 Kriegstagebuch der 3 Pz Gr. 07.10.1941.
21 TsAMO RF, op.8583, d.47, pp. 97-103.
22 Boucsein, op. cit., p. 76.
23 Stoves, op. cit., p. 255; apparently, the counterattacking Soviet tanks were of the BT type and/or T-26s.
24 "Historical log book of the 920th Rifle Regiment", TsAMO RF, op.481005, d.1, pp. 1-3.
25 "Combat dispatches and summaries of the headquarters of the 31st Army", TsAMO RF, op.8583, d.46, pp. 24-44.
26 Stoves, op. cit., p. 255.
27 "Historical log book of the 920th Rifle Regiment (119th Rifle Division)", TsAMO RF, op.8583, d.1, pp. 1-3.
28 "Operational summaries of the 199th Rifle Division headquarters", TsAMO RF, op.8583, d.50, pp. 120-127.
29 "Historical log book of the 119th Rifle Division", TsAMO RF, F.1083, op.1, d.1, pp. 60-84.
30 "Operational summaries of the 119th Rifle Division headquarters", TsAMO RF, op.8583, d.50, pp. 120-127.
31 Kriegstagebuch der 3 Pz Gr. 07.10.1941.
32 Stoves, op. cit., p. 255.
33 Ibid.

34 "Operational summaries of the 119th Rifle Division's headquarters", TsAMO RF, op.8583, d.50, pp. 120-127.

35 Kriegstagebuch der 3 Pz Gr. 07.10.1941.

36 TsAMO RF, F.208, op.2511, d.216, p. 40.

37 "Operational summaries of the headquarters of 31st Army", TsAMO RF, op.8583, d.47, pp. 97-103.

38 Kriegstagebuch der 3 Pz Gr. 07.10.1941.

39 Ibid.

40 Manteuffel, op. cit., p. 198.

41 Boucsein, op. cit., p. 76.

42 Ibid.

43 Wolfgang, op. cit., p. 150.

44 Kriegstagebuch der 3 Pz Gr. 07.10.1941.

45 Ibid.

46 "Operational summaries and dispatches of Heeresgruppe Mitte headquarters", TsAMO RF, F.500, op.12462, d.757, pp. 148-236.

47 Kriegstagebuch der 3 Pz Gr. 07.10.1941.

48 TsAMO RF, F.208, op.2511, d.216, pp. 37-42.

49 "Combat dispatches and summaries of the headquarters of the 31st Army", TsAMO RF, op.8583, d.46, pp. 24-44.

50 TsAMO RF, F.1158, op.1, d.11a (files of the 49th Guards Rifle Division).

51 "Combat dispatches and summaries of the headquarters of the 31st Army", TsAMO RF, op.8583, d.46, pp. 24-44.

52 "Operational dispatches and summaries of Heeresgruppe Mitte headquarters", TsAMO RF, F.500, op.12462, d.757, pp. 148-236.

53 Kriegstagebuch der 3 Pz Gr. 08.10.1941.

54 Boucsein, op. cit., p. 78.

55 "Historical log book of the 119th Rifle Division", TsAMO RF, F.1083, op.1, d.1, pp. 60-84.

56 "Operational summaries of the headquarters of the 119th Rifle Division", TsAMO RF, op.8583, d.50, pp. 120-127.

57 "Operational dispatches and summaries of Heeresgruppe Mitte headquarters for 08.10.1941", TsAMO RF, F.500, op. 12462, d.757.

58 Kriegstagebuch der 3 Pz Gr. 08.10.1941.

59 "Combat dispatches and summaries of the 31st Army headquarters", TsAMO RF, op.8583, d.46, pp. 24-44.

60 Ibid.

61 Kriegstagebuch der 3 Pz Gr. 08.10.1941.

62 "Operational summaries of the headquarters of the 31st Army", TsAMO RF, op.8583, d.47, pp. 97-103.

63 TsAMO RF, F.386, op.8583, d.63, pp. 46-47.

64 Kriegstagebuch der 3 Pz Gr. 08.10.1941.

65 Ibid.

66 Manteuffel, op. cit., p. 197.

67 "Combat dispatches and summaries of the headquarters of the 31st Army", TsAMO RF, op.8583, d.46, pp. 24-44.

68 Kriegstagebuch der 3 Pz Gr. 08.10.1941.

69 Ibid.

Chapter 5

1 Ibid.

2 "Combat dispatches and summaries of the 31st Army", TsAMO RF, op.8583, d.46, pp. 24-44.

3 Kriegstagebuch der 3 Pz Gr. 08.10.1941.

4 "Combat dispatches and summaries of the 31st Army", TsAMO RF, op.8583, d.46, pp. 24-44.

5   TsAMO RF, F.208, op.2511, d.216, pp. 7-183.
6   It was these numerical designations that are indicated in the German intelligence summaries, although the 54th Regiment according to the TsAMO RF belonged to the 25th Rifle Division, which was operating under the command of Odessa Military District's Coastal Army, while naturally no other documents at all were preserved on the 18th Regiment.
7   "Intelligence summaries of Heeresgruppe Mitte headquarters", TsAMO RF, F.500, op.12462, d.623 (Vol. 2), pp. 4-49.
8   Ibid.
9   "Operational dispatches and summaries of Heeresgruppe Mitte headquarters", TsAMO RF, F.500, op.12462, d.757, pp. 148-236.
10 Boucsein, op. cit., p. 78.
11 "Operational dispatches and summaries of Heeresgruppe Mitte headquarters", TsAMO RF, F.500, op.12462, d.757, pp. 148-236.
12 Kriegstagebuch der 3 Pz Gr. 09.10.1941.
13 TsAMO RF, F.208, op.2511, d.216, p. 46.
14 "Combat dispatches and summaries of the 31st Army", TsAMO RF, op.8583, d.46, pp. 24-44.
15 Kriegstagebuch der 3 Pz Gr. 09.10.1941.
16 Ibid.
17 Ibid.
18 Ibid.
19 Ibid.
20 Ibid.
21 Boucsein, op. cit., p. 79.
22 Wolfgang, op. cit., p. 151.
23 "Combat dispatches and summaries of the 31st Army", TsAMO RF, op.8583, d.46, pp. 24-44.
24 "Operational summaries of the 31st Army headquarters", TsAMO RF, op.8583, d.47, pp. 97-103.
25 Kriegstagebuch der 3 Pz Gr. 09.10.1941.
26 Ibid.
27 Stoves, op. cit., p. 256.
28 Ibid.
29 Ibid.
30 Kriegstagebuch der 3 Pz Gr. 09.10.1941.
31 TsAMO RF, F.208, op.2511, d.216, p. 48.
32 "Operational summaries of the 31st Army headquarters", TsAMO RF, op.8583, d.46, pp. 97-103.
33 Kriegstagebuch der 3 Pz Gr. 09.10.1941.
34 "Operational dispatches and summaries of Heeresgruppe Mitte headquarters", TsAMO RF, F.500, op.12462, d.757, pp. 148-236.
35 Ibid.
36 Ibid.
37 "Intelligence summaries of Heeresgruppe Mitte headquarters", TsAMO RF, F.500, op.12462, d.623 (Vol. 2), pp. 4-49.

Chapter 6
1   "Operational dispatches and summaries of Heeresgruppe Mitte headquarters", TsAMO RF, F.500, op.12462, d.757, pp. 148-236
2   Kriegstagebuch der 3 Pz Gr. 10.10.1941.
3   Ibid.
4   "Operational summaries of the 31st Army headquarters", TsAMO RF, op.8583, d.46, pp. 97-103.
5   Kriegstagebuch der 3 Pz Gr. 10.10.1941.
6   "Operational summaries of the 31st Army headquarters", TsAMO RF, op.8583, d.47, pp. 97-103.
7   TsAMO RF, F.208, op.2511, d.216, p. 55.
8   Kriegstagebuch der 3 Pz Gr. 10.10.1941.
9   Ibid.

10   TsAMO RF, F.208, op.2511, d.216, p. 55.
11   Stoves, op. cit., p. 256.
12   Kriegstagebuch der 3 Pz Gr. 10.10.1941.
13   Ibid.
14   Ibid.
15   "Operational dispatches and summaries of the Heeresgruppe Mitte headquarters", TsAMO RF, F.500, op.12462, d.757, pp. 148-236.
16   Ibid.
17   Stoves, op. cit., p. 256.
18   Boucsein, op. cit., p. 80.
19   TsAMO RF, F.208, op.2511, d.216, p. 55.
20   Stoves, op. cit., p. 256.
21   Kriegstagebuch der 3 Pz Gr. 10.10.1941.
22   "Intelligence summaries of Heeresgruppe Mitte headquarters", TsAMO RF, F.500, op.12462, d.623, pp. 1-24.
23   TsAMO RF, F.208, op.2511, d.216, p. 55.
24   Kriegstagebuch der 3 Pz Gr. 10.10.1941.
25   "Operational dispatches and summaries of Heeresgruppe Mitte headquarters", TsAMO RF, F.500, op.12462, d.757, pp. 148-236.
26   Ibid.
27   "Operational dispatches and summaries of Heeresgruppe Mitte headquarters", TsAMO RF, F.500, op.12462, d.757, pp. 148-236.
28   Boucsein, op. cit., p. 80.
29   Stoves, op. cit., p. 257.
30   "Intelligence summaries of the Heeresgruppe Mitte headquarters", TsAMO RF, F.500, op.12462, d.623, pp. 1-24.
31   TsAMO RF, F.1158, op.1, d.11a (files of the 49th Guards Rifle Division).
32   Kriegstagebuch der 3 Pz Gr. 11.10.1941.
33   Ibid.
34   Ibid.
35   TsAMO RF, F.208, op.2511, d.216, pp. 7-183.
36   "Operational summaries of the Western Front", TsAMO RF, F.208, op.2511, d.160, pp. 83-84.
37   Kriegstagebuch der 3 Pz Gr. 11.10.1941.
38   Ibid.
39   Ibid.
40   TsAMO RF, F.208, op.2511, d.216, p. 56.
41   Kriegstagebuch der 3 Pz Gr. 11.10.1941.
42   Stoves, op. cit., p. 257.
43   Kriegstagebuch der 3 Pz Gr. 11.10.1941.
44   The town of Pogoreloe Gorodishche and its railroad station are in the Zubstov District of Tver' Oblast.
45   Kriegstagebuch der 3 Pz Gr. 11.10.1941.
46   Ibid.
47   Ibid.
48   Ibid.
49   Manteuffel, op. cit., p. 197.
50   Kriegstagebuch der 3 Pz Gr. 11.10.1941.
51   TsAMO RF, F.208, op.2511, d.216, p. 56.
52   Kriegstagebuch der 3 Pz Gr. 11.10.1941.
53   Strauss, Franz Joseph, *Geschichte der Panzer-Regiment 3*. Neckargemünd 1977. Kurt Vowinckel Verlag, p. 335.
54   Manteuffel, op. cit., p. 197.
55   Ibid., pp. 198-203.
56   "Western Front", TsAMO RF, F.208, op.2511, d.217, p. 183.

Index

INDEX OF PEOPLE

von Bock, Generalfeldmarschall Fedor vi, 21, 68, 94, 106, 114
Bormann, Leutnant 45-46, 105, 118
Budennyi, Marshal S.M. 23-24, 90

Danhauser, Oberst 44-45, 82, 88

Eckinger, Major 60, 67, 137
Enckevort, Oberleutnant 150-151, 153

Gayen, Leutnant 64, 137, 141
Guderian, Generaloberst Heinz Wilhelm 22, 42, 58, 84, 113
Guliaev, Major N.A. 20, 51-52, 102

Hoepner, Generaloberst Erich 22, 58, 84, 88, 113
Hoth, Generaloberst Hermann vi, 21, 23, 31-35, 37-40, 50-51, 54-55, 60-61, 64, 68, 76, 81, 83-84, 88, 94, 106-107, 113-115, 129

Jäger, Leutnant 149, 151, 153

Kesselring, Generalfeldmarschall Albert 22, 39, 68, 138
Knorr, Leutnant 149-150, 152

Koll, Oberst 33, 47, 50, 60, 63
Konev, Colonel General I.S. iii, vi, 19, 22, 24, 30, 32, 36, 82, 93, 114, 140

Landgraf, Generalmajor 32, 36, 82
Löwe, Major 36, 62, 69

Manteuffel, Oberleutnant Hasso 83, 89, 100, 156-163, 165

Polenov, Major General Vitalii Sergeevich 91, 102-104, 108, 112, 120-121
Pollex, Oberleutnant 38, 83, 122, 146

Raus, Generalmajor Erhard vi, 47, 63, 94, 132
Reinhardt, General der Panzertruppen Georg-Hans vi, 21, 31, 34, 41, 54, 87, 94, 114-115, 119, 122, 129-130, 132-133, 136-139, 144-147
Rittau, Generalmajor 37, 59, 67-69

Schröeder, Hauptmann 80, 87, 90
Strauß, Generaloberst Adolf 21, 32, 34, 106-107, 113, 117, 122, 129-130, 138

Zhukov, G.K. x, 82, 91-92, 140

INDEX OF PLACES

Aleshkovo 61, 66-67, 70, 74
Andreevskoe 102-104, 109, 123

Baranovo 86, 109, 139
Baturino 20, 42, 50, 54, 56, 60-61, 75
Belyi xi, 20, 24, 27-28, 30, 33, 37, 39-40, 42, 48, 50-51, 54-55, 58, 60-66, 70-74, 76, 79, 81, 83, 87, 101, 104-107, 111, 114, 126, 129-130, 132, 142

Berlin 29, 38, 40
Bogoroditskoe 82, 137, 144
Bol'shaia 51-52, 86, 90-91, 123, 144
Bol'shaia Kosha 86, 90-91, 123
Bol'shevo 30, 101-102
Bol'shoe Krasnoe xi, 124-125
Boloshevo 116, 134
Bolshevo 121, 125, 133
Bor 24-25, 30, 33, 35, 55, 62, 64-66, 76

Borki 47, 54, 56, 62, 72
Briansk 23, 36, 58, 73, 134
Bykovo 73, 107, 116
Byshovo 49, 55, 61, 64

Chemenovo 80, 86, 88-89
Chernovo 74, 83, 87

Dnepr River 24-28, 30, 32-33, 36-37, 41, 44,
    46, 51, 54-55, 58-60, 63-66, 68-73, 75-77,
    79-80, 82-85, 87-90, 104-109, 111-112,
    114-115, 117-119, 121, 124-125, 128, 130,
    132-133, 149
Dugino xvii, 103, 109, 119, 132-133

Efremovo 46, 49, 52, 55, 61, 64

Fedino 79, 87, 90
Frolovo 51, 54, 59

Glushkovo 60, 63, 70, 74, 84, 107
Gorodok 87, 90, 114
Griaznoe 68-69, 72-73, 89, 136
Gzhat' River 140-141
Gzhatsk xi, xvi, 27, 91, 103, 108, 112-115,
    117, 122, 128, 130-131, 139, 141, 147

Hill 220 37, 44-46, 82, 89, 105
Hill 220.5 82, 89, 105
Hill 229.5 71, 78, 80, 86

Iartsevo 49, 54, 153
Iukhnov xi, 58, 68
Ivashkovo 66, 76, 84, 103-104, 136, 141

Kalinin 25, 27, 113-115, 122, 138, 140, 145,
    147-148
Kamenets 54, 59, 65, 68, 79, 104, 109, 115,
    119, 122
Karavaevo 81, 83, 102, 104, 123-124
Karmanovo 130, 137, 139, 141
Kasnia River 119, 127, 132
Kholm-Zhirkovskii 28, 30, 33, 41-42, 46, 51,
    56-57, 59-65, 67-74, 76-80, 82-84, 86-89,
    101, 104, 106-107, 111, 113, 115, 121, 125,
    132, 138, 146
Kniazh'e 63-65, 67, 72
Kokosh' River 44, 47-50, 54-57
Komary 51, 66, 70, 72, 79, 81, 84, 107, 130
Koshkino 83-84, 89
Kostino 68, 85, 121

Krapivnia 50-51, 56, 75
Krasnoe xi, 108, 120, 124-125, 136
Krasnyi Kholm 130, 132-133, 139, 147

Leningrad 24, 26-27, 45, 82, 91, 114, 120,
    125
Liady 52-53, 55, 102
Liapkino 33, 63-64, 72-73, 80
Lipitsy 83, 104, 117, 119, 127
Lukino 66-67, 70

Mamonovo 55, 57, 62
Mezha 47, 71, 105
Mikhalevo 51, 102, 109
Minsk 19, 87, 107, 124
Mitkovo 117-118, 128
Mol'nia 66, 83, 101-102, 107, 115-116, 121
Moscow i-ii, x-xii, xvi-xvii, 19-20, 23-30, 32,
    36-37, 82, 87-88, 90-92, 101, 112-114, 122,
    126-127, 134, 146, 153, 155
Mozhaisk 68, 121, 153

Nemoshchenka 103-104, 110
Nevel' 31, 34, 36
Nikol'skoe 62, 137, 141
Noviki 69, 79, 81, 90
Novodugino 101, 103, 108, 111, 121, 139,
    149

Olenino xi, 90, 103, 105, 110, 112, 118, 126,
    131, 133, 138
Osmiaia River 45-46, 48-49
Ostashkov 27, 85, 90, 112, 114, 129
Otpisnaia 69, 79, 90

Peno 85, 90, 144
Petrakovo 105, 118, 120
Pigulino 65, 68, 117, 128
Pochinok 45, 53, 62
Podol'sk i, xi, xiii, 124
Pogoreloe 62, 124, 145-148, 165
Pokrov 111, 117, 126, 131
Prechistaia 34-36, 38, 55
Pyzino 120, 123-124

Repino 53, 56, 66
Ripshevo 24, 35, 38
Rzhev x-xi, xvi-xvii, 27, 32, 42, 74, 82, 90-91,
    101, 103, 105, 107, 112-115, 119, 121-122,
    125-126, 129-133, 135-139, 144-145,
    147-148, 155

Samykino 119, 121, 124, 133
Selizharovo 90-91, 108
Shchesna River 127, 132-133, 139
Shelepy 37, 43-45, 49, 55
Skachkovka 51, 61, 64
Skachkovo 49, 54, 56
Smetishche 46, 49-50, 55, 75-76
Smolensk i-ii, xi, xv-xvii, 19-20, 23-24, 26-28,
    31, 51, 71, 87, 107, 113, 122, 124, 143, 149
Smolensk Oblast i-ii, xi, 20, 24, 143, 149
Sokolovo 90, 108, 120
Spas-Demensk 58, 64, 66, 68-69, 75, 83,
    107-108, 113, 121-122, 130
Staritsa 132, 145-147
Staro-Selo 44-45, 49
Stepankovo 123-124
Svity 51, 54-56, 62, 66
Sychevka i, v, x-xi, xv-xviii, 23-24, 27, 30,
    53, 69, 73-75, 88, 91, 100-104, 106-107,
    111-121, 123-129, 131-137, 139-144,
    146-147, 154

Tesovo 117, 119, 121, 125, 128, 132
Tikhanovo 59-60, 67, 69-70, 76-77, 82-84,
    86, 89
Torbeevo 75, 117, 121
Toropets 25-26, 28, 34
Tver' xvi, 20, 25, 59, 165
Tver' Oblast 20, 25, 165
Tychkovo 77, 82, 89, 106

Ust'e 72, 76, 80, 106

Valutino 90-91, 101-102, 109-110
Varvarino 101, 103-104
Vasil'evo 25, 60, 72, 109, 126, 131
Vazuza River xv-xvi, 109, 111, 117, 121,
    140-141, 143-144
Velizh 33, 35, 37-38
Viaz'ma i, vi-vii, x-xi, xiv, xvi-xvii, 20, 23-25,
    27-30, 32-33, 38, 40, 54, 58, 63-66,
    68, 70-71, 73-75, 77, 79-89, 91, 99-101,
    104-108, 113-115, 117-119, 122, 124,
    127-129, 132-133, 136, 146, 154-155
Viaz'ma River 77, 83-84, 89, 105-106, 115,
    117, 127
Vladimirskoe 104, 113, 120, 132, 142
Volga River xv, 26, 37, 137-138, 141, 145, 147
Volochek 80, 104, 109, 148
Volynovo 61, 66, 79
Vop' River 31, 39, 44, 47-48, 50-57, 59, 62-63
Voskresenskoe 83, 86, 88, 108, 117, 148
Votria River 47-48, 57

Warsaw 27-28, 58

Zamosh'e 50, 53, 91
Zaplav'e 90-91, 112
Zelenaia Roshcha 120, 125, 131
Zheltoe 81, 90, 104
Zhidkii 37, 45, 54
Zhuchki 120, 128, 131, 136
Zlatoustovo 130, 139, 141
Zubtsov xi, xvi-xvii, 76, 126, 130-133, 137,
    139-141, 143-145, 147

INDEX OF GERMAN MILITARY UNITS

Army Groups
Heeresgruppe Mitte viii, x-xi, 19, 21-22,
    24-26, 29-32, 36, 39-40, 45, 68, 72, 81,
    88, 91, 101, 106, 111-115, 119, 122, 126,
    129-130, 132, 139, 155-165

Panzergruppe
Panzergruppe 2 22, 24, 37, 42, 58, 113
Panzergruppe 3 i, vi, x, 21, 23-25, 27-28,
    30-31, 33-34, 36-42, 45, 47-48, 50-51,
    54, 56-60, 62-64, 66-69, 71-73, 75,
    79-88, 92, 94, 100, 106-107, 111-115,
    117, 119, 122, 124-126, 128-130, 132,
    134, 136-138, 143-146, 148, 155-156,
    158-165

Panzergruppe 4 x, 22, 24, 37, 42, 58, 66, 79,
    88, 107-108, 113, 130

Armies
2. Armee 22, 24
4. Armee x, 21, 24, 30, 43, 68
9. Armee x, 21, 24, 30-43, 55, 57-58, 60,
    63-64, 69, 73, 80-82, 88, 106, 111,
    113-114, 117, 119, 122, 129-130, 132-133,
    136, 138, 148
16. Armee 41, 114, 129

Brigades
900. Lehr-Brigade (mot.) 22, 24, 60, 80,
    106-107, 111, 113, 121, 130

Corps

V Armeekorps 21, 28, 34-38, 40-41, 47-48,
    51, 53-57, 59-60, 62, 65-66, 69, 72-73,
    79-80, 88-89, 104, 106-107, 111, 114, 119,
    121, 124-125, 127-128, 132-133, 136, 138,
    143
VI Armeekorps 21, 28, 32-37, 40, 47-48, 51,
    54, 56-57, 59-60, 62, 64-66, 70-73, 79, 83,
    86-87, 106, 111, 117, 124, 126, 129-130,
    138
VIII Armeekorps 21, 26, 31, 33-34, 41,
    48-49, 55, 60, 83, 104, 119, 124, 128
VIII Fliegerkorps 35, 37-40, 42-43, 55,
    60-61, 65, 71, 73, 75-76, 79, 83-84, 89,
    108, 113, 119, 122, 132-133, 136, 139,
    143-146
XXIII Armeekorps 21, 33-35, 39-40, 60, 72,
    88, 107, 134, 138
XXVII Armeekorps 21, 33, 40, 106
XXXXI Panzerkorps 21, 28, 30-31, 34-36,
    38, 40-42, 45, 49, 54-57, 59-60, 62, 64-66,
    69-70, 72-73, 75-76, 79-81, 83, 86, 88,
    90, 104, 106-107, 111, 114-115, 117, 119,
    121-122, 125, 127-130, 132-133, 135, 139,
    141, 145, 147
LVI Panzerkorps 21, 28, 30-31, 33, 36-38, 41,
    45, 49, 51, 54-56, 62, 65-70, 72-73, 75-76,
    79, 81, 83, 86, 88-89, 104, 106, 112-113,
    115, 117, 122, 125, 128-130, 132-133, 136,
    138-139, 143, 147

Divisions

1. Panzer-Division 21, 23, 31, 33, 35-38,
    45-46, 48-51, 54, 56, 58, 60-67, 70-73,
    75-76, 79, 81, 84, 86, 104, 107, 109, 111,
    115, 117, 119, 121, 125, 132, 134-137,
    139-141, 143-147, 157
5. Infanterie-Division 21, 35, 39, 48, 50, 59,
    62, 65, 69, 72, 79-80, 83, 87, 90, 107, 111,
    114, 117, 119, 121, 125, 133, 138
6. Infanterie-Division 21, 30, 35, 38, 41, 45,
    56, 62, 70, 72, 77-79, 81-84, 86, 90, 107,
    110, 115, 117, 121, 125, 130, 132-133, 137,
    139-140, 142, 144, 146, 148
6. Panzer-Division 21, 31-33, 36-38, 40-42,
    44-45, 47, 50-51, 54-57, 59-60, 62-65,
    67-71, 73, 79-80, 83-88, 90, 107, 113, 117,
    121-122, 124, 129-131, 138-139
7. Panzer-Division 21, 24, 33, 35, 37-38,
    44, 46-47, 50-51, 54-57, 61, 63, 65, 68,
    70, 72-74, 76, 79-80, 83-87, 89-90, 100,
    104, 107, 112-114, 117, 119, 121-122, 124,
    131-133, 136-138, 143, 146-149, 156

10. Panzer-Division 22, 113, 117, 119, 122
14. Infanterie-Division (mot.) 21, 24, 30,
    32-33, 35, 38, 40, 55, 59, 64-65, 75-76, 81,
    87, 106-107, 115, 117, 121-122, 129-132,
    139, 145, 147
19. Panzer-Division 22, 106, 111, 113
26. Infanterie-Division 21, 35, 38-39, 42, 45,
    47, 51, 55, 60, 71-72, 79, 110, 118, 127, 134
28. Infanterie-Division 21, 124
35. Infanterie-Division 22, 35, 38, 39, 46,
    48-50, 59, 62, 65, 69-70, 72, 79-81, 83,
    86-87, 90, 107-108, 111, 114, 117, 119, 121,
    124, 130, 133, 138, 147
36. Infanterie-Division (mot.) 21, 30, 33-36,
    38, 41, 54-56, 60, 62-63, 66, 70, 72, 79,
    81, 84, 86, 90, 107-108, 117, 119, 121, 125,
    128, 137, 139, 145-146, 148
102. Infanterie-Division 21, 155, 158, 160,
    162-165
106. Infanterie-Division 22, 31, 35, 45, 48,
    50, 53-55, 60, 62, 65, 68, 72, 79-80, 83, 87,
    90, 106-107, 114, 119, 121, 133
110. Infanterie-Division 21, 35, 39, 42, 47,
    54, 56, 62, 71-72, 79, 110
129. Infanterie-Division 21, 30-31, 35, 37,
    41, 42-52, 55-56, 59, 61-65, 67, 69-74,
    76, 78-80, 82-83, 85-89, 105-106, 108,
    113-115, 117, 121, 124, 128-130, 132-133,
    138-139, 141, 147
SS *Reich* Division 22, 122, 130

Regiments

Panzer-Regiment 1 67, 137, 139, 141
Artillerie-Regiment 73 60, 75, 104
Schützen-Regiment 113 60, 63, 67, 75, 104,
    109, 137, 139, 141
Artillerie-Regiment 129 44, 82-84, 106, 108,
    117
Infanterie-Regiment 427 37, 44, 46, 48, 55,
    64, 74, 76-77, 84, 89, 113, 117, 128, 130
Infanterie-Regiment 430 71, 77-78, 80

Miscellaneous

Kampfgruppe von Hey 111, 132, 137, 141,
    143-144
Aufklärungs-Abteilung 4 50, 60, 75, 139
Aufklärungs-Abteilung 5 130, 133, 139, 145,
    147
Luftflotte 2 22, 39, 84, 137-138
Luftwaffe 20, 35, 38-39, 41-42, 44, 50, 56,
    65, 73, 79, 105, 107, 111, 121, 126, 131,
    135, 146

INDEX OF SOVIET MILITARY UNITS

Fronts

Briansk Front iii, 19, 23, 36, 58
Reserve Front iii, 19, 23, 36, 58, 66, 81, 86, 90-92, 101, 103, 118, 140, 153
Western Front ii-iii, vi, 19-22, 24-27, 30, 32, 36, 58, 61, 66, 72, 81-82, 89-93, 101, 103-104, 111-116, 118-119, 121, 128, 140, 144-145, 153, 160, 165

Groups

Group Boldin vi-vii, 81-82, 93, 115, 118, 127, 153
Group Polenov 91, 103, 112

Armies

16th Army 22, 58, 115, 153
19th Army vii, 20, 22, 57-58, 82, 89, 113, 115, 118, 153
20th Army vii, 20, 22, 57-58, 82, 89, 113, 115, 118, 153
22nd Army 22, 112, 123
24th Army vii, 20, 22-23, 57-58, 82, 89, 113, 115, 118, 131, 153
27th Army 91, 108, 121
29th Army vi, 22-23, 43, 58, 93, 109-110, 112, 118, 131-133, 161
30th Army 20, 22-23, 51, 57-58, 61, 74, 101-103, 108, 111-112, 115, 118, 123, 126, 131, 133, 153
31st Army 23, 81, 85-86, 90-91, 101-104, 108-109, 112, 115, 118-121, 123, 126, 128, 131-133, 135-136, 139, 143, 145, 148, 160-164
32nd Army vii, 20, 22-23, 57, 81-82, 89, 91, 108, 113, 115, 118, 153

Divisions

5th Rifle Division 90-91, 102, 121, 124

18th Leningrad People's Militia Rifle Division 120, 125, 136
18th Rifle Division 86, 103-104, 109, 115, 121, 123, 142, 144
48th Rifle Division 103-104, 109, 115, 121, 123, 136, 142, 144
49th Guards Rifle Division 158-160, 162, 165
107th Motorized Rifle Division 61, 65-67, 70, 72, 74-75, 82, 89, 116, 142-143, 153, 158
110th Rifle Division 85-86, 90-91, 102, 108, 112, 121, 123-124
119th Rifle Division 43, 50, 85, 90-91, 102-105, 110, 112, 118, 121, 123-124, 131, 136, 157, 161-162
126th Rifle Division 133, 139-140, 142-143
220th Rifle Division 103-104, 109, 115, 121, 123, 136, 142, 144
242nd Rifle Division 116, 133, 142
247th Rifle Division 90-91, 102, 104, 108, 112, 120-121, 123-126, 128, 131, 133, 136, 140, 142, 144
249th Rifle Division 90-91, 102, 121, 123-124
250th Rifle Division 66, 104-105, 115, 131, 133
251st Rifle Division 20, 51-52, 102, 115, 123, 133, 142

Brigades

128th Tank Brigade 81-82, 127

Battalions

20th Separate Reconnaissance Battalion 67, 70, 74, 142

Miscellaneous

Stavka ix, xi, xiii, 32, 36, 58, 90, 112
Supreme High Command ix, 58, 90